GUIDE TO FLY TYING

GUIDE TO FLY TYING

Dick Talleur

For Charlie —
Best wishes for fly tying mastery .

Dick Talleur

STACKPOLE
BOOKS

Published by
STACKPOLE BOOKS
5067 Ritter Road
Mechanicsburg, PA 17055
www.stackpolebooks.com

Printed in China

First edition

10 9 8 7 6 5 4 3 2 1

Jacket design by Wendy A. Reynolds
All photos by Dick Talleur

Library of Congress Cataloging-in-Publication Data
Talleur, Richard W.
    Guide to fly tying/Dick Talleur.
    p.   cm.
    Includes bibliographical references (p.   ) and index.
    ISBN 0-8117-0987-6 (hardcover)
    1. Fly tying   I. Title.
    SH451.T287   2000
    688.7'9124—dc21

                                                                99-29969
                                                                CIP

CONTENTS

Preface vii

1   Vises, Tools, and Materials 1

2   Hooks 11

3   Thread 14

4   Flank-Feather Wings 21

5   Wulffmanship 38

6   Tippet Wings 47

7   Spinners and Spents 56

8   Down-Wing Dry Flies 62

9   Clump-Wing Dry Flies 71

10 Parachutes 76

11 Small and Smaller 84

12 Variants 91

13 Soft-Hackle Wet Flies 95

14 Winged Wet Flies 103

15 Nymphs 113

16 Stonefly Nymphs 127

17 The Hornberg 133

18 New and Novel Woolly Buggers 137

19 Unmuddling the Muddler .143

20 The Pseudo Sculpin 150

21 Marabou Streamers 153

22 The Bucktail or Hairwing Streamer 158

23 Matukas and Meatballs 169

24 Featherwing Streamers 177

25 A Very Edible Crayfish 182

Bibliography 187

Index 189

PREFACE

In the late 1970s, I wrote *Mastering the Art of Fly Tying.* It was published in spring 1979 and stayed in print for just over twenty years. I was amazed at that book's durability and the countless positive comments I received. *Guide to Fly Tying* was conceived as a second edition of *Mastering,* but by the time I was finished adding, updating, and revising, I found I had written a new book. I hope this one will meet with similar approval from the fly-fishing and tying community. Since the publication of *Mastering,* many astounding changes have occurred in fly fishing and tying. New techniques and methods have evolved. Hundreds of new products have been introduced, and there have been near-incredible advances in the genetic development of fowl for hackle feathers and other fly-tying applications.

Despite this explosion in tying and fishing products and technology, the fundamentals are unchanged. You can still catch a lot of fish on an Adams, a Hare's Ear, a Mickey Finn streamer, or a Muddler Minnow, and they are still tied pretty much the same way. However, there are many refinements that enhance both the tying and the fishing, and these are what make this new book necessary.

This book not only explains and refines the techniques involved in tying the various fly types covered in the first book, but also explores some interesting and useful new methods and procedures, often using new materials. This will greatly expand the tier's repertoire and the angler's arsenal. The book also includes some basic criteria you might apply in assessing new materials as they come along. Innovations are occurring so fast that catalogs and periodicals are having trouble staying current and giving accurate appraisals, and advertising would have you believe that all these products are wonderful.

The first few chapters include a lot of information and photographs that may, to the more experienced tier, seem redundant. This was done in order to update the material covered in the original book and so that the book would be essentially complete in itself and beginners wouldn't have to go to other sources to find the basics.

While you're going through the tying procedures presented here, let your own imagination and talent shine through. You may come up with your own ways of doing certain things, and they may be better than mine. For this, I'd be pleased and gratified.

Yours for tying mastery and enjoyment,

Dick Talleur

CHAPTER 1

Vises, Tools, and Materials

VISES

It's a bit risky to get specific about fly-tying vises these days. There has been quite a lot of volatility in that field, with several top-of-the-line products vacillating on and off the market, and it's difficult to keep up with all the changes. I am compelled, therefore, to take a more generic approach.

There are many good vises on the market that vary in design and features. There is also an enormous price range, and usually, as the old saying goes, you get what you pay for. I'll add the following caveat, however: If you spend top dollar, be sure you do get what you pay for.

Vise Design

It isn't necessary to spend a small fortune on a vise that will hold a hook securely. What does justify a higher price tag is functionality, which refers to both features and dependability. Besides holding the hook absolutely immobile, there are only a few requisites for a vise to be highly versatile and functional. They are:

• Revolving or rotating capability. This refers to the ability to revolve the hook and view it from the rear. The vise also needs to have an angle adjustment feature so that the entire assembly and the hook shank can be positioned horizontally and in a straight line.

• Adjustable collet angle. This means the ability to increase or reduce the angle at which the entire sleeve-collet-head assembly is positioned, from vertical to horizontal. The sharper the angle, the better the access to the hook from the rear, which makes tying on small hooks much easier. The horizontal position is helpful when tying on large hooks. Having an adjustable collet angle allows you to rotate the assembly to inspect and work on the back side of the fly. Streamer and salmon fly tiers find this feature most valuable.

• A wide range of chuck or jaw settings to accommodate hooks of different sizes (referring to the wire thickness). One vise, the Hunter's Multi Head (HMH), from the Kennebec River Fly & Tackle Company, offers

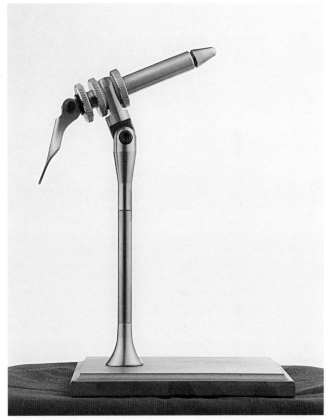

The classic lever-cam vises of the D. H. Thompson Company set the design criteria for an entire generation of vises.

the unique feature of changeable jaws that facilitate tying on the entire spectrum of hooks, from largest to smallest.

Vises also differ in how they hold the hook. Many use the traditional lever-cam design. Some use a wheel that, when turned, pulls the jaws backward into the collet, thus clamping down on the hook shank. Other models use a lever mounted near the jaws to effect closure. One vise, the Regal, employs a unique spring-loaded method of closure in which you operate a lever to open the jaws, and the spring exerts the required pressure to close them.

All of these technologies work. They are all designed to do one thing: to hold the hook securely. How well

1

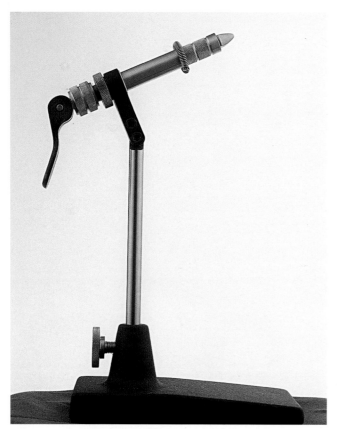

The Hunter's Multi Head (HMH) vise, with its interchangeable jaws, is rich in features.

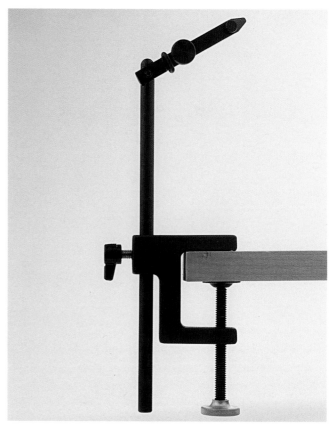

An economical model from Griffin makes a good starter vise.

they work depends on the quality of manufacture and your willingness to understand and properly adjust the tool. The specific design is secondary to function and features. Don't let high-tech appearances or hype sway you. Decide what you want from your vise, try out as many as you can, and choose the one that you're happiest with.

Pedestal Base versus C-Clamp Mount

Whether to buy a vise with a pedestal base or a C-clamp mount depends on your personal preference. Each style has its own advantages. The C-clamp mount is more solid; if properly secured, it's immobile. It gives you the ability to adjust the height of the vise, and it's usually a bit cheaper.

The pedestal base is much more adaptable and can be set on any flat surface, thus it's great for traveling. The base has no obstructions that would interfere with lap drawers. The pedestal base does not give you the ability to adjust the height of the vise, but this isn't usually a major problem. If you need to change your height relative to the vise, a common adjustable office chair solves the problem. The matter of stability shouldn't be a problem, either, provided that the base is of sufficient size and weight. Some vises offer a conversion kit so that you can use either kind of mount.

Rotary Vises

Vises also can be rotary and stationary. True rotary vises are those that are intended to be used in a fully rotating mode. Stationary, standard-design vises may have a rotating or revolving capability, which is useful and desirable, but it's not the same as true rotary operation.

Rotary vises have their advantages and disadvantages. Manufacturers claim that they ease, improve, and speed up certain operations, such as wrapping floss bodies on large hooks. Also, when feeding such materials out of a bobbin, no twists are introduced, as there are during conventional wrapping with bobbin-mounted materials.

The standard bearer for true rotary has been the Renzetti line of vises. Andy Renzetti is a master machinist, and his products are of excellent quality and fine precision. There are several models to choose from, with a considerable range of prices.

There are certain technical disciplines associated with the true rotary vise and its operation in that mode. The design is such that the shank of the hook can be aligned on a true axis with the main shaft of the vise. Thus the hook can be rotated 360 degrees with the shank maintaining a straight, horizontal position. The assembly is designed to turn freely so that you can spin the hook and apply materials without hand wrapping.

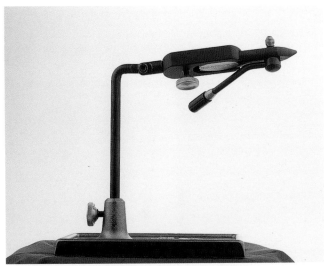

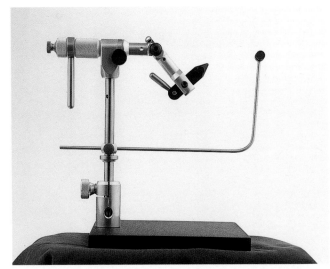

The Regal, with its spring-loaded jaws, incorporates a unique design.

Andy Renzetti has long set the standard for true rotary vises.

In theory, that sounds like a great advantage. However, in order to use true rotary, you have to secure the thread, which means knotting it with either a few half hitches or a three-turn whip finish. Then the thread is draped off the front of the hook by means of a device called a bobbin rest. After the operation is completed, the bobbin is retrieved from the bobbin rest, which is moved out of the way until it's needed again. Some tiers have adjusted to this, and it doesn't bother them. I find it a bit awkward and time-consuming, and I don't like having to tie a knot at an intermediate point, as I often like to reduce thread buildup by unwrapping tie-in wraps after completing an operation, such as when making a two-layer floss body. The knot makes that impossible.

Even so, there are those who swear by these tools. Many tiers of highly cosmetic full-dress Atlantic salmon flies feel that they can achieve greater precision in such operations as applying ribbing tinsel or shaping a floss body. Master saltwater tiers, such as Bob Popovics, use the rotary feature to apply various coatings. These great masters of the art spent a lot of excruciating hours at the vise developing such skills, however. Their fine flies are not just a result of the design of the vise.

There are a couple of other problems with rotary vises. When the rotating feature is not being used, which is most of the time, you have to work around a lot of machinery. This inhibits clear access to the hook from the rear. And it can be difficult to align the hook shank with the center of the shaft so that it will revolve on a true axis and not wobble around.

Rotary vise manufacturers have tried to address these problems with innovations in design. Ron Abby, proprietor and designer of the Dyna-King line of vises, has a recent entry in the rotary market called the Barracuda

which features a removable hook-centering device that greatly simplifies setting the hook shank in perfect alignment. This is aided by an adjustable jaw barrel, which allows the entire jaw assembly to be slid up or down as desired. These are giant steps in the right direction.

The top-of-the-line Renzetti has several adjustment features that enable the tier to simulate the posture of a conventional vise when the rotating feature isn't in play. This helps unclutter the area behind the jaw mechanism, allowing easier access from the rear. A crank assembly that mounts on the rear of the vise increases speed considerably. This works better with C-clamp mounting, as a pedestal base tends to move about while you're cranking.

Although I don't use the true rotary vise, I don't speak against it. I recommend that you thoroughly try it out for yourself. Consider how often you would use the true rotary feature. If a rotary vise seems to best suit your tying needs, then it may be the design for you.

Travel Vises

Taking a fly-tying vise on a trip is no problem unless you're flying. Then the added weight and bulk can become a bit unwieldy, especially with a pedestal base. Miniature travel vises reduce this problem somewhat, although their functionality can be questionable. In order for a vise to comfortably accommodate fly-tying tools, certain dimensions are critical, especially the distance between the front of the jaws and the upright shaft on which the assembly is mounted. If this does not allow sufficient working room, tying becomes difficult. Before buying a travel vise, tie some flies with it—the flies you'd normally tie for your fishing locales. If you find this uncomfortable, take your regular vise on your trips.

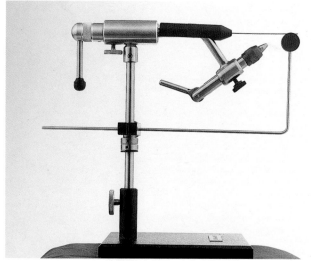

The Dyna-King Barracuda, built and designed by Ron Abby, is a top-quality new entry in the rotary market.

OTHER TOOLS

After years of tying, and having played around with dozens of gadgets, I believe that a small assortment of practical and essential tools is all the fly tier needs. Few special-purpose tools enable you to do things better, easier, or faster than you can do them by hand. In fact, some of them make the task more difficult.

I'm reminded of my days at AT&T Headquarters in downtown Manhattan. In the summer, when the weather was nice, we often encountered street vendors hawking various products. One that intrigued me was a vegetable slicer. He could slice up carrots, cucumbers, potatoes for French fries, and all sorts of stuff with bewildering wizardry. It was very impressive. I finally ended up buying one of those things. However, in practice, I found it cumbersome, and before long, it was stashed in the back of a drawer and I was back to my paring knife. It occurred to me that all this guy did was slice veggies for show all day, every day. I don't prepare food that way; I might slice one or two cukes a week. Get the message?

I now have a drawer that contains a whole bunch of fly-tying gadgets that complicated, rather than simplified, my life. Rather than do likewise to yours, I'll omit lengthy descriptions of them. I'll make mention of some, and if you want to give them a try, you're on your own. Just remember; when you're at a big fly fishing show, and you see a guy doing neat-looking tricks with some StarWars vise, cute dubbing spinner, or bizarre hackle pliers, keep in mind that he slices those cucumbers many hours a day.

Here is some information on tools that are indispensable, or nearly so.

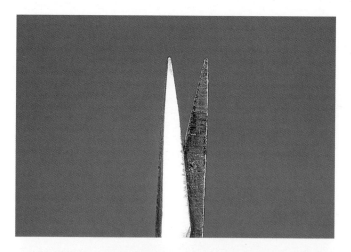

Scissors for fine work must have fine-tipped blades that meet precisely from both front and side.

Scissors

Most tiers have at least two pairs of scissors. People who tie a wide range of flies, from small drys to large saltwater streamers, may have quite an assortment. Scissors are specialized tools and should be treated as such. In other words, don't cut a big bunch of synthetic hair with your fine-tipped dry-fly scissors.

Scissors used for the most delicate and precise sort of work must have tips that come to a sharp point and are precisely matched to perform efficiently. The blades must be thin when viewed from the sides for close-in cutting. Better-quality scissors have a screw, rather than a rivet, at the axis so that they can be tightened. Whether the blades are straight or curved is a matter of personal choice.

Such delicate scissors are easily damaged. A few indiscreet cuts of heavy or tough material can ruin them. At the very least, the tier must avoid cutting any heavy stuff with the tips of the scissors, but rather should work well down into the blades. Keep a second, sturdier pair on hand. They need not be expensive. Nail clippers also are useful for cutting thick quills, oval tinsel, plastic

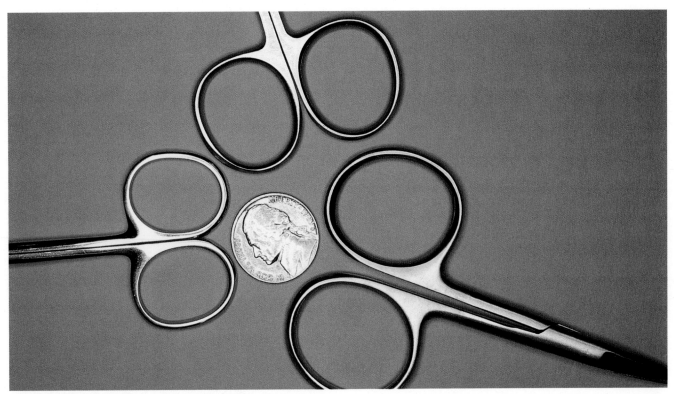

The size of a scissors' finger loops is your choice.

wraps, and similar materials. Some scissors have tiny serrations along one blade. This helps the blades grip and shear materials and is particularly helpful for trimming spun hair, which has a tendency to slip when being cut.

When choosing scissors, there's also the matter of fit—the size of the finger loops as well as overall length. Many tiers keep their scissors in their dominant hand at all times, with the fourth finger through one of the loops. In order to do this without getting stabbed, the scissors must be long enough to extend beyond the palm. I need 4-inch scissors, but for those with smaller hands, 3½ inches may suffice.

The size of the finger loops is a matter of personal preference. Some people like oversize finger loops. I feel that a closer fit gives me more precise control, and overly large finger loops are uncomfortable when the scissors are resting in the palm of my hand. Try several models to see what feels best.

It's possible to sharpen most scissors and thus extend their useful life. You'll need a very fine stone. Open the blades as wide as they will go. Draw each blade across the stone without altering the bevel—the angle of the cutting edge. If one of the blades is serrated, you can touch it up a bit, but too much sharpening will remove the serrations.

Some good scissors are offered today at reasonable prices, although I advise against buying very cheap ones. They may look nice at first glance, but closer inspection usually turns up various imperfections, and you won't get the metal quality found in better scissors. When I bought a bargain-priced pair several years ago, they dulled quickly, and when I tried to sharpen them, the blades virtually disappeared.

Bobbins

The fly-tying bobbin is a most useful tool, as it replaces several tedious operations formerly done by hand, eliminates a lot of knot tying, and maintains tension on the thread. The most important thing is that the tip of the tube be perfectly smooth or it will cut the thread, which is a nightmare.

I see a lot of bobbins every year while teaching, and I've seen brand new ones with bad tube mouths. When I see someone constantly breaking thread with moderate tension, or if I notice thread fraying all the time, I immediately suspect that bobbin. If you encounter such problems and despair of your heavy-handed technique, borrow a bobbin that's known to work well. Get an experienced tier to help, if possible. You may find that it's not you, but the tool—in which case you return it, of course. Bobbin tubes may develop sharp edges over time simply through wear from the action of the thread. Some bobbin manufacturers use ceramic tubes or inserts to prevent this. The Griffin Company offers a well-designed bobbin that has a little ceramic doughnut in the tip, as well as plastic bushings that fit into the hole that goes through the spool to prevent the spool from coming into contact with the frame of the bobbin.

Most new bobbins need to have the tension adjusted. The bobbin should be able to hang in suspension without feeding out thread by virtue of its own weight. The thread should feed out readily and smoothly, but under a modicum of tension applied by the tier. To achieve the proper tension, mount a spool of thread in the tool and carefully bend the limbs of the wishbone until the bobbin behaves as desired. Bend the limbs uniformly on each side so that the thread spool is centered when mounted.

Bobbin Threader

A bobbin threader is used to draw the tying thread through the tube of the bobbin. Essentially, it consists of a sharply pointed loop of fine wire that's fitted into some sort of handle. Lacking this, you can get by with a piece of fairly stiff monofilament, doubled over. Dental floss threaders make great bobbin threaders, especially for mounting bulky threads, flosses, stretch nylon, and other such materials.

Bobbin Holder

A bobbin holder holds the bobbin and thread out of the way when you're working on something that doesn't directly involve them. I find the tool to be much more of an interference than the thread and bobbin, but some tiers find them helpful. With a true rotary vise, the bobbin holder is a necessity when the rotating feature is being used and comes with the vise as standard equipment.

Hackle Pliers

The primary function of hackle pliers is to grip a feather while wrapping it to form a hackle. There are a number of designs on the market today, some of which are quite a departure from the basic or conventional. Though I'm a strong advocate of innovation, gadgeteering is evident here. You only need simple hackle pliers with a firm but gentle grip, comfortable size and shape for handling, and sufficient weight to hold a feather in position when hanging suspended. This last is important, as quills are stiff and will try to unwrap themselves unless tension is maintained. After thirty-five years of fly tying, I still prefer English hackle pliers, which meet all of these criteria. Adding a small piece of heat-shrink tubing to one of the jaws improves the grip and lessens the possibility of breaking feathers. A word of caution: Avoid miniature pliers, as they're harder to handle and lack sufficient weight. You can work on small flies just as easily with normal-size pliers; it's the size of the jaws that counts, not the overall size of the tool.

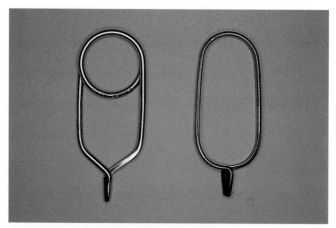
Two models of classic English-style hackle pliers.

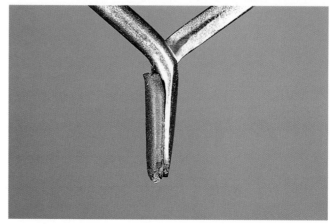
The jaws of a pair of typical hackle pliers can be enhanced by the addition of a piece of heat-shrink tubing.

Some people use spring-loaded electronics clips as hackle pliers. For general work, they are too light and the wrong shape. Nevertheless, they don't cost much and are handy for certain operations, such as twisting and wrapping peacock herl.

Hackle Gauge

In dry-fly tying, proper sizing of hackle—that is, assessing barb length as related to hook size—is very important. Once you gain some experience, you'll be able to eyeball a feather and tell what size it is, but as a beginner, you may need the assistance of a hackle gauge. I recommend a model with a small peg or pin around which you can bend the feather to simulate its being wrapped around the hook. A hackle gauge that can be attached to the post of the vise is most convenient.

Bodkin

Also called a dubbing needle, a bodkin is simply a sharp-pointed instrument used for such tasks as picking out fur bodies and applying head cement. My favorite consists of

Tweezers come in handy. Different designs serve different purposes.

a hardware-store item called a pin vise, which enables you to change points any time you choose. An alternative to a bodkin for picking out and fuzzing up fly bodies is to use a little piece of "male" Velcro, the side with the tiny hooks. It works great and never cuts the thread.

Tweezers

A good pair of tweezers can be blessedly useful on a fly-tying desk. I have several pairs of different design. The ones I treasure most are a flat-nosed pair made by a company called Tweezerman. They are very good quality and well worth the rather high price I paid for them. The quality is recognizable, because they are the most often pilfered of all my tools at public tying events. These tweezers have tips a little over $1/8$ inch across, which are cut at an angle. They are useful for everything from picking up stray hooks to flattening quills to crimping materials.

Hair Evener

A hair evener, or stacker, helps you to quickly and effectively align the tips of bundles of hair. A number of designs are available. The most important consideration is that the inside diameter of the tube be of adequate size. Those with narrow tubes only work with small bunches of hair and are ineffective for calf tail hair which is crinkly and requires a generous-size tube. You can operate on smaller bunches with a wide-tube stacker, but not vice versa.

Hair Packer

A hair packer is a specialized instrument used when spinning deer or similar hair. As the bunches are tied in place, the packer is used to compress the hairs, which improves the appearance and performance of the fly. It's a low-cost item, but you can make a serviceable one from the housing of a ballpoint pen.

Whip Finisher

The most effective knot for tying off the thread after completing a fly is the whip finish. It is sometimes used during intermediate steps as well. The whip finish is easily done by hand, but it's even more easily and quickly done with a good tool. I particularly like the Matarelli whip finisher, which at this writing comes in two sizes. The larger model is much more versatile and easier to work with.

Half-Hitch Tool

There was a time when the half hitch was frequently used in fly tying. The elderly gentleman who got me started didn't use a bobbin; he secured each operation with a half hitch or two until the end, where he did a whip finish by hand. Today, thanks mainly to the bobbin, half hitches are practically a thing of the past, though there are occasions where you might want to use them. Making half hitches by hand is simple, however, and a half-hitch tool is not really necessary.

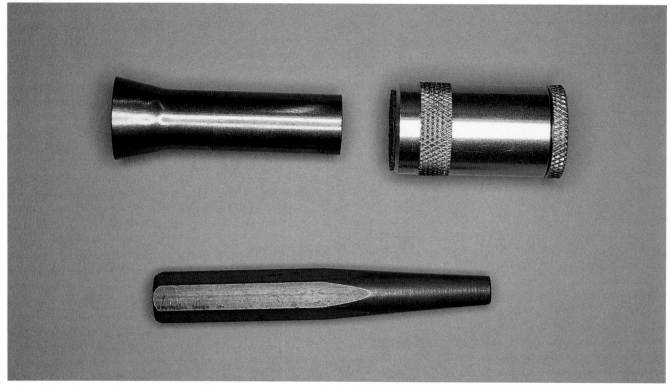

Two useful tools. Top: *a hair packer;* bottom: *a stacker, or hair evener.*

Materials Clip

A materials clip is an adjunct to the vise that holds certain types of materials out of the way while subsequent operations are being performed—for example, it's used to secure ribbing tinsel while you tie the body of the fly. Many vises come equipped with materials clips. In any case, it's a useful and low-cost add-on.

Hackle Guard

Some beginners find a hackle guard useful. Its purpose is to hold the completed hackle of a dry fly out of the way while you finish off the fly. If the proportions of the fly were reasonably good, and the hackling fairly well done, there would be no need for the hackle guard. I don't even recommend it for beginners, who should instead work on learning good technique.

Dubbing Twisters

Several different types of dubbing twisters are available. These devices may be of some practical use, such as for spinning tough-to-handle dubbing materials. Some tiers need such tools, although I prefer to do my twisted-type dubbing with spinning loops, hackle pliers, and adroit technique.

There are other devices that serve specialized purposes in fly tying. You'll undoubtedly find out about them as you go along, and it's your decision as to which, if any, of them will be helpful. As stated earlier, I'm all for innovation, but only in the interest of improvement and progress. Essentially, my rule is not to use a tool for any task that I can do just as well by hand.

Adhesives and Protective Coatings

Though I don't advocate overdoing it, the use of adhesives and protective coatings can be most helpful. In some cases, they are actually part of the tying process. Head cement or lacquer is most commonly used. With modern synthetic waxed threads and well-tied whip-finish knots, fly heads could be left unfinished with minimal danger of their coming apart. But then you'd have to be careful not to damage the thread with forceps or some other tool when unhooking fish. And flies simply don't look as pretty without a nicely finished head. So I vote for lacquer or cement of some type. In fact, I use two coats on larger flies with more prominent heads.

Probably the next most widely used adhesive is wax. A lot has changed with regard to the need for wax. Back when tiers used silk thread, proper waxing was a necessity. The great tiers still practicing when I was just a beginner used silk thread almost exclusively and were very wax-conscious. The list includes Helen Shaw, Ray Bergman, Ray Smith, Walt and Winnie Dette, and Harry and Elsie Darbee. The Darbees made their own wax. The recipe may be found in that most entertaining book, *Catskill Flytier,* along with a hilarious note about a lady who thought the stuff was homemade candy, and got her false teeth stuck in it. The first recipe consisted of resin, beeswax, and lard. Later, castor oil was substituted for the lard. The resin provided the tackiness, the beeswax served as a preservative, and the castor oil texturized the stuff.

Even with such powerful waxes, all of those people used a head coating. The Darbees preferred a glue called Ambroid, thinned with acetone. It was very good stuff, and I used it for years. The acetone caused the glue to penetrate well into the thread, despite the resistance of the wax.

I don't use wax very much. I'm fortunate enough to have smooth, somewhat moist hands. As a teacher of fly tying, however, I encounter people who have rough, dry hands. A little wax is most beneficial to these folks. Still, I'm not a fan of really sticky waxes. The judicious use of a less-tacky wax should be all you need.

The typical cements and lacquers of today require some form of solvent, such as acetone, methyl ethyl ketone (MEK), toluol, or lacquer thinner. The last is a mixture of chemicals and varies somewhat in formula. One brand I use contains methanol and toluol and is meant to be used with various wood and metal finishes. It is not compatible with rubber, plastic, asphalt tile, linoleum, brushes with synthetic bristles, and most automotive and similar specialty lacquers. Pretty potent stuff.

Be sure to buy the right thinner for whatever lacquer or cement you use. This is important. Though a general lacquer thinner may seem to work on a particular product, it may actually be changing the formula, so it's best to use the one that's recommended.

These solvents often contain toxic substances, so when you use a solvent, be sure to have proper ventilation and protection. If you frequently get a lot of this stuff on your hands, wear protective vinyl or rubber gloves.

A favorite coating of mine is a Veniard product called Cellire, which is not a lacquer, but a celluloid varnish. It comes in white, yellow, red, black, and two consistencies of clear—thin for fly heads and heavy for rod wrappings.

I recommend using the Veniard varnish thinner, Unitit. I have found that while a general-purpose thinner will cut Cellire, the varnish doesn't harden as well and the luster is lessened.

Properly thinned and applied, Cellire renders a beautiful finish. When tying cosmetic flies for framing, I suggest a coat of clear, two coats of black, and another coat of clear, allowing for thorough drying time in between. For fishing flies, two coats of whatever color you prefer will do the job.

Cellire is also good for making painted eyes. The following procedure will give the best results with any brand of head lacquer.

1. Apply a coat of clear cement, and let it dry completely.
2. Lay the fly on its side.
3. With a cylindrical object of some kind, such as the butt end of a small drill bit, pick up a droplet of yellow or white Cellire and transfer it to the head of the fly. If the substance is of the right consistency, the droplet will spread into a near-perfect circle without having the applicator actually touch the head of the fly. Do this on both sides.
4. After the Cellire has completely dried, dot on black pupils with an applicator of smaller diameter.
5. When the pupils are dry, apply a clear coat as protection.

I should say, in fairness to other manufacturers, that I would follow the same procedure for finishing heads and making painted eyes with any brand of head lacquer.

Most head finishes, Cellire included, are hard and brittle when dry, although there are a few that are described as flexible. The most well known is Dave's Flexament, a product of renowned fly tier Dave Whitlock. This is a clear compound that dries to a tough, rubbery finish. It has adhesive qualities and helps hold the fly together. It can also be used to perform repair jobs, such as mending splits in jungle cock feathers.

The thinner is generally available in fly shops where Flexament is sold. You'll need to keep a supply on hand, as it seems to evaporate quickly, and Flexament needs to be kept from getting too thick.

Nail polishes can also be used as head finishes. Some seem to work quite well, and the range of colors is practically limitless. I use metallic colors, such as pearl, to finish heads on certain flies. Painting up fly heads is not what the manufacturers of nail polishes have in mind, and many of them don't form the best kind of coating for flies. You'll have to experiment. Sally Hansen products are pretty good, and the clear Hard-as-Nails is quite popular as a head finish.

Nail polish bottles also come in handy, with a built-in applicator in the cap. I trim out most of the bristles with a razor blade to reduce the brush to a better size for fly-tying applications.

When it comes to head finishing, there's nothing stronger or more durable than epoxy. The mixing process is a bit tedious, however, and then there's the long drying time. Even the five-minute variety requires a number of hours before you can fish the fly. The proportions have to be right, and epoxy won't set properly in overly cold temperatures. When buying epoxy, be sure to get the clear type. Avoid the two-part finishes intended for coating rod wrappings, as they are low in viscosity. Epoxy applied over waxed thread doesn't penetrate as well as some other finishes. For security, you might first apply a coat of well-thinned, clear lacquer and allow it to dry completely.

Cyanoacrylate superglues are extremely strong and fast drying and can be used to protect quill bodies and other delicate components. Zap-A-Gap is a popular brand among fly tiers.

Manufacturers have recently been offering coatings and adhesives with water-based finishes. These products, made by companies like BT's Flyfishing Products, Rainy's, and Lac Loon, are truly solvent-free or have only a little denatured alcohol to help keep them from freezing during shipping. They can be thinned and cleaned up with plain water.

I've experimented extensively with the BT product which comes in red, yellow, black, and two types of clear—hard and flexible, the latter called AquaFlex.

Although I was a bit skeptical at first, I've found that the water-based products compare favorably with the solvent-based ones. I'm delighted with the appearance and consistency they produce, as well as the short drying time.

Most of all, I'm intrigued with the properties of AquaFlex. I have been using it in place of epoxy and those messy silicone bath tub sealants, and the results are superb. I've been able to encase heads having stick-on eyes by blobbing on two generous coats, allowing complete drying between them. The finished coat is very tough, with a consistency akin to surgical tubing. I've also had great success repairing splits in jungle cock eyes with this product.

Aside from durability over time, the only question I have is how the BT finishes will behave when applied to waxed threads. As mentioned, solvent-based lacquers, if properly thinned, penetrate such heads. I'm not sure this is the case with water-based ones. I'm also not sure how much it matters. As a precaution, you might do as was recommended with epoxy.

With water-based products, make sure the finish is absolutely dry before exposing the fly to water. Once the compound has hardened, it's impervious to water, but until then, the slightest amount of wetness will wash it away.

The BT bottles tend to stick shut when stored for any length of time. As a preventative measure, you can rub a thin smear of Vaseline around the rim now and then, as I do with cans of Barge Cement, the adhesive I use for resoling waders. Otherwise, the bottles can be opened with wide-jawed pliers or by immersion in hot water for a few minutes.

Rainy's Water-Based Popper Paint works well on bass poppers. It can be applied to foam poppers without destroying them and also works very well on balsa wood.

Water-based rod-wrap finishes are now available and will probably be standard soon. A water-based epoxy is just around the corner. Ah, technology! I think water-based is the way we should be going, and I'll be awaiting new developments with hopeful anticipation.

CHAPTER 2

Hooks

There are many hooks on the market today. The most important thing is to select the best hook for each type of fly you tie. That's not very difficult, once you understand a few simple points. When choosing a hook, there are several essential considerations in determining the quality:

• Good metallurgy—neither so soft that the hooks bend, nor so hard that they are brittle.

• Well-formed eyes—no open spots or rough, sharp edges.

• Sharp points as they come from the package.

• Properly formed points, relative to the diameter of the wire.

• Small barbs that do not substantially weaken the hook at that spot.

HOOK DESIGN

There are also several considerations related to design. The following are those that I feel are the most important:

• Dry-fly hooks should have a model perfect bend, which means that the shape of the bend describes a semicircle. This best accommodates the standard dry-fly structure, with the tail extending straight out from the rear of the hook.

• Turned-down and turned-up eyes should be formed at an angle of 30 to 35 degrees. This enables the use of knots that form behind the eye, such as the improved turle, allowing the leader to come straight out through the eye without offsetting the positioning of the fly or causing it to be held at an angle.

• Ultrashort hooks, where the gape is almost equal to the shank length, don't engage well, especially if the hook has a turned-up eye.

• Longer hooks need to be made of heavier wire so they will resist bending under the strain of fighting a large game fish.

• Wire diameter should bear a relationship to the type of fly being tied and to the size of the hook, which is determined by the gap, or gape. Dry-fly hooks need to be light, whereas hooks for sunken flies should be

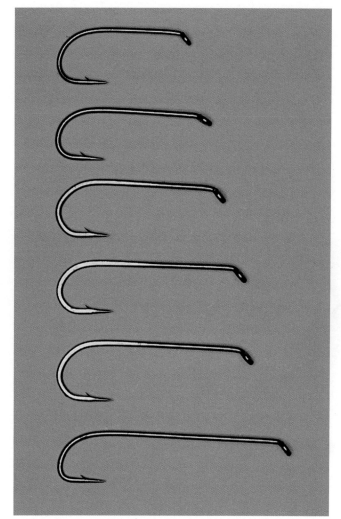

Comparison of shank lengths. From top: *standard, 1XL, 2XL, 3XL, 4XL, 6XL, 7XL (there is no 5XL).*

heavier so that they contribute to the sink rate and minimize the need for adding weight.

• Hooks for streamers and certain other types of flies work best, from a tying standpoint, if they have a looped eye.

• Though not a functional necessity, wet flies, nymphs, streamer flies, and salmon flies seem to look and

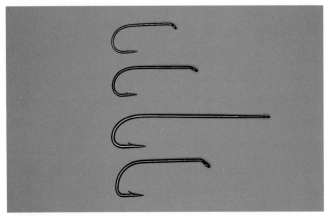

Comparison of shapes or bends. From top: *model perfect, sproat, modified sproat, Limerick.*

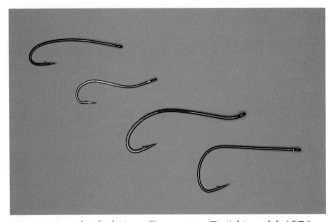

Some unique hook designs. From top: *Daiichi model 1270 curved-shank; Daiichi model 1770 swimming nymph; Daiichi model 1870 Gary Borger larva; Daiichi 2720 wide-gap stinger.*

ride better on hooks with compound bends, such as sproat, improved sproat, or limerick.

• Very fine-wire hooks should have shorter points with small barbs. The fineness of the wire allows such points to penetrate effectively with modest pressure so that fine leader tippets can survive strikes and hookups. Conversely, heavier wire hooks require longer points, as the diameter of the wire inhibits penetration if the points are too stubby. Resharpening also becomes a problem with such a design.

• The barb should be small on all hooks to aid penetration and lessen the probability that the hook will break during debarbing. Such hooks can often be used without debarbing, while still allowing for easy release of the fish.

A looped eye is formed by running the wire that forms the eye down the hook shank a little way, rather than closing the eye by simply forming a circle. The looped eye appears a lot on Atlantic salmon hooks, partly due to tradition and partly for functional reasons. With the eye formed in this manner, there's no chance of

having a rough edge or poorly closed eye, which eliminates one source of disaster when playing a large, acrobatic fish.

Looped eyes can be turned up, turned down, or straight. The main thing is that the wire that runs down the hook shank, called the return wire, must be tapered down to nothing so that there's no bump where it ends. Unfortunately, not all manufacturers follow this procedure. Watch out for looped-eye hooks with untapered or poorly tapered return wires.

Some hooks have tapered eyes, where the metal that forms the eye has been reduced, or tapered. This is a nice touch, especially on dry-fly hooks. It allows the inside dimension of the eye to be properly sized while minimizing the bulk of the outside of the eye, thus eliminating a bit of metal. A tapered eye isn't essential, but it's definitely nice to have. Eyes on which the metal isn't drawn down are known as ball eyes, particularly if they are straight and not turned down or up.

Turned-down eyes are the most popular, and understandably so. If properly formed, they will accommodate just about any of the commonly used fishing knots, a very valuable feature. Straight eyes will accommodate only those knots that form in front of the eye, such as the improved clinch. They are particularly good with the Duncan Loop, an increasingly popular knot that allows a fly more freedom of swing. This knot is used mostly with streamers, large nymphs, and saltwater flies.

Turned-up eyes are mainly used by salmon fly tiers, although they can be used in general tying. For a while, they were favored by the mini- and microfly tiers, as they had better hooking characteristics than the turned-down eyes. The recent advent of down-eye hooks in very small sizes with oversize gapes has offset this, however.

HOOK FINISHES

Tradition and habit continue to govern hook finish. Most hooks are still coated with bronze lacquer, a rather subdued, relatively inconspicuous natural color that doesn't draw undue attention to itself.

The black Japanned finish still predominates with Atlantic salmon-fly hooks. The initial purpose was to inhibit corrosion, as salmon are sometimes fished for in brackish waters. Today's regular bronzed hooks would probably be fine for the salmon angler, but I'm not going to tangle with tradition.

The saltwater set prefers a silver metallic finish. Stainless steel is still popular, despite the hassles over its resistance to biodegrading. Nickel and tinned finishes are duller, which is probably good, but saltwater fly fishers seem to like the sheen of stainless.

Over the last few years, I've seen a definite improvement in hook quality. Still, it's advisable to be on the

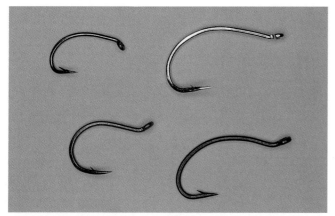

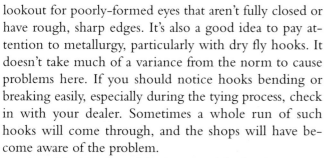

Other unique hook designs. Top left: *Partridge model K4A grub/shrimp;* top right: *Daiichi model 1155 heavy wide-gap, gold;* bottom left: *Daiichi model 4253 salmon egg, red;* bottom right: *Partridge model K2B Yorkshire sedge.*

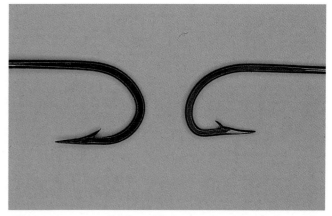

These two streamer hooks are from the same manufacturer and are listed as being the same size. Size is determined by gape, or gap.

lookout for poorly-formed eyes that aren't fully closed or have rough, sharp edges. It's also a good idea to pay attention to metallurgy, particularly with dry fly hooks. It doesn't take much of a variance from the norm to cause problems here. If you should notice hooks bending or breaking easily, especially during the tying process, check in with your dealer. Sometimes a whole run of such hooks will come through, and the shops will have become aware of the problem.

As with threads and leader materials, hooks are encumbered by an arcane and inaccurate system of sizing and classification. It's the "X " thing again—2X long, 3X fine, and all that. The X allegedly stands for "extra." The main problem with the system is that there is no benchmark. If all manufacturers could agree that the standard wire diameter of a size 12 dry fly hook be established as, let's say, 20 thousandths of an inch, the shank length from the beginning of the bend to the beginning of the eye at $3/8$ inches, and the gape (gap) at half the shank length, or $3/16$ inches, that would at least give the tier a point of reference.

Regrettably, there has, to my knowledge, been no movement towards standardization. I sympathize with the manufacturer's problems. Redesigning and retooling would be costly, and besides, whose hook would be designated as "standard"? So, the fly tier simply has to cope. The bright side is that there are a lot of excellent hooks out there and fewer mediocre ones all the time.

If you're a serious dry-fly fisherman, you might want to invest in a good micrometer for measuring wire diameters of hook shanks. (In one case, I found that a hook designated as 4X fine had about the same diameter as that of another manufacturer's 1X fine.) A good "mike" also comes in handy for measuring the diameter of leader materials, which often vary considerably from the diameter printed on the label.

As to the fair number of special hook designs we've seen lately, I am very much in favor of innovation, provided it isn't for its own sake. I particularly like the innovations in nymph hooks that enable graceful shaping and enhance the swimming effect.

CHAPTER 3

Thread

In addition to many old favorites, there are a number of new threads available, some of which are very good for special applications, such as tying very large or small flies, spinning or stacking hair, and even as body material.

Throughout the 1970s and into the 1980s, Danville's prewaxed tying thread was far and away the most widely used. It was a nylon version of the prewaxed silk thread developed by Herb Howard, a well-known commercial tier and entrepreneur of the 1950s and 1960s. The first product that significantly challenged the Danville empire was Uni-Thread, introduced at the very first fly tackle dealer show in Hershey, Pennsylvania in 1986. I well remember this, as the owner of the company, Jean-Guy Cote of Saint Melanie, Canada, recruited me to demo the stuff. To my pleasant surprise, it behaved very well indeed and did not have the attributes that bothered me with the Danville. I switched, and for general tying, I've pretty much stuck with Uni ever since.

The thing I found the most bothersome about the original Danville thread was its tendency to untwist and spread out into tiny individual fibers that would fray, break, and get caught on the hook point. To control this tendency and to counteract the slipperiness of the nylon, Danville applied a fair amount of wax to the thread. This caused wax buildup in the bobbin tube and, to some degree, interfered with the application of head lacquers and other finishing adhesives. Their current product, Flymaster, seems to be waxed more conservatively.

The basic Uni-Thread product is polyester. It feels and behaves a lot like the old silk that everyone was using 40 years ago, for which reason it found favor with some of the old traditionalists, notably Walt Dette and Helen Shaw. Unlike nylon, which has no memory, polyester holds its twists very well and retains its more-or-less round configuration, which enhances the material's natural strength. Polyester doesn't need to be waxed, but Uni-Thread 8/0 and 6/0 can be purchased either waxed or plain, the waxing being very moderate.

Another advantage of Uni-Thread products is the high-quality spools. They don't have rough spots, and they retain their labels, so that one can easily tell waxed from unwaxed, 6/0 from 8/0, and so forth. In the world of fly tying products, which is notorious for user-hostile packaging, this is truly a God-send.

Unfortunately, the system for rating the thickness of threads is arcane and badly-outdated. The higher the number, the finer the thread—in other words, 8/0 is finer than 6/0. Or at least, it's supposed to be. But the system is not only inaccurate and badly flawed, it is also abused by certain suppliers in order to represent their threads as being finer than they really are, and thus possessed of a higher strength-to-diameter ratio.

In order to evaluate a thread's quality and potential applications, there are only a few absolute criteria:
- Tensile strength overall.
- Tensile strength as related to thickness.
- Shape of cross section under tension—the relative flatness or roundness.
- Displacement, or bulk.

These qualities vary depending on the kind of fly you're tying—you need finer thread for smaller flies, flatter thread where smoothness is important, wider thread for covering area on large hooks, and strong thread for spinning deer hair and tying down resistant materials. Related to these criteria are several behavioral considerations whose impact may not be quite so obvious:
- Limpness or stiffness. Limper threads better enable certain techniques, such as soft, or gathering wraps. Some threads don't behave well without a lot of tension and tend to loosen, unwrap, and jump off the hook when softer wraps are used.
- Texture and slipperiness. Some threads are made of slippery material and don't accept dubbing as well as others. The old silk threads had a pleasant texture and were preferred by the more traditional tiers of yesteryear, most of whom didn't use bobbins and were very particular about the feel of their threads. Some of the

modern products, notably the polyester ones, have a similar texture.

• Memory. This is somewhat related to limpness but also refers to the tendency of some threads to untwist. This can be desirable when extreme flattening is wanted, but it must be controlled or the thread will spread too much and individual filaments will be isolated.

• Resistance to abrasion. Some delicate threads don't tolerate much contact with anything, including rough fingers. Using bobbins with the smoothest of tubes helps counteract this.

• Stretchiness. A little stretchiness is okay, but threads that are too stretchy can cause problems. They tend to perform poorly under moderate tension, and in extreme cases, they can retract so much after being tied off that the whip finish is lost.

There are also a few desirable packaging considerations. The spool should be a standard-size, to properly accommodate bobbins, and smooth, with no rough or protruding edges. It should have a slot in which to stash the tag end of the thread for storage and a label that stays in place.

Learn about the threads that are available, see how they perform, and use what best suits the application at hand. If you'd like a more in-depth analysis of threads, see the article by Chris Helm and Bill Merg in the Summer 1996 issue of *Fly Tyer* magazine. The authors do an excellent job of assessing the characteristics of the more important and popular threads available in the late 1990s, with specific data on strength, diameter, construction, and other such details. The article also comments on the inaccurate rating system, as I do here, and refers to a unit of thread thickness, "denier," which, ideally would replace the current number system.

THREAD MANAGEMENT

Effective thread management is the key to successful fly tying. There are very few operations in fly tying that don't involve the thread, so developing these skills is most essential. Following are four basic and essential thread management techniques.

The Pinch Wrap

This one is perhaps the most critical of all thread management techniques, as it enables you not only to affix things exactly where they are placed, but also to execute some of the more challenging procedures, such as winging a wet fly. That being a prime example, I'll use a simple Catskill-style wet-fly wing to demonstrate the pinch. The photos show two opposing goose quill sections, set back-to-back. These will compose the wing.

1. Set the winging sections on top of the hook, centering them over the shank.
2. While maintaining the position of the feather sections, bring the thread directly upward on the near side of them, sneaking it in between your left thumb and forefinger (the reverse for lefties). This is done by slightly opening the fingers at the tips.

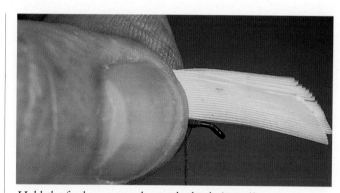
Hold the feathers centered atop the hook (step 1).

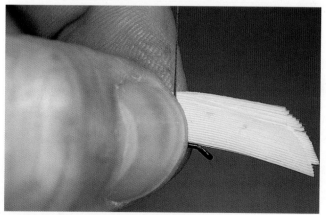
Sneak the thread up between the left thumb and forefinger (step 2).

3. Now bring the thread over top of the feather sections, all the while controlling the materials with the pinch.
4. Sneak the thread between the thumb and forefinger again, coming down the far side. This causes a loop of thread to form over the winging strips.
5. While pinching everything together, apply thread tension directly downward, snugging that loop of thread around the winging sections. Be sure that the winging sections are held straight and centered on the hook shank. Keep your left forefinger pressed firmly against the back of the hook, so that thread torque won't carry the material down around the far side.
6. Repeat this move several times, one atop the other.

A useful variation of the pinch is executed as follows: Instead of applying thread tension downward after positioning everything, bring the thread back up between the fingers again, as though you were setting up a second pinch. Then apply tension by pulling upward instead of downward. This may be helpful when trying to control hard-to-handle materials.

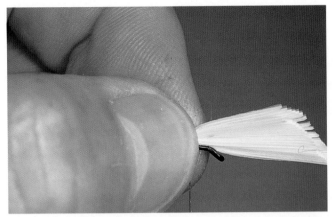

Come down the far side and apply thread tension downward (steps 4 & 5).

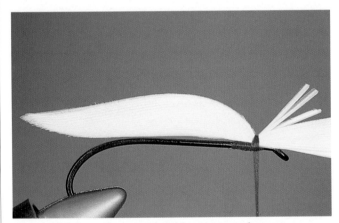

The result of a well-executed pinch wrap procedure.

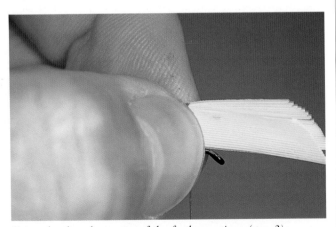

Bring the thread over top of the feather sections (step 3).

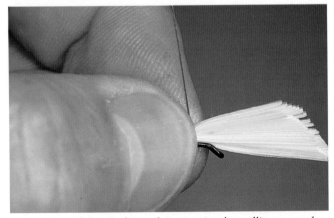

A variation of the pinch, applying tension by pulling upward.

The Slack Loop

This technique, also called the gathering wrap, is used both singly and in sequence. It's primarily used to affix materials to the hook when a pinch wrap would be ungainly, as when materials are already in place that could be messed up by being pinched, such as a hairwing on a caddisfly imitation that has palmered hackle already in place.

1. Cut off, clean out, and stack (even up the tips of) a small bunch of hair. Hold it in position on top of the hook, as shown.
2. Sneak the thread up and over, with moderate tension; you virtually lay the thread over the material.
3. You now can tighten by pulling down, continue around the hook and tighten by pulling up, or take one or two more slack wraps and tighten them all at once. The specific situation dictates what will work best.

Hair held in position on top of the hook (step 1).

The soft wrap (step 2).

The result of a well-executed slack loop sequence (step 3).

The Hair-Spinning Wrap

This procedure is essentially the same as for the slack loop. This wrap is used to spin bunches of hair, as is commonly done on Muddler heads, spun and trimmed bodies on dry flies, bass bugs, and so on. There's some debate over whether to spin hair over a bare hook or a thread base. Both will work. It's a bit easier with bare wire, but I think a more durable result is obtained when a thin thread base is in place. It's your call.

1. Tie on with some fairly strong thread. Then cut, clean out, and manicure a small bunch of soft, pulpy deer hair—the kind that lends itself to being spun. Try to work nearer to the butt than the tip end of the bunch, as that's where the best spinning hair is located.
2. Hold the bunch on top of the hook and take two thread wraps, each precisely on top of the one before. Use moderate tension—just enough to keep them in place.
3. As you begin the third thread wrap, apply firm tension and let go of the hair. It will be spun around the hook, and with luck, it will be even. Sometimes it needs to be tweaked a bit in order to even out the distribution and fill in bald spots.

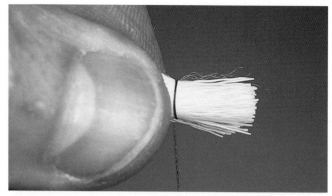

The gathering wraps, under moderate tension (step 2).

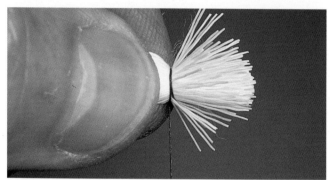

Tension is applied (step 3).

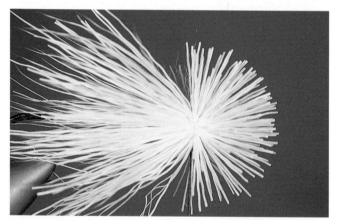

Firm tension spins the hair around the hook (step 3).

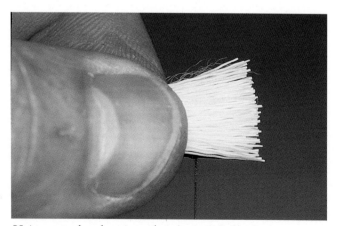

Hair prepared and set into place (steps 1 & 2).

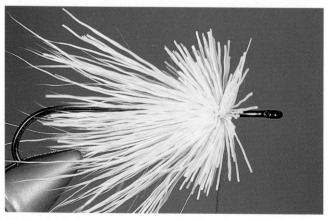

Hair is stroked upward and ready for trimming.

The Distribution Wrap

This is an interesting and useful technique in which a certain amount of tactile sensitivity is required. A little practice takes care of that, so don't be intimidated. Essentially, the purpose of the distribution wrap is to get materials to "walk" around the circumference of the hook, either partially or completely, in a controlled manner. The appropriate amount of tension and precisely where and how it is applied vary with the type and amount of material. A common application is that of tying legs onto a nymph.

1. After tying the fly up to the point where the legs go on, select the desired material. Here, I'm using cock ring-necked pheasant tail tips.
2. Hold the fibers in position against the far side of the hook with the left forefinger, but don't use the pinch technique.
3. Sneak the thread over the top under moderate tension. As it begins to come into contact with the material, allow some of the fibers to get tied in while the rest march ahead, impelled by the torque action of the thread, deploying evenly as they go. The idea is to affect about a 180-degree distribution around both sides and the bottom.

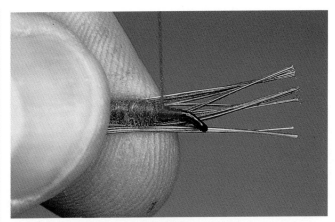

Begin the sneaky first wrap (step 3).

Continue the sneaky wrap (step 3).

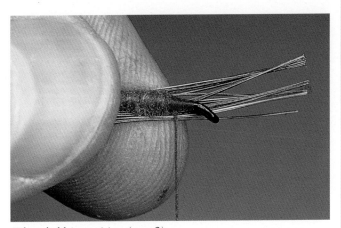

Fibers held in position (step 2).

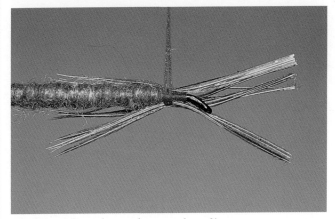

Further continue the sneaky wrap (step 3).

4. Follow up with another wrap or two under moderate tension. Inspect the results, and if necessary, adjust the distribution with your fingers before locking in the legs permanently.

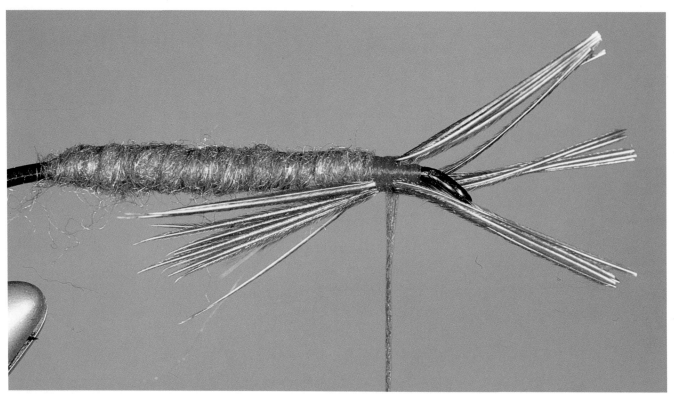

The result, side view.

The result, bottom view.

CHAPTER 4

Flank-Feather Wings

In *Mastering,* I used the Quill Gordon as a pattern lesson for typical, or Catskill classic, dry-fly tying. Perhaps the most important technique covered was the wood duck wing, which is fashioned from the flank feather of that bird. Here I will use the more ubiquitous Hendrickson as the prime teaching pattern instead, as the distribution of the Quill Gordon has been reduced by environmental degradation of various types. The Quill Gordon is presented later in the chapter, however, along with two other patterns that feature flank-feather wings but incorporate variations in the other components.

The flank-feather wing, and others of similar construction, are used on many popular flies. For example, the Wulff-type wing is tied in exactly the same manner, except that it is made of hair instead of feather. Winging the dry fly is perhaps the most challenging of all techniques for the beginner, and its mastery signifies a major advancement in a tier's career.

The insects that inspired the design of the various Hendrickson patterns are of the *Ephemerella* group. The archetypal Hendrickson dressings were designed to imitate *Ephemerella subvaria,* according to the late Art Flick, who was credited with originating the Red Quill, which imitates the male *E. subvaria.* The basic Hendrickson is attributed to the late Roy Steenrod of Livingston Manor, New York, who dates back to the legendary Theodore Gordon. Al Hendrickson was often Roy's fishing partner on the Beaverkill, hence the name of the pattern and of a productive and popular pool not far downstream from the junction of the Beaverkill and Willowemoc at Roscoe.

The dressing for the body of the original Hendrickson, as Roy designed it, had what was described as an elusive pinkish cast. He used a dubbing described as "the urine-burned fur from a vixen red fox." Try finding that in a fly shop or catalog! In reality, the color varies, as does the color of the natural from watershed to watershed. When an *E. subvaria* hatch is under way, the larger females do have a pinkish or lavenderish tint—a sort of rosy glow—just as they come off the water. This fades

quickly, but it's present at the time the trout have a shot at these morsels and is therefore of some importance.

Fortunately, this dubbing can be synthesized rather easily, and close approximations can be purchased in most fly shops. The one I liked best is no longer available. It was a synthetic fur called Andra Spectrum, a superb blend created by Dr. Fred Horvath in the 1970s. A close match can be obtained by mixing small amounts of soft, easily dubbed light pink, lavender, and pale gray fur. I play with the quantities until I like what I see. The exact kind of fur matters little; what does matter is the texture. For dry flies, I like dubbing that packs smoothly, without the spinning loop technique, and can thus be easily shaped. It can be natural, synthetic, or a mixture of the two. I pay less attention to its floating properties, leaving that to the hackle and tail and today's chemical enhancements.

NECK, OR CAPE, HACKLE

Rooster neck, or cape, hackle is used for this fly. Recent years have seen the development of what is known as genetic hackle—that grown and cultured specifically for the fly tier. A brief look at the development of hackle follows.

History

There are references to cock's hackles throughout British writings of the past several centuries. Frederick Halford, whose work was published around the turn of the twentieth century, is still known as the ultimate dry-fly purist. His patterns were exquisitely delicate and beautifully conceived. He was attentive to color to the point of fanaticism and was very concerned with such matters as the effect of floatants on the color of the finished fly. Halford used the best hackle then available, and he did remarkably well with it.

As a correspondent of Theodore Gordon's, Halford was instrumental in the development of dry-fly fishing in America. Gordon did not change a lot of what Halford had done, except to adapt his techniques to imitating the insects he observed on the streams he fished. The Quill

Gordon, of course, is the most well-known and enduring of these dressings.

I have seen Quill Gordons tied by the originator, and the hackle he had to work with was, by today's standards, very low-grade. This was a constant headache for him. Still, he managed to put together many functional and gracefully dressed flies.

Since the 1920s, a number of people have raised chickens expressly for their feathers—what we now call genetic hackle. Among them was Chip Stauffer, of northeastern Pennsylvania, who kept a small flock of birds that were very good for their time. He didn't kill his birds; he plucked them once a year.

Chip gave me some very interesting samples of his feathers, and a number of flies he had tied. He had some very pretty colors—grays, gingers, and such. The hackles were all on the larger side; a 12 was a small one. The barbs were quite stiff, and there was little web. If one liked tying variants and spiders, they were just the thing. And the tailing material was great.

Chip shared his feathers with cronies, people like Preston Jennings, and Art Flick, who took some broodstock and maintained a small flock of his own. I do not know if Chip did a lot of egg-swapping, but I assume he must have done some, as this would have been necessary to maintain a healthy gene pool.

In the 1930s, the Darbees and the Dettes—Harry and Elsie and Walt and Winnie—began a commercial tying business in the Roscoe, New York area, and were soon raising their own birds. The partnership didn't survive all that long, and when the two couples went their separate ways, so did the chickens. Harry and Elsie kept their flock in the backyard of their house on the Willowemoc near Livingston Manor, which also served as a shop. They produced a variety of colors, including buffs, gingers, browns, and barred rocks, but they were most noted for their gray birds, their duns.

As with Chip Stauffer's hackles, the quality was very good compared to what else was available in that era, and so the world beat a path to the Darbee's door. I remember a wealthy New Yorker paying Harry $60 for a prime dun neck in the 1960s. Most of us were tying with imported necks that seldom cost more than $5, and some less than $1.

Meanwhile, something extraordinary was happening in, of all places, Minneapolis. An attorney named Andy Minor had put together a flock of birds, acquiring breeders from various sources, including the Darbees. A meticulous man, Andy kept the flock rather small and scrupulously recorded every selective mating. His birds improved over time by several orders of magnitude over those from whom he had acquired his breeders.

In the late 1960s, Buck Metz of Belleville, Pennsylvania, began to assume a significant role in the hackle culture game. With the family's large egg and meat production farm at his disposal, Buck was able to grow quality hackle on a fairly large scale for the first time. I'm not sure where Buck's brood stock came from, but his feathers were welcomed with enthusiasm by tiers, myself included.

At about the same time, Andy Minor decided that he should arrange for the continuity of his work. Through a mutual friend, Howard West of the 3-M company, he was introduced to Ted Hebert, who happened to own a small farm in Laingsburg, Michigan, not far from Michigan State University. Some fertilized eggs changed hands, and Ted soon proved to be a most able custodian of the unique birds. Eventually, most of the brood stock was transferred to the Michigan farm. Over a period of more than a quarter of a century, under the watchful eye of Ted Hebert, the Minor birds improved even more.

Meanwhile, a California fly tier named Henry Hoffman was diligently scouring the county fairs for barred rocks, or grizzlies, as they are called, that appeared to have brood stock potential for hackle. Almost unheard of east of the Rockies, Henry meticulously refined and cultivated a most unique line of grizzlies that set a new standard in several categories of hackle quality, most significantly in the small-hackle department.

As the popularity of fly tying grew, people began to find out about Henry, and before long, he became almost a marked man. Tiers all over America and across the seas became fanatical in pursuit of his feathers. The best year Henry ever had yielded only 2200 saleable pelts, which at that time (the mid-1980s) was probably no more than 10 percent of the demand. I well recall being in Blue Ribbon Flies, in West Yellowstone, Montana, when a shipment from Henry arrived. Craig Matthews, the proprietor, took one look at the return address and hustled the box into the back room. It was almost like a drug deal. Thanks to fortunate timing and embarrassing persistence, I came away with one cape and one saddle.

Heretofore, saddles had found very little favor with dry fly tiers, and for good reason: they simply didn't have the characteristics for dry fly hackling. Henry changed all that, and with remarkable impact. His saddles not only enhanced the tying of the standard dry flies, but they enabled and inspired new designs. The Stimulator, a Pacific Northwest pattern, is a prime example.

In the late 1980s, an interesting young man appeared on the scene who would have an enormous impact on the raising of chickens for hackle. Tom Whiting, a fresh Ph.D. in poultry genetics in hand, proceeded to buy the Hoffman Supergrizzly flock and move the operation to western Colorado.

A comparison of hackle quality. Left: *a Hoffman grade 1 Supergrizzly;* right: *a so-so grizzly, which was labeled grade 1 dry fly.*

By the time of the sale, Henry had acquired some brown and cream birds and was slowly breeding in the grizzly quality. Tom began a rapid expansion of that program, carefully applying his knowledge of genetics and related sciences. Both the grizzlies and the other colored birds continued to improve, something most of us thought was impossible. The saddles in particular went through amazing development, and before long, hackle was being sold as much by the foot as by the pelt.

As the Whiting Farms birds set new standards of quality, Buck Metz decided it was time to cash in on his many years of hard work and sold his flock to Umpqua Feather Merchants, the large Oregon-based distributor. In addition to selling them on the general market, Umpqua uses the birds to supply its offshore commercial tying operation.

The latest major development, at this writing, is the merging of the Whiting and Hebert flocks. In 1997, Tom and Ted completed a deal under which the Hebert/Minor strain was transferred to Whiting Farms in the form of fertilized eggs. The transition went very well, and now Tom has lots of big, brawling, healthy duns, browns, and gingers. He tells me that the Hebert birds are so tough and aggressive that he's worried about putting the roosters in with his Hoffman-strain chickens.

Unless some bizarre form of genetic engineering occurs, the merging of the Hoffman and Hebert flocks puts Whiting Farms well out in front of the parade for the foreseeable future. Besides the exquisite dry fly hackle,

Tom is now raising birds that yield prime feathers for streamers, saltwater flies, salmon and steelhead flies, and all sorts of flies.

One last point of interest before we leave the historical portion of this narrative; both Tom Whiting and Ted Hebert became adept at dyeing pelts to enhance color. Ted did some unbelievable work with hair dyes that resulted in gorgeous coachman browns, straw creams, olive duns, and such. Tom and his staff also do excellent dye jobs, producing everything from jet black to lovely shades of gray. The good news is that these new processes do not affect feather quality, unlike the destructive processes of years past. These results should put to rest the outdated arguments against the use of dyed hackle.

What to Look for in Necks

Several characteristics constitute quality and value in a dry-fly neck, or cape.

• Fine, flexible quills.

• Stiff, strong, relatively web-free, barbs (the stiff tines that form the hackle). Web refers to softness along at the base of the barbs along the quill.

• High barb count on the quill, especially in the "sweet spot"—the area used to form hackle.

• Consistency of barb length, which is what determines size.

• Equal barb length on both sides of the quill.

• Beautiful coloration or sheen.

• Long "sweet spots," meaning quality throughout a large portion of the feather. (The sweet spot is the portion of prime quality and consistent size (barb length) on a feather.)

I consider quill fineness and flexibility the most important attribute. If the quill characteristics are first-rate, I can do a reasonably good job of applying hackle to a fly, even if the other points of quality are less than ideal. Fine, flexible quills enable close packing of barbs, do not get in their own way, and have much less of a tendency to twist or roll. With such feathers, tying is a joy instead of work.

Feathers that lie along the edges of capes and saddles tend to be somewhat asymmetrical, with longer barbs on one side of the quill than on the other. This is more prevalent on saddles than on capes. If the disparity is minor, the hackle will be suitable, but any significant difference in barb length will result in a messy, inefficient hackle. This is an important factor when purchasing capes and saddles. If you buy one through the mail and it lacks quality in this regard, send it back.

On small flies, it's possible to form an adequate hackle with one cape feather, given exceptional quality in all of the above attributes. This is rarely true on sizes larger than 16, however, even with the best of feathers. Usually two are required, and they must be matched precisely for uniformity of size.

Now let's tie a Hendrickson. If you don't have any nice wood duck flank feathers in your inventory, you can use dyed mallard or teal flank feathers, keeping in mind that they won't yield quite the same results.

There are three different methods for tying the wood duck wing, depending on the feathers at hand:

• Using one fairly large feather with a centered quill and a neat, uniform tip.

• Using two opposing sections cut from fairly large left and right feathers.

• Using two small feathers back-to-back.

The traditional Catskill classicists preferred the second method, as there was no quill to create bulk behind the tie-in spot of the wing. There are ways of dealing with this problem, however. Though the wood duck has made a remarkable comeback, it's still somewhat limited and fairly pricy, and you don't want to waste anything usable. The first method is the easiest, fastest, and most commonly used, so we'll start with that one.

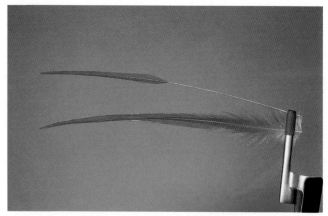

A high-grade dry-fly hackle, before and after being stripped back to the sweet spot.

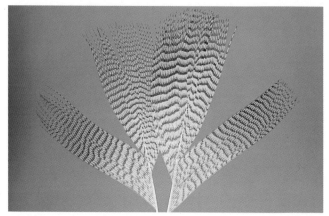

Two opposing wood duck feathers with sections suitable for winging.

Two small wood duck feathers suitable for being used together for wood duck wings.

Pink Hendrickson (female, E. Subvaria)

Hook	Standard dry fly, Daiichi model 1180 or comparable, size 10-14.
Thread	8/0 Uni-Thread or comparable, tan or light gray.
Wings	Wood duck flank.
Tail	Medium gray hackle fibers or substitute.
Body	Pink Hendrickson dubbing.
Hackle	Medium gray.

[Note: All tying instructions in this book are written for right-handers. If you're left-handed simply reverse the hand directions.]

1. Tie on just rear of the eye, and wrap a thread base on which to mount the wings, using two or three very neat layers of thread. The wraps should be next to one another. End up with the thread hanging about 25 to 30 percent of the shank length to the rear of the eye.

2. Select a good-size wood duck flank feather that has a fairly well-centered quill and is more-or-less even across the tip. Strip off the junky stuff and short fibers along the sides until it resembles the one in the photograph.

3. Inspect the feather, taking note of the quill. If it extends far enough out toward the tip that it would be involved in the wing, it should be pruned out by snipping the quill outside the tie-in spot. Don't go any further toward the butt than is absolutely necessary; you want to lose as little feather as possible.

4. Now fold and stroke the feather toward the tip, bringing all usable fibers together. Hold the delta of the feather—the part nearest the butt—with your left thumb and forefinger. With your other thumb and forefinger, stroke the fibers toward the tip and slightly downward so that the feather is folded and all of the fibers are evened up. This manipulation, if done properly, compensates for the small variations in the length of the fibers from the center to the edges.

5. When you're happy with the configuration of the bunch, measure the wing length. The wings should be just about equal to the length of the hook shank, from the eye to the beginning of the bend. This assumes that you're using a standard dry-fly hook, on which the shank is twice the gap. Adjust your grip so that you can cover the tie-in point with your fingers, which will allow you to execute the pinch wrap.

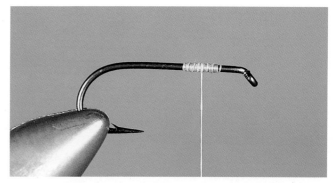

Tying on and forming a thread base for the wing (step 1).

A prime wood duck flank feather stripped of the waste material along the sides (step 2).

The feather was prepared for winging by notching out the center quill (step 3).

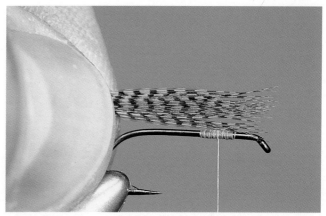

The wood duck fibers are drawn together and measured against the hook shank for wing length (steps 4 & 5).

6. Set the winging bunch atop the hook at the thread position, centering them with the shank. Roll your gripping fingers back a bit and sneak the thread in between them, bringing it straight upward.

7. You are now about to execute the most important thread management technique in fly tying: the pinch wrap. Roll your gripping fingers forward a bit, catching the thread, the hook, and the material. Now sneak the thread downward on the far side of the hook while controlling everything by pinching, applying pressure with the thumb and forefinger. This prevents the torquing action of the thread from pushing the winging material to the far side of the hook shank.

8. Maintain the pinch as the loop of thread disappears between your thumb and forefinger and tightens around the wing material. Pull straight downward until the pinch wrap is snugged up. Don't allow anything to slip.

9. Add two or three more pinch wraps, executing them just like the first one.

10. Carefully let go with your left hand, and inspect what you've done. If the wing is not tied on in the proper location, about 25 to 30 percent of the shank length to the rear of the eye, adjust or retie.

11. When you're happy with the tie-in, take a few wraps to the rear, but don't lock down the material completely. Now gently stroke the fibers directly upward, as though you were standing the wing up. This allows any errant fibers that slipped down around the hook on the back side to be restored to position atop the hook.

12. Lock in the winging material with some firm thread wraps just behind the wing, keeping everything smooth and neat.

13. With your right thumb, crimp the wood duck fibers into a virtually upright position to give them some memory.

The wood duck being set into position for tie-on (step 6).

The wood duck tied in place (steps 7–12).

Crimping the wing material to create memory (step 13).

14. Regrip the winging material, and while holding it upright or slightly beyond, wrap a dam of thread at the base, jamming it in against the front until the winging bunch stands up straight by itself.

15. With your scissors at an oblique angle, taper-cut the butt material. This sets things up for a properly shaped body later on.

16. While holding the winging fibers up out of the way with your left hand, bring the thread ahead of the wing by passing it beneath the thorax.

17. Looking down from above, separate the material into two equal bunches. You can divide them with anything that's handy—a dubbing needle, toothpick, or whatever.

18. Take hold of the wings-to-be and spread them with your fingers. This also builds in memory.

The wing butts trimmed, and the thread in position to form the wing (steps 15 & 16).

Dividing the winging bunch into equal portions (step 17).

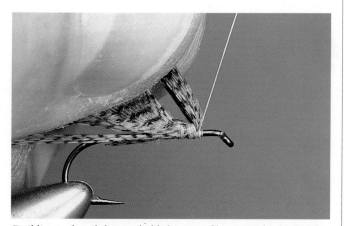

Building a thread dam to hold the wing fibers upright (step 14).

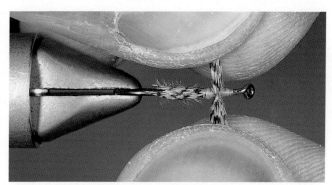

Separating the divided bunches (step 18).

The completed thread dam holds the wing fibers upright (step 14).

The divided bunches separated (step 18).

19. Now you will execute the first of the two thread procedures that establish, position, and secure the wings. I call it the X-wrap. Start with the thread ahead of the wings, and pass it back through the notch between the wings.

20. Bring the thread underneath the hook, up behind the wings, and back through the notch, ending up with the thread ahead of the wings on the far side of the hook. One X-wrap is usually enough, but if you feel that you need a second one, simply repeat the process.

21. The second thread procedure is the figure eight. It begins just like the X-wrap, but once the thread has passed below the plane of the hook to the rear, you bring it counterclockwise around the base of the feather until the wing base is encircled completely. Then pass the thread back between the wings and bring it directly down behind the near wing on the front side of the hook. During this operation, you must hold on to the far wing firmly and keep moderate but steady tension on the thread. Don't let go of the far wing until the thread is hanging straight down behind the near wing, with tension being maintained by the weight of the bobbin.

22. Repeat the process with the near wing, encircling the feather at the base. Don't let go of the near wing until the thread is hanging straight down behind the far wing, with tension being maintained by the weight of the bobbin.

23. Repeat the entire procedure, putting another figure eight on top of the first one, following all instructions carefully. That should lock the wings in place permanently.

The X-wrap (steps 19 & 20).

The figure eight (steps 21–23).

The figure eight (steps 21–23).

The X-wrap (steps 19 & 20).

The finished wing, angle view.

24. If you didn't do so earlier, taper-cut the wing butts on a long slope, then cover them neatly with thread, wrapping rearward to the bend.

25. The tail needs to be fanned out a bit, which can be achieved by one of two methods: wrapping a tiny ball of thread—just two or three turns—precisely to the rear of where the tail fibers are tied on or slipping a couple turns of thread under the tail after tying it on. Either method will cause the barbs to spread a little. The body dubbing will hide the thread. The less contrast between the thread and the dubbing, the less of a problem hiding the tail-spreading wraps.

26. Select the tailing material. If you have feathers with long, stiff barbs that will make good tails, you can gather them from the quill in one of two ways: If the feather is symmetrical, (if the barbs are the same length on either side of the quill) you can fold the feather by stroking all barbs to one side and gather the tailing bunch from the barbs thus concentrated. If the feather is not symmetrical, you should work with only one side at a time or the tips of the tailing bunch won't match up well. To fold the feather, stretch the quill between your two hands, and stroke the barbs downward and slightly rearward until they all lie to one side of the quill. Then take hold of a small bunch by the tips and either cut or pull them from the quill. Keep in mind that you'll need the thumb and forefinger of your tying hand free to manipulate the feather. It's helpful to attach a pair of hackle pliers to the butt end so that you can hold on with the lower fingers of your right hand.

27. The tail should be the length of the hook shank or a tiny bit longer. The fly should be able to rest on the tips of the tail and the hackle, with the point of the hook clearing, or barely touching, the surface on which it rests. Gauge the length, then tie in the bunch precisely atop the hook, forcing the fibers back against the thread ball.

The taper-cut wing butts bound down, thread in position for the tailing procedure (step 24).

The tailing bunch (step 26).

Measure the tailing material for length (step 27).

Tie it in place (step 27).

28. Ideally, the tail butts should dovetail with the wing butts to create a perfectly smooth underbody. Unfortunately, they aren't always long enough to do that. With a fur body, minor nonlinearities in the underbody can be hidden with discreet dubbing, but with quill bodies, that's tough. One advantage Micro Fibetts provide over natural feathers is adequate length for configuring the underbody. In any event, apply a couple layers of thread, wrapping almost to the wing and back to smooth everything out.

29. Whatever the texture of your dubbing material, tease it out and apply it in small wisps, with the fibers lying parallel to the thread as closely as possible. Spin it on in very small quantities, gradually building up and shaping a "worm" of material on the thread so that it will form the desired body shape. The most common mistake is to apply too much material; refer to the photo for proportions.

30. As you wrap the dubbed material, respin as necessary to keep it tight and well packed. If you find that you need to remove a bit of it, back off a wrap or two, pick off the excess, and respin. If you must add a bit, do so before you run out so as to maintain shape and continuity. Remember, the body should end just behind the wing so that the hackle positioned behind the wing is not wrapped over any body material.

Dubbing should be teased out before being spun onto the thread (step 29).

Spinning on the dubbing (step 29).

Wrapping the body (steps 29 & 30).

The tail in place, underbody wrapped, thread in position for dubbing the body (step 28).

The completed body. Note the thread position (step 30).

31. The rule of thumb is that the hackle on a conventional dry fly is one and a half times the gape of the hook. This is measured by flexing the feathers into a simulation of the wrapped position and observing them in relation to the gape. Inexperienced tiers may find a hackle gauge helpful here. However, the hackle gauge doesn't take into account any buildup resulting from the winging process, so a feather that measures, for example, a full size 12 on the gauge may come out somewhat oversize on the fly, depending on how much buildup has occurred. Here, I have selected two cape feathers that are equal in barb length. Prepare the feathers by stripping off all waste material nearest the butt end of the quill until only the sweet spot remains.

32. Lay the feathers together spoon style, and tie them in by the butt ends, pretty side forward, against the bottom of the hook just behind the wing, keeping in mind that the idea is to distribute the hackle fairly evenly behind and in front of the wings. Leave the tiniest bit of bare quill exposed, as this will permit the feather to rotate into proper position with regard to the hook shank before any barbs peel off.

33. Try to smooth out the areas fore and aft of the wing with discreet thread wraps, but avoid creating unnecessary bulk. The thread should end up near the front but not crowding the eye.

34. One of the feathers will be just in front of the other. This one is wrapped first. Hold it by the tip with your hackle pliers, and begin to wrap over and away. The wraps should abut each other, working forward. Don't leave spaces in between; the second feather will find the little niches on its own. Start behind the wing, and when you reach the rear of the wing, cross over underneath. Then continue on to the thread position.

35. Tie off the first feather with a series of firm wraps, but use no more than necessary. Keep in mind that the second feather will further secure this one. Before wrapping the second feather, trim any stray barbs from the first one.

36. Wrap the second feather as you did the first. If a wrap doesn't appear to seat properly, back off and do it over again, perhaps varying the angle or tension a bit. The idea is to balance out the hackle fore and aft of the wings.

The hackle feathers tied in. Note the tiny length of bare quill at the tie-in point (steps 31 & 32).

The first hackle feather is wrapped rearward of the wing (step 34).

The first hackle feather completely wrapped, tied off, and trimmed (step 35).

The second hackle feather is wrapped through the first (step 36).

37. When you reach the thread position, tie off the second feather. Trim off any errant barbs before doing the whip finish.

Tying off the second hackle feather (step 37).

Remove the fly from the vise and set it on your tying table. Does it balance properly, with the hook barely clearing or just touching the surface? If not, try to assess what needs to be adjusted when you tie the next one.

Hendricksons vary considerably in color. Besides the variations in *E. subvaria,* there are two other closely related mayflies in the greater Northeast that are commonly called Hendricksons and occur within the same general time frame. So you might want to use different colors than called for here. It's best to know what the bugs look like where you fish.

The tail on a conventional dry fly serves dual purposes of balance and flotation, but I'm not sure what image it conveys to the fish. It certainly doesn't look like the tails on a natural insect. Possibly it serves to represent the dragging shuck of a semiemergent dun.

You may need to use a substitute for the hackle tail because it's getting harder to find good tailing barbs. The traditional material comes from the long-barbed feathers around the edge of a cape, commonly known as spade hackles or throat hackles. Many generations of breeding for small hackle has had a negative effect on these precious feathers, and on many capes, they have all but disappeared. This is a shame.

The finished fly, side view.

An acceptable substitute is a packaged synthetic material known as Micro Fibetts, although they're not as good as prime hackle barbs. If I had to take a wild guess, I'd have to say that they are nylon paintbrush bristles. They come in a wide assortment of colors, so they can be matched pretty closely with the hackle. Micro Fibetts must be spread in order to create a snowshoe effect. This is true for natural hackle barbs as well, but it's an absolute must with the synthetics. If they're tied in a bunch, they'll simply wick up water, and the rear end of the fly will be sunk. If they're spread properly, however, the snowshoe phenomenon provides adequate flotation.

Note that I've described the hackle as medium gray rather than dun. By this, I hope to reduce the ambiguity and confusion over all the variations of dun. In America, it is accepted that dun is gray and medium dun is medium gray. Then we get into the many shades, subtones, and overtones—pale watery dun, dark dun, rusty dun, olive dun, honey dun. These can be very beautiful, but describing them accurately is virtually impossible; you have to see them.

The finished fly, angular view.

The Red Quill is the ever-popular Art Flick pattern of the thirties that is still a good match for the male *E. subvaria* Hendrickson. The males are a little smaller, so I usually tie the Red Quill in size 14. You can use a slightly darker shade of gray for the hackle and tail if you wish, but that's not critical. Except for the body, all components are the same as for the female.

Red Quill

Hook	Standard dry fly, Daiichi model 1180 or comparable, size 10-14.
Thread	8/0 Uni-Thread or comparable, tan or light brown, size 14.
Wings	Wood duck flank.
Tail	Medium gray hackle fibers or substitute.
Body	A stripped quill from a brown rooster cape.
Hackle	Medium gray.

1. Tie the wings and tail following the instructions for the Pink Hendrickson. In the photo, I'm using Micro Fibetts for the tail to ensure sufficient butt length to smooth out the underbody. Take particular notice of how the tail butts and wing butts are integrated to form the base.
2. Tie in a stripped quill by the tip end, trimming back a little to obtain the desired thickness. Then bind the excess smoothly along the hook shank, integrating it with the underbody. Stop just short of the wings.
3. Wrap the quill, each wrap abutting the previous one. Tie off as neatly as possible, leaving space for the hackle, as was done on the Pink Henderson. As quills are round and hard, the tie-off and trimming can be a bit problematical. You can flatten the tie-off spot with a pinch or two from a pair of fine-nosed pliers, if you wish. Also, you can bind the excess quill along the far side of the hook, working behind and then in front of the wing before cutting off the tag. Trim on a slope to avoid creating a stump.

The tail tied in (step 1).

The quill tied in, underbody formed (step 2).

The quill being wrapped (step 3).

The butts of a bunch of Micro Fibetts taper-cut (step 1).

The completed quill body (step 3).

4.   Complete the fly by applying hackle, and whip-finish.

You need to coat the finished body with something, as these flies are rather fragile. Stand the finished fly on its nose and apply a thin layer of Zap-A-Gap or similar superglue. Don't get any of it on the tail or wings. I suggest you tie as many flies as you want, then do all the reinforcing at one sitting.

Years ago, inexpensive stripped quills in strung bundles were readily available. The quills were fairly thick compared with those on a modern genetic cape, producing attractive segmentation. The color ranged from medium brown to ginger, which accommodated several highly popular flies.

I haven't seen these stripped quills for a while, so I checked with Leila Wilder, coproprietor of Hunter's Angling Supplies along with her husband, Nick. She told me that now and then she is able to buy a batch, but supplies are inconsistent and often hard to track down. Therefore, unless you can locate a supplier, you'll need to strip your own quills. This is easy enough: Simply remove all barbs from the large feathers found at the rear of a medium brown cape. I prefer to strip a lot of quills at one sitting and preserve them by placing them in a small bottle with a mixture of one-quarter hair conditioner and three-quarters water. This also keeps them soft and pliable. When you're ready to use them, simply dry each quill on a paper towel. If you wish, you can flatten a quill a little by laying it on a hard surface and drawing a dull-edged object over it, such as the outside of a scissor blade.

Although the Quill Gordon natural is not so common these days, you may sometimes encounter good hatches on smaller streams that have escaped pollution and other forms of environmental degradation. Therefore, it's still useful to know how to tie the imitation. The Quill Gordon is tied the same way as the Red Quill, except that the body is made from the stripped quill of a frond taken from the eyed portion of a peacock tail feather.

These quills stubbornly resist being stripped of their herl, and you may be tempted to use fronds from down the stalk, which can be cleaned off with a thumbnail. However, these lack the light-and-dark segmentation that characterizes the body of this fly, although they do make nice bodies for other mayfly patterns. There are three methods for stripping peacock eye fronds:

• Simply rub off the fuzz with the coarse side of an ink/pencil eraser. This produces good results, but it's slow and a bit tedious.

• Bring some water to a boil in a small saucepan. Drop in a teaspoonful of paraffin, and allow it to melt and spread over the surface of the water. Take the pan off the burner, and immerse a whole peacock eye, withdrawing it slowly (about two or three seconds). The paraffin will coat the feathers and will harden in a minute or so. Individual

The hackle feather tied in (step 4).

The completed fly.

fibers can then be removed and stripped with a thumbnail. This produces good results, but it's a bit messy.

• Pour a little Clorox into a sauce dish. Prepare a stop bath by mixing a heaping tablespoon of baking soda with a cup of water, and have it at hand. Swish the peacock eye around in the Clorox. The herl will soon be eaten off the quills. The instant you can see that the quills are bare, immerse the eye in the stop bath. Then rinse with water. This method is quick and convenient, but the quills come out somewhat brittle, and some of the coloration and breadth can be lost. Immersion in a solution of one-quarter hair conditioner and three-quarters water helps counteract the brittleness.

Before going to the trouble of stripping these quills, first determine whether they have good contrast. Early on, I observed that if I squeezed the eye of a peacock tail feather between the thumb and forefinger and looked at it from the back side, it would emit a pale-colored flash if it had good contrast. I thought that I'd originated this technique, but while restudying Jim Leisenring's *The Art of Tying the Wet Fly,* first published in 1941, I found that he had used exactly the same technique. Leisenring also describes another method for cleaning peacock quills. You grab a quill with hackle pliers, lay it on a piece of cardboard, and draw it under a needle. This will work, but it is slow, tedious, and fraught with peril, as these quills break fairly easily. Also, it's necessary to change directions several times during the process, holding the quill first by one end, then by the other. Try it if you wish.

Quill Gordon

Hook	Standard dry fly, Daiichi model 1180 or comparable, size 12-14.
Thread	8/0 Uni-Thread or comparable, greenish olive, tan, or light gray.
Wings	Wood duck flank.
Tail	Light to medium gray hackle fibers or substitute.
Body	A stripped peacock quill.
Hackle	Light to medium gray.

The segmented effect is best achieved when the dark edge of the peacock quill lies to the rear during wrapping. This means that the quill should be tied in that way. The fronds from either side of the main center quill have the dark edges on opposite sides. This is easily compensated for, as you can tie them in by either the butt or tip end. When tied in by the tip end, segmentation will result, with the reticulations progressively wider with each wrap. The same effect can be achieved with a quill tied in by the butt end simply by controlling the width of the reticulations by overlapping a bit. I prefer the butt-end tie-in, as the contrast is more vivid.

An interesting "quill" body can be formed by taking three moose mane hairs, two dark and one light, and wrapping them all at once. This works best if the light-colored one is rearmost throughout the procedure, although it will come out all right otherwise, so long as the order in which the hairs are wrapped is maintained throughout—in other words, no crossovers. This body also requires the superglue treatment. A number of years ago, I designed a fly pattern that incorporates this body. I call it the Teal-Winged Adams Quill. This is one of the most useful general patterns I've found. I've used it to simulate, if not match, a number of stream insects, and it also serves as a good probing fly. I tie it in sizes 8 to 16. If you can tie the other flies in this chapter, you can tie this one as well.

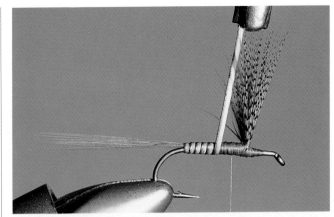

A peacock quill being wrapped.

The completed body.

The finished fly.

Teal-Winged Adams Quill

Hook	Standard dry fly, Daiichi model 1180 or comparable, size 8-16.
Thread	8/0 Uni-Thread or comparable, black or brown.
Wings	Barred teal flank feathers, tied wood duck style.
Tail	Mixed brown and grizzly hackle fibers.
Body	Moose mane "quill" effect.
Hackle	Mixed brown and grizzly hackle fibers.

The mixed tail on this fly can be a little difficult to tie properly. I have developed two methods that both work well. For either method, start by selecting two feathers, a brown and a grizzly, with long enough barbs for tails.

• *Method 1.* Match up the tips of the barbs so that they're even, and simply remove them all in one operation. Then tie them on in the usual manner.

• *Method 2.* Remove a bunch of barbs from one or the other sufficient for half a tail. Tie it on with just two turns of thread. Select an equal bunch from the other feather. Hold it on top of the first bunch with your left hand, and get the tips even. Then hold both bunches together and back off the thread wraps, thus untying the first bunch. Roll the two bunches between your fingers a bit to mix them, then tie them on as one.

Two opposing teal sections convex-to-convex.

The finished wing, angular view.

Starting the mixed tail, using method 2.

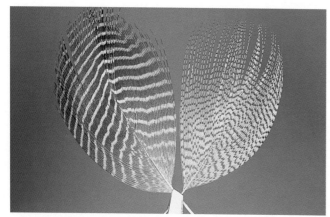

A comparison of barred flank feathers, teal on the left, mallard on the right.

Adding the second tailing bunch, per method 2.

The completed tail.

The first hackle wrapped—in this case, the brown.

The moose mane fibers tied in.

The completed fly.

The completed body.

The hackle feathers tied in.

CHAPTER 5

Wulffmanship

The Wulff dressings are unique and imminently practical flies dating back to 1931. They were designed by Lee Wulff for the brawling freestone rivers of the mountainous Northeast. Lee found that the delicate Halford-type dry flies that had traditionally produced on the placid chalk streams of England and Normandy did not adapt well to typical American conditions, and he set about to solve the problem. I would say that he did so admirably.

The Wulff family has grown considerably since the advent of Lee's two original dressings, the White Wulff and the Gray Wulff, which I believe were the only ones he actually originated. I would guess that there are two dozen Wulffs at this writing, and that may be a conservative estimate.

The only tricky aspect of Wulff tying is doing the wings, but once you've learned that, it becomes pretty easy. Tying Wulff wings follows the same procedure as for the flank-feather wings, except that it's applied to a bunch of hair. The two combined techniques, the X-wrap and the figure eight, are the same as for the wood duck flank wing.

Wulff wings can be made from calf tail, which was Lee's favorite, as well as bucktail. Smaller Wulffs require finer hairs, such as calf body hair or certain kinds of goat hair. There are a few important considerations involved in preparing and handling the material.

Understanding how to properly use a stacker is the key. This enables you to work with less bulk, as once stacked, all of the hairs become part of the wing silhouette. The penalty you pay for not cleaning out the bunch and evening up the tips can be rather harsh, as unmanageable bulk at the tie-in point gets really nasty.

No matter what type of hair you're working with, selection is all important. With calf tail, for example, length is not the primary criterion. More important are texture and relative straightness—relative, because no calf tail has really straight hairs. As to texture, some tails have much stiffer hairs than others, and though they may be usable on larger hook sizes, they're not pleasant to work with.

Calf body and goat hair, which can also be great Wulff winging materials, tend to be somewhat straighter and a little softer than calf tail hair, and a lot more manageable. The only drawback is that they tend to be on the short side. If you can find some that runs about an inch (25 millimeters) in length, buy it and treasure it.

Bucktail or, more properly, deer tail, as we probably don't know for sure what sex the animal was, may not appear to be a viable winging material, but it actually works quite well. Here again, selection is important. You'll want the smaller, finer-textured tails for making Wulff wings. These hairs run much straighter than calf tail and result in a somewhat different look. Lee sometimes chided me about my wings, saying that they were too neat. Lee liked rough-looking flies, and who would argue the point with him? Not me, for sure, but I still prefer to make them at least somewhat tidy. With calf tail, even the neatest wings are still quite bushy.

Lee also used calf tail for his tailing material, and judging from the number of fish he caught, it obviously worked. However, I prefer a straighter hair, such as bucktail, moose body, or woodchuck tail. I advocate stacking these hair bunches, because I feel that the neater the tips, the better the balance. On smaller hook sizes, I prefer to use feather barbs for tailing. I don't worry about the color of the tail all that much. If it doesn't quite match the wing color, no big deal.

In consideration of the types of currents in which Wulffs are fished, I use somewhat more hackle than with more delicate, insect-specific dry flies. Either cape or saddle feathers will work, but I prefer high-quality saddles. The barb strength and count, along with the very narrow quills, have virtually revolutionized the way we tie Wulff-style hackles. It's now possible to dress a medium to large Wulff with a single feather of this type, as the ultrafine quill causes the hackle to pack densely, and the high barb count yields a generous amount of hackle per turn. All that's required is to leave enough space behind and in front of the wings. You can use two feathers, either saddle or cape, and may need to do so out of necessity when the hackle requires a mix of brown and grizzly. With the long saddle feathers, it's often possible to wrap them both at the same time, but that doesn't always work, and it's not a procedure I would recommend for the beginning tier. If you do want to give it a try, don't use hackle pliers. The feathers have to slip around a little between your fingers in order to compensate for small but significant differences in circumference.

When gauging these high-grade saddle feathers for size, you must flex them into the wrapped position and observe the barbs carefully. The barbs are so stiff, and lie at such a severe angle along the quill, that when they are actually wrapped into a hackle, they come out a size or two larger than they first appeared. This is somewhat true of cape feathers as well, but to a lesser degree.

There are several sources of trouble that cause more wing-related headaches than everything else combined. Probably the worst mistake is trying to use too much material.

Using too much hair for the wings causes the wing butts to be thicker than necessary. This gets you into trouble when it comes to hackling the fly, not only because of excess bulk, but also because of asymmetry. There is no wing butt material ahead of the wings, which means that the hackle has two unequal diameters around which to travel. There is also a bit of a problem with hairwings that results from the presence of the wing butts on top of the hook. This causes there to be two different planes, or levels, on top of the hook shank. There is also a difference in diameter, but that could be compensated for by simply building up in front with discreet thread wraps. That, however, won't effectively solve the two-level problem. Unless the wing butts are really bulky, the problem may be so minor that it can simply be ignored, but in extreme cases, you might want to do something to reduce the disparity. Some careful thread work to simply smooth things out may be sufficient, but on larger flies, you need to shim up the front a little.

If the problem isn't too severe, the disparity can be compensated for quite effectively by tying in the hackle feathers by the quill butts ahead of, rather than behind, the wing and on top of, rather than beneath, the hook, thereby using the quill butts to compensate for and balance out the wing butts. Hold the feathers under moderate tension with your left hand. Then lock in the quills with neat, tight thread wraps, working rearward. When you reach the wings, move the feathers downward and bind the quills to the near side of the hook, wrapping back to the front of the body. Then wrap forward again, and trim short of the eye. Neaten and even up as necessary with some discreet thread wraps. The idea is to create as even and flat a base as possible. Then wrap the

feathers and finish off the fly in the usual manner. This alternative method for tying in hackle feathers may seem tricky, but with a bit of practice, you'll master it.

In more severe cases, a supplemental material can be used as a shim. I prefer a smooth, fine yarn such as polypropylene. On large flies, it can be used as it comes from the package. On smaller flies, it can be reduced. This process should be done after the winging bunch has been stood up but before the wing is configured.

A second mistake is not manicuring the winging bunch properly and thoroughly. It's important to get rid of all the junk and short stuff in the bunch and to work with only those hairs that will contribute to the formation of the wings. One of the most useful tools in working with hairs is a little fine-toothed comb. It can be used to clean out the trashy stuff, the shorties and the underfur, and to unlock the kinky hairs so that they can be evened up in a stacker.

Proper preparation is especially important with calf tail, which can be difficult to stack. You'll need that fine-toothed comb, as well as a wide-tubed stacker. The first thing you should do when you buy a new calf tail is to thoroughly comb it; you'll be amazed at the junk that you remove. Remember: you can stack small bunches of hair with a big stacker, but you can't work on big bunches with a small one. This is especially true with calf tail, because of its kinky texture, which causes the hairs to billow out and bind inside the tube. Combing toward the tip ends a few times will unlock the hairs bound together by the natural twists in the material.

A third mistake is not sizing the wings properly. Tiers often have a tendency to make the wings too tall. Hairwings are somewhat heavier than other types of dry fly wings and too long a wing will cause the fly to tip over on its side on the water. Assuming a standard length hook, the height of the wing should be equal to the length of the hook shank.

The pattern presented here is the Ausable Wulff, originated by Francis Betters, the proprietor of a fishing-supply shop on the west branch of New York's Ausable for many years. The unique flies he designed are ideal for this rather intimidating yet always exciting stream.

The body material was originally the orangy or amber fur from an Australian opossum. That's still the standard recipe. If you have trouble finding it, however, don't hesitate to use a substitute. There are several beautiful dubbing mixes on the market today that work at least as well as the original material. One I like in particular is sold under the brand name of Ligas Scintilla. There are several shades that are similar to the opossum, and to each other. Use whatever looks right, as there is a lot of variation in the shade of the natural material.

Fran Betters ties the body of this fly by applying the dubbing in such a way that allows the thread color to shine through a bit. Using a liquid fly floatant helps. On larger flies, it helps to use the spinning-loop, or double-thread, dubbing method, rather than the single-thread. This is something I usually don't recommend on dry flies, but in this case, it does serve a purpose. The spinning-loop method of dubbing is presented here, but you can use the simple single-thread method if you prefer. The spinning-loop method usually produces a thicker body, which is desirable on flies of this type.

Fran used Danville hot orange thread, which is fluorescent. You can substitute something else, but for authenticity, it should be similar to the Danville product. Uni-Thread Fire Orange is nice.

Ausable Wulff

Hook	Standard dry fly, Daiichi model 1180 or comparable, size 8-14.
Thread	Bright red or hot orange 6/0 or 8/0.
Wings	White calf tail or substitute.
Tail	Woodchuck tail, moose body hair, or brown bucktail.
Body	Orangy or amber Australian opossum fur or substitute.
Hackle	Brown and grizzly mixed.

1. Tie on just rearward of the eye and create a thread base on which to mount the wings, ending up with the thread about 25 to 30 percent of the shank length to the rear of the eye, depending on how you want to deploy the hackle, front and back. I prefer 30 percent, as I like plenty of hackle in front of the wings.
2. Cut off a small bunch of the hair, and prepare it by cleaning out the junk, combing out the tips, and stacking them or evening them up manually.
3. Hold the winging bunch in your left hand, and measure the length against the hook shank. Then set it onto the thread base and tie it in place, using either a series of pinch wraps or a couple of soft gathering wraps, followed by some securing wraps. Before locking the bunch down completely, gently stroke the hairs into an upright position a few times. This allows any hairs that have rolled off to the far side to be brought back on top, where they belong. It is important that all of the hairs are squarely on top of the hook.

Comb out both the butts and tips of the winging hair (step 2).

Evening up the tips in a wide-tubed stacker (step 2).

The hair tied in (step 3).

4. Take a few more firm wraps, then trim off the butts on a long slope. It's easier to do this before standing the wings upright. Now wrap to the rear and back, covering the sloped wing butts; this helps stabilize this slippery hair.

5. With the hair thus secured so that it won't slip under pressure, crimp it into standing position with your thumb, thus creating some memory. Then, holding the hair upright with your left hand, build a dam of thread against the front. You'll need quite a few wraps in order to position the wing directly upright, but don't use more than necessary. As you're building this dam, run the thread toward the eye and back now and then, smoothing things out so that you don't create a bump that will interfere with wrapping hackle later on.

6. Now form the wing, following the instructions for the flank-feather wing. Divide the hair into two equal bunches using a dubbing needle, toothpick, or other implement. Then take hold of the two bunches with your thumbs and forefingers, and spread them so that they assume a winglike attitude.

7. Shape, position, and secure the wings with the X-wrap and figure eight sequences as described for the flank-feather wing. Sometimes, with larger Wulff-type wings, a double-wrap figure eight is helpful. You simply put a second wrap of thread 360 degrees around the base of the far wing immediately after the first one, before crossing back between the wings. Work with the tube of the bobbin pointing downward. Follow the same procedure with the near wing, applying tension throughout. The only tricky part is that you have to let go of the wing for a moment in order to position the thread for the second encirclement. If you're careful to keep the thread tight to the base of the wing, it won't slip off the end of the hair.

8. Wrap neatly to the bend. Then cut a small bunch of hair for the tail, and prepare it as you would a winging bunch. Gauge the length; it should be equal to or slightly longer than the hook shank.

9. Here's a little trick that will help you obtain a smooth, shapely underbody. Before tying the tail hair in place, precut it on a taper that complements the wing butts. Then lay it in place precisely on top of the hook, and tie it on as you would a winging bunch.

10. Cover the tail butts with thread, wrapping almost to the wings and back to the bend.

The butts trimmed and bound down (step 4).

The hair bunch standing up (step 5).

The finished wing, front view (steps 6 & 7).

Integrating the slope-cut tail butts with the wing butts (steps 8–10).

11. To perform the spinning-loop, or double-thread, method of dubbing, start by exposing a few inches of thread, and spin on a slightly tapered layer of fur, as shown. Work progressively with small, teased-out wisps. Try to be precise, as it is difficult to adjust quantities with a spinning loop after it is formed.

12. Just beyond where the fur ends, grab the thread with your hackle pliers, and hold it under tension. Form a loop by running out some more thread and wrapping it over the hook right where the dubbed thread is positioned. Then wrap forward to where you want the body to end. Make sure you leave space for plenty of hackle behind the wings.

Spinning on the dubbing (step 11).

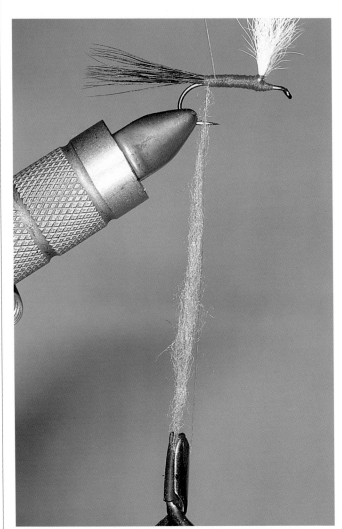

Forming the spinning loop (step 12).

13. Let the hackle pliers hang. Then spin them in a clockwise direction until the dubbing is tightly configured. The behavior of the material will tell you when you've spun it enough.

14. Now wrap the body, using the hackle pliers throughout. If you find that you have some material left over, tie it down where you want the body to end, let the hackle pliers hang so that the material unspins, then trim off the excess and secure the tag end with some tight thread wraps. Leave space for the hackle to follow.

15. Dry-fly-grade saddle hackles are best for such flies. It's important that the two feathers be equal in barb length. While sizing them, keep in mind that the diameter of the wing butt increases the length of the hackle proportionately, and the wing butt on a Wulff is thicker than most. Strip back to where prime quality begins, as covered in the flank-feather wing chapter.

The dubbing after it has been twisted (step 13).

The body in place (step 14).

16. If you see a need to shim up in front of the wings with the hackle quills, do so now. Hold the feathers under moderate tension with your left hand, then lock in the quills with neat, tight thread wraps, working rearward. When you reach the wings, move the feathers downward and bind the quills to the near side of the hook, wrapping back to the front of the body. Then wrap forward again, and trim short of the eye. Neaten and even up as necessary with some discreet thread wraps.

17. Wrap the first hackle, beginning at the front of the body, crossing over at the thorax, and continuing on to the tie-off point, leaving adequate space for tying off the second feather and doing the whip finish. Don't skimp on the hackle on these flies. Before wrapping the second feather, take care of any trimming and neatening required by the tie-off of the first feather.

18. Wrap the second hackle, integrating it neatly with the first one. If you notice any conflict with the hackle already in place, back off a turn, and rewrap with a slight adjustment.

19. Tie off the second feather, neaten up, and do a whip finish. If your fly looks rough, don't worry—their originator liked them rough.

Once you can tie this type of fly, it's useful to learn the Royal Coachman body so that you'll be able to tie the Royal Wulff and several similar patterns. The Royal Coachman body uses peacock herl, a wonderful material used in many historic killer flies. It can be purchased either in bundles or by the tail. For streamer fly tying, where peacock is frequently used in a different manner, you'd be better advised to use the shapely fronds off the tails. For this application, the bundled material works fine. The Green River Wulff, or SteppenWulff, as I call it, uses the Royal Coachman body. I was introduced to this fly on the Green River in Utah. It was a huge hit with the big browns on the freestone rivers of New Zealand, especially when dressed with (can you believe it?) a bright red wing!

Using the hackle quills to shim up in front of the wings (step 16).

The hackles, ready for wrapping (step 16).

The finished fly (steps 17–19).

SteppenWulff, or Green River Wulff

Hook	Standard dry fly, Daiichi model 1180 or comparable, size 8-14.
Thread	Black 6/0 or 8/0.
Wings	White calf tail or similar hair.
Tail	Same as for the Ausable Wulff, or white, such as calf tail or bucktail.
Body	Two short sections of peacock herl with a bright green belly band in between.
Hackle	Mixed brown and grizzly, preferably Hoffman saddle.

1. Tie in the wings and tail in the same manner as for the Ausable Wulff.
2. Select four or five peacock herl fronds, even up the tip ends, cut them back a little to get rid of the most fragile portion, and tie them in by the tips. In securing them, form a thread loop as though you intended to do a spinning-loop dubbed body. The loop should be about as long as the fronds.
3. Wrap back over the threads to the rear, locking in the loop so that it doesn't matter which end you use. Then cut off one side of the loop and trim it to the length of the peacock. Be sure that both the peacock and the thread are side by side at the bend of the hook, with no space between the two, or the thread will come across the peacock and may cut it. If you find it easier to simply tie in another piece of thread instead of doing the loop process, you may do so.
4. Pick up the tag end of thread, and start twisting it and the peacock fronds together. Don't take too many twists at first, as the thread might sever the herl.
5. Wrap the twisted herl and thread around the hook, forming a small ball of herl. If you run into difficulty with the twisting, you can use an electronics clip or regular hackle pliers.
6. Bind the herl and thread to the hook, covering it neatly, creating space and a thread base for the center portion of the body. Leave the herl hanging to the front, as it will be used to form another bump, which is the third segment of the body.
7. For the belly band, you may use any floss or flosslike material you happen to have on hand. On larger hook sizes, you can even use yarn if you wish. At the front end of the thread base just created, tie in a short piece of this material.

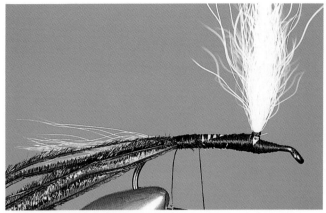

Wings and tail completed, peacock herl tied in, reinforcing thread in place (steps 1–3).

The first body segment completed (steps 4–6).

The base wrapped for the belly band, with the material tied in (step 7).

8. Wrap a little belly band, working to the rear and then forward, forming a double layer. Secure it and trim off the excess.

9. Wrap the thread forward a bit, then pick up the herl and thread, retwist, and make another little ball, staying well behind the wings. Then tie off and trim the peacock.

10. From here on, it's the same as for the Ausable Wulff.

Not all hairwing flies are part of the Wulff pack, but the winging techniques learned here will enable you to tie a wide variety of patterns. Hairwing dry flies are wonderful in the proper environment. They work great in faster water, and sometimes even in slower currents. They can be used as strike indicators by suspending a nymph or something below the main fly on a dropper. Once in a while you might hook two fish at once, one on the dropper and one on the hairwing—always a thrill.

The belly band in place (step 8).

The completed body (step 9).

The completed fly (step 10).

CHAPTER 6

Tippet Wings

The Adams has been written up many times, but no fly better illustrates the techniques involved in tying the hackle-tippet wing. Most of the tying steps are the same as for the flank-feather wing. For the Adams, you merely need to learn about the winging material and how to use it. After that, you can learn some of the innovative designs that incorporate this type of wing.

The original Adams was tied by Len Halliday, a noted pre-World War II tier from Michigan. It had a yellow egg sac, and the wings were tied spent. The version that's considered standard today omits the egg sac and employs upright wings. However, the addition of that egg sac can sometimes make a world of difference astream, and I have my own way of tying it.

For the wing material, the pattern calls for small feathers, or tippets, as they are often called, from a barred rock cape. Until fairly recently, rooster, or cock, feathers were the order of the day, but many tiers, myself included, have switched to hen grizzly. There are several reasons for this. These days, it's hard to find cock grizzly broad and webby enough to make good-looking wings. And who wants to burn two good-quality dry-fly hackles to make a set of wings, with such capes running upward of $50? Also, rooster quills sometimes have a distinct tendency to twist when tied on, but with hens, this is much less the case.

If you do happen to have a grizzly cock neck that has softer, webbier feathers, by all means, use it. Otherwise, search for a hen cape that has fairly well-defined barring, is light in shade, and has tippets that are well

A pair of hen grizzly tippets.

shaped for winging. Whiting Farms' pelts are excellent for this purpose.

The conventional technique is to strip off the barbs until all that remains are those that will actually form the wings. I've found, however, that simply folding back the barbs nearest the butts works better, as this gives you something to hold on to and helps keep the quills from rotating and skewing the wings. Another benefit is that if you miscalculate and make the wings too short, you can easily back off and repeat the folding-back process, whereas once you've stripped off material, it's too late. If you prefer to strip the quills bare, go ahead, but I think you'll find my method to be preferable.

You'll need soft, smooth-packing dubbing for this pattern. It can be natural or synthetic. Silk dubbing works extremely well, especially for smaller flies.

Adams

Hook	Standard fine-wire dry fly, sizes 10-18.
Thread	Black 6/0 or 8/0.
Wings	Grizzly (barred rock) tippets, soft rooster or hen.
Tail	Mixed brown and grizzly.
Body	Gray dubbing, finely packed.
Hackle	Mixed brown and grizzly.
Egg sac	Yellow Uni-Stretch, polypropylene yarn, or similar (optional).

1. Tie on up front, and lay down a neat foundation, with the thread ending up about one-quarter of the shank length to the rear of the eye.
2. Choose two small feathers that match up properly with the hook size. Strip off the fuzzy stuff nearest the butts, but leave lots of material in place—more than you think you'll need to form the wings.
3. With your left thumb and forefinger, hold the feathers convex-to-convex, so that they curve away from each other, with the tips perfectly even and pointing toward the hook eye. Then fold back the barbs until what remains in front of your fingers is exactly what's needed for the wings. The wing height should be equal to the length of the hook shank.
4. Hold the folded-back barbs in such a manner as to expose the quills at the point where the thread will intersect them. Set the feathers atop the hook, with the point of exposure positioned exactly where the wings should be located. Tie them in place with several pinch wraps, followed by several securing wraps. Try to keep them centered.
5. When the wings are almost, but not quite, locked in, gently stroke them upright. This helps set the wings in perfect position and alignment, as it corrects for any slipping or rolling that may have occurred during the tying-in process.
6. Gently crimp the wings into an upright attitude, then lock them in that position with a few thread wraps tight to the front of the quills.
7. Slope-cut the butts and excess material, then neatly bind it down as you wrap to the rear. This forms a smooth, nicely tapered underlayer and establishes the shape of the finished body.

Tying on the tippets (steps 3 & 4).

This is how the tippets appear after being tied on (step 4).

The tippets trimmed and standing upright (steps 5–7).

8. From here on, the procedure is the same as for any standard dry fly. For instructions on tying the mixed tail, refer to the Teal-Winged Adams Quill at the end of the chapter on flank-feather wings. Remember to spread the tailing fibers a little, and balance out the hackle fore and aft of the wings.

Two high-grade neck hackles stripped to their sweet spots. Note that the Hoffman Supergrizzly has lost considerably less material than the brown. This is typical of these feathers.

The tail in place.

A closer look at the hackle feathers, showing the sweet spot, or usable length.

The body in place.

The completed Adams.

The optional egg sac can be tied in several ways. I've seen it made out of a small bunch of dubbing or a turn of narrow yellow chenille. My method is simple and works great on dry flies.

1. Cut off a short piece of yellow Uni-Stretch, polypropylene yarn, or something similar. You won't need much in the way of diameter, so if the material you've chosen is overly thick, reduce it as appropriate. Tie in the yarn just behind the wing.
2. While applying tension by pulling on the yarn from the rear, bind it down along the hook shank, working to the rear.
3. At the very bend, double the yarn by folding it forward, and take a few turns of thread over it at that spot.
4. Adjust the size of the egg sac by pulling forward on the tag end of the yarn, thus tightening the little ball at the rear until it resembles the one in the photo.
5. Cut off the excess yarn. The wraps used to tie the egg sac will serve double duty as tail spreaders.

The yarn doubled back (step 4).

The egg sac adjusted to proper size (step 5).

The yarn that will form the egg sac tied in (steps 2 & 3).

The finished egg sac.

Some hackle tippets, such as the grizzlies used to make Adams wings, are well shaped and can be used as they come from the pelt. Others require some reshaping. The most efficient means for doing this is with a wing burner. This tool is simply a doubled-over piece of metal, typically thin brass stock, the ends of which have been machined into winglike shape. The feather is placed inside the device with the quill centered. The excess barb material that sticks out around the edges is then burned away with a butane lighter.

There are a number of such tools on the market, including models for making caddis wings and nymphal wing cases. Some of the ones designed for making mayfly-type wings are shaped to emulate the more or less exact conformation of a mayfly wing. This produces a nice cosmetic effect but isn't a necessity from a fishing standpoint. I make my wings symmetrical, with the quills centered. They seem to work just fine.

As I'm not totally happy with any of the burners currently available, I simply make my own. With my design, the quills hang out the bottom of the tool so that they can easily be centered. I use thin, flat brass sheets that can be purchased in hobby shops. You'll need a small pair of metal-cutting scissors, or tin snips, and a fine file or a grinding bit for a 1/4-inch drill or Dremel tool. Begin by cutting off a 5- to 6-inch piece of brass stock, and fold it double. With the tin snips, cut from the folded end lengthwise almost to the other end, leaving enough material to form the wing silhouette. Cut the brass into a winglike shape, as shown. Refine the shape and smooth out the edges with the file or grinding wheel. By adhering to a symmetrical shape, and by making it so easy to center the quills, this burner allows you to do two wings at once. Just make sure the quills are aligned and centered.

With winging feathers, there are limits on what will work. Ideally, these feathers should be webby, soft, and have fairly fine quills. Although feathers whose barbs or quills are too stiff may look nice, they have negative aerodynamics and are almost impossible to tie on straight. They will twist your leader in no time. Gamebird body feathers are notorious for this. Size also has a bearing on how these wings perform. They can't be too tall or too wide. I don't tie cut-wings larger than a size 10, and that's pushing it.

A representative pattern that uses such wings is the Pale Morning Dun, which is a major hatch out west. The color of the body varies slightly from one watershed to another. Typically, it's a yellowish shade with a hint of pale olive or green.

Two tippets with lots of web at the centers.

A tippet being shaped with a wing burner.

The result.

Pale Morning Dun

Hook	Standard fine-wire dry fly, size 16-18.
Thread	Light olive, fine.
Wings	Pale gray hen cape feathers.
Tail	Pale watery dun (light gray).
Body	PMD shade dubbing, finely packed.
Hackle	Pale watery dun (light gray).

1. Tie on up front, and lay down a neat foundation, with the thread ending up about one-quarter of the shank length to the rear of the eye.
2. Choose two hen cape feathers that are somewhat larger than what you would select if you were going to use them as is. Strip off the fuzzy stuff nearest the butts, but leave lots of material in place—more than you think you'll need.
3. Shape the feathers in the wing burner.
4. Hold the feathers convex-to-convex, with the tips perfectly even and pointing toward the hook eye. Then fold back the barbs until what remains in front of your fingers is exactly what's needed for the wings. The wing height should be equal to the length of the hook shank.
5. Follow the Adams instructions for tying on and configuring the wings and finishing the fly.

Now for some innovation. Years ago, I learned through frustrating experience that standard dry flies aren't always the answer, however well tied and matched to the naturals on the water. Trout learn about our flies, sometimes very quickly. It's often necessary to show the fish something a little different than the traditional tackle-shop selection that passes over their heads on a daily basis.

The wings tied on (steps 4 & 5).

The steps for completing the PMD.

The steps for completing the PMD.

One answer is what I call the cut-wing thorax style, a design introduced in the first edition of this book. Here, I've added a couple refinements. One of those refinements has to do with how to separate the hackle and create space for the thorax. Originally, I cut a fairly wide V out of the bottom of the hackle—about 60 degrees—but I've found that it works better to simply fold the hackles out of the way and dub in the thorax with the X-wrap technique. I also wrap the hackle differently than on conventional flies, which is enabled, to a large degree, by the fine quills on modern genetic hackle feathers. This is demonstrated below.

The dressing for the Pale Morning Dun Cut-Wing Thorax is the same as for the original Pale Morning Dun. Choose a very thin-quilled feather for hackling; a dry-fly-grade saddle is probably the best choice, although cape hackles will also work okay. This type of fly will float lower on the water than one with a conventional hackle. Since one of the design objectives is to present a well-defined wing silhouette, it's advisable to make the wings a little longer than usual, one or possibly two hook sizes.

The steps for completing the PMD.

The steps for completing the PMD.

Pale Morning Dun Cut-Wing Thorax

1. Follow the steps for the Pale Morning Dun up to, but not including, the hackle. Leave a little bit of extra space between the front of the body and the wings to accommodate the dubbing.
2. Select a thin-quilled feather, and tie it in as you would for any dry-fly hackle.
3. Wrap the hackle feather with alternating turns fore and aft of the wings. Keep it concentrated around the base of the wings as much as possible. This sets up the thorax. When finished, tie off the feather in front of the wings, and neaten up the area with discreet trimming. The thread is now hanging just ahead of the wings.

Note how the hackle is concentrated at the thorax position (step 3).

4. Spin a small amount of the same dubbing used for the body onto the thread, keeping it thin and tightly packed.

5. With your fingers, spread the hackle barbs directly underneath the wings into a V. If you find that you need to remove a few barbs by cutting out a small wedge, that's okay, but be conservative, and trim as closely as possible.

6. Bring the dubbing back through the V, behind the wings and hackle, then over and around the hook. Continue by bringing the dubbing back through the V, crossing the first wrap.

7. Repeat the X-wrap. This will spread the hackles out to the sides, so that they become virtual outriggers. It's best to get the job done with just two X-wraps; more than two may make things messy. On larger flies, you might need a third, however.

8. When all is in place, complete the fly with a whip finish.

Because of the way hackle deploys around a hook, you'll probably need to do a little repositioning with your fingers in order to get both sides of the hackle to protrude straight out to the sides, with the wings centered. This is normal.

So what's the design objective here? There are several. One is to create a more circular, and thus more realistic, light pattern. Another is to unclutter the image around the thorax. Yet another is to maintain the wings in a natural position, important in slow, placid waters. This fly has produced well for me and several of my angling acquaintances.

Passing the dubbing back beneath the spread hackle (step 6).

Passing the dubbing forward beneath the spread hackle (step 6).

The finished fly, side view.

The dubbing is spun on and in position to begin wrapping the thorax (step 4).

The finished fly, bottom view.

The finished fly, front view.

CHAPTER 7

Spinners and Spents

Certain stream insects, mayflies in particular, are often more of a benefit to the angler when they are dead or dying than during emergence. The Latin term is imago, but fly fishers call these insects spinners or spents. These terms are used pretty much interchangeably, but in proper parlance, the spinners are the insects still hovering about in the air, and the spents are those spread-eagled on the surface. There's also a form called the semispent, which is a mayfly lying on the water with one of its wings sticking upward at an angle. There are times when trout are selective to this form.

Spinner falls are usually an evening occurrence, and some are nocturnal. The most famous is that of the huge Michigan night caddis, which is not actually a caddisfly but, in fact, a very large mayfly, *Hexagenia limbata*. Their emergence and egg depositing both happen at night.

Weather can alter both spinner and spent-fly activities, sometimes radically. I've experienced this many times while anxiously awaiting a Hendrickson mating flight. As evening approaches, I can see the bugs becoming active in the trees along the river bank. Then, just as they begin to venture forth, the wind comes up. The skittish spinners dive back into the foliage and stay there until conditions are more hospitable, which might well be the next morning. Evening spinner falls are usually the norm, but if conditions are ideal, the bugs will change the game clock. These delicate yet persistent creatures didn't survive virtually unchanged for millenniums without being adaptable.

It's interesting to consider why trout like spinners so much. It seems that there would be little nutrition left by the time these insects have completed their mating ritual and the female has released her eggs. And yet trout can make a living this way. Sure, they like to chow down on sumptuous morsels when the smorgasbord is rich with goodies, but when times are lean, they can do quite well on lesser fare. Actually, the hollow body of a spent fly is a pretty healthy mouthful compared with some other dietary items. Trout are very good at finding and feeding on minute items. In fact, they are capable of seeing the egg sacs on ovipositing females and can be selective to them.

Another factor has to do with availability and ease of capture. The trout are well aware that these insects aren't going anywhere, except down their throats. They can lie in the most comfortable places in the slower pools and feed at their leisure. Just watch the riseforms; you'll see what I mean.

The obvious problem with imitating spent flies is that of emulating their transparency or, at least, their translucency. Until some amazing technological breakthrough comes along, there is no way that I know of to make a hook transparent. Thus, tiers must resort to other artifices. Extended bodies are sometimes used, especially on larger flies, but I've yet to find a design for this that is problem-free enough for my liking. Tiers also use body materials that transmit a halo effect when lying on the water with light coming from above, relying, to a large extent, on the wings to create a realistic effect. This is an attempt to get the trout to focus on a certain part of the fly so that what is obviously counterfeit isn't noticed. As fly tiers, the challenge is to do this within the bounds of practicality. The flies must float, hold form, and be reasonably durable. I remember one character who was fanatical about strict imitation and was always dreaming up the most bizarre tying stunts. He made spent fly wings out of cellophane wrappers from cigarette packages, trimmed to shape. He did well to get a half-dozen casts out of one of those things, let alone a half-dozen trout.

Which is not to say that I'm anti-innovation; quite the contrary. In fact, I've tried many materials in an effort to better emulate spent wings, including pre-formed and die-cut various plastic sheet material and several types of synthetic yarns. I encountered a number of problems and vexations. Because of their lack of air flow, plastic wings spin tippets horribly, and they aren't very durable. Synthetic yarns don't hold form and get all messed up during fishing. One of the most annoying things about polypropylene yarn wings, which were all the rage for a short while, is that when you do manage to catch a trout, the yarn gets tangled in the fish's teeth.

I hope this rather negative prologue hasn't discouraged you. Actually, tying successful spent imitations is quite simple, as you're about to see. My objective in sharing my experiences with all that other stuff was intended to set you up for the revelation that simple spent patterns tied with user-friendly materials work just fine. It's an exercise in practicality.

A pattern that works for a number of spents is the Rusty Spinner. It can be tied in an assortment of sizes and shades. The example presented here is tied on a size 12 hook and uses a shade of dubbing that suggests the *E. subvaria* Hendrickson spinner.

As a preliminary to tying this fly, read the instructions for the Pale Morning Dun Cut-Wing Thorax in the previous chapter. The methods of deploying the hackle and constructing the thorax are virtually the same for the spent fly. Dedicated Catskill-style purists may find it somewhat painful to use this hackle-wrapping technique. It will not look nice and neat. Don't worry; everything will come out fine once the thorax operations are completed. Use the softest true dry-fly-grade dubbing you can find, or you'll have trouble when X-wrapping around the wings.

Rusty Spinner

Hook	Standard dry fly, Daiichi model 1180 or comparable, size 8-16.
Thread	8/0 Uni-Thread or comparable; brown.
Wings	Pale gray or white hackle, tied spent.
Tail	Individual fibers, either long hackle barbs or Micro Fibetts.
Body and thorax	Very fine, tight-packing, dry-fly-grade rusty-colored dubbing.

1. Select and prepare one large feather for the wings. This should be somewhat oversize compared with standard hackle, but not so much so as variant hackle.
2. Tie on near the front and wrap a thin thread base. Then tie in the feather about one-third of the shank length back from the eye.
3. Wrap the feather as you would the hackle on a thorax dun, crossing back and forth and maintaining a narrow vortex. Tie the feather off, then cut a little V out of the top and bottom hackles.
4. Wrap to the bend, passing the thread through the hackle at the thorax.

The hackle wrapped in concentrated fashion, similar to that for the PMD Cut-Wing Thorax (step 3).

A V is cut out top and bottom (step 3).

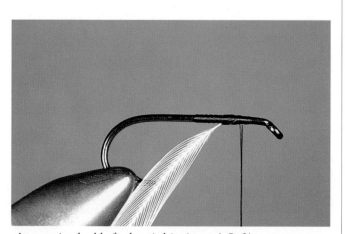

An oversize hackle feather tied in (steps 1 & 2).

5. To tie the tail, tie three long barbs or Micro Fibetts on top of the hook at the bend. Work the thread between the center and farthest fibers, separating them. Then come under the hook and pass the thread up between the nearest and center fibers, separating them too. The tail should resemble the one in the photograph. The separation of the tails can be reinforced by wrapping a very thin skein of dubbing between them as you begin the body.

6. Spin on a thin skein of dubbing, applying more than you would for just the body. Repeat the tail separation, then wrap to the base of the hackle.

7. Be sure that the hackles are out of the way, creating a path for the thorax. Then dub in the thorax with the X-wrap technique. Pass the dubbing through the spread hackle fibers beneath the hook, take one turn in front of the hackle, then pass the dubbing back through the hackle again.

8. Configure the wings by executing exactly the same procedure on top of the hook. Spread the hackle fibers, then X-wrap the dubbing into place as shown, ending up ahead of the wings. If at any time during this process you need to add more dubbing, spin it on in a continuous skein, keeping it very thin. If you see that you need to repeat either or both of the X-wraps in order to configure the wings as desired, go ahead and do so.

9. Whip-finish, then adjust the deployment of the wings with your fingers, if necessary.

Continue the body dubbing to form the thorax, working back and forth through the V cuts, top and bottom (steps 8 & 9).

Continue the body dubbing to form the thorax, working back and forth through the V cuts, top and bottom (steps 8 & 9).

The finished fly, top view.

Forming the split tails (step 5).

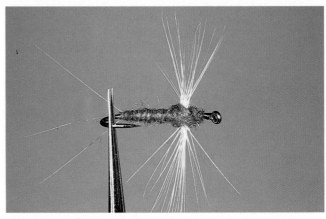

The finished fly, bottom view.

One of the truly unique spents we encounter, especially here in the Northeast, is that of the *Ephemera guttulata,* the eastern green drake. It was once thought that the green drake dun and spinner were two different flies because of their remarkably different appearance. I recall a case where a young man convinced an older angler of the truth about *E. guttulata* by capturing some duns, putting them in a cage, and watching the metamorphosis.

Many tying tricks have been tried in an effort to create a spent green drake imitation that closely resembles the natural. A lot of these dressings feature extended bodies. I've yet to find one that is effective enough that I'm willing to put up with the problems inherent in extended bodies.

There are a couple versions of the Coffin Fly pattern. This one is fairly simple, but you can take your pick.

When using Uni-Stretch, there are times when you'll want it to behave as thread, and other times when you'll want it to behave like floss. Spin the bobbin clockwise to tighten it into a threadlike configuration, and the reverse, when you want to flatten the material to use it like floss.

Coffin Fly A

Hook	Long-shank dry-fly hook, such as Daiichi model 1280, Mustad model 94831, Partridge model H1A, or Tiemco model 5212, size 6–10.
Thread	White Uni-Stretch, mounted in a bobbin, then black thread, 8/0 or 6/0.
Tails	Black or dark gray Micro Fibetts, three or four for each individual tail.
Body	Uni-Stretch.
Thorax	Black dubbing.
Wings	Very large grizzly, tied spent.

1. With the Uni-Stretch mounted in a bobbin, tie on about one-third of the shank length back from the eye, and wrap to the bend.
2. Use three or four Micro Fibetts to obtain sufficient thickness. When wet, they will stick together and behave as one. When working on the tail, keep the Uni-Stretch tightened into a threadlike configuration. Tie on the center tail, then make a bump.
3. Tie on the two side tails in such a manner that the bump spreads them. Reinforce this spreading by taking a wrap of Uni-Stretch between each of the outer tails and the center tail.
4. Flatten the Uni-Stretch so it's flosslike, and wrap the body. It will be necessary to reflatten the material periodically, because wrapping it out of a bobbin puts twists in it.
5. When the body is built up to the desired dimensions, tie off the Uni-Stretch, and tie on black thread. You are now in the thorax area.

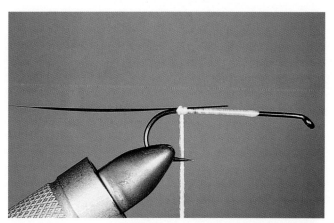

The tails in place, Uni-Stretch positioned to begin forming the body (steps 1–4).

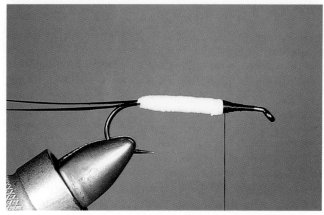

The completed body, Uni-Stretch exchanged for black thread (steps 4 & 5).

6. Tie in two huge grizzly feathers, as you would for a typical dry-fly hackling procedure.
7. Dub the thorax.
8. Wrap the hackles over the thorax, tie them off, and trim top and bottom to create a spentwing effect. Whip-finish.

This fly isn't a particularly good floater, so a good supplement is advised. Drying with a powder desiccant is helpful. Fortunately, most *E. guttulata* spinner action occurs in slower waters, so this dressing is feasible from a flotation standpoint The Uni-Stretch isn't translucent, but it's reflective and it has that waxy look of the natural. In short, it works.

Feathers tied in for winging (step 6).

The thorax dubbed on (step 7).

A silhouette view of the completed fly, after the winging feathers are wrapped and trimmed (step 8).

Coffin Fly B

Hook	Long-shank dry-fly hook, same as for Coffin Fly A.
Thread	White 8/0 or 6/0, then black 8/0 or 6/0.
Tails	Black or dark gray Micro Fibetts, three or four for each individual tail.
Body	White dubbing, soft dry-fly grade, ideally with shine or brilliance.
Thorax	Black ostrich herl; omit if badger hackle is used.
Wings	Very large silver badger, white, or grizzly, tied spent.

1. Tie on up front, wrap to the bend, and tie on the center tail.
2. With a bit of dubbing, create a small bump; then tie in the outer tails on either side, spreading them.
3. Dub the body, using either the spinning-loop or single-thread method, as you prefer. Stop about one-third of the shank length back from the eye.
4. Tie in the hackles.
5. If you're using white or grizzly, tie in two strands of ostrich herl, wrap them both at once to form a thorax, then wrap the hackles through the herl. If you're using badger, omit the thorax.
6. Whip-finish, and trim top and bottom.

These dressings can be adapted to imitate other large spents. The main thing is to find places where these hatches occur and to get in on the sometimes-incredible fishing they generate.

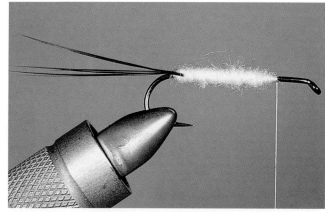

The dubbed body in place. Note proportions (step 3).

Feathers tied in, ostrich herl thorax in place (steps 4 & 5).

The split tails in place (steps 1 & 2).

Silhouette view of the completed fly.

CHAPTER 8

Down-Wing Dry Flies

Down-wing means a wing made that lies in repose along the top of the hook. Two important stream insects, the caddisfly and the stonefly, carry their wings in this manner. Certain land-based insects, notably the grasshopper, do likewise.

These flies are not hard to tie, especially now that we have great dry-fly saddles. This is significant because many of them have palmer-style hackle, which is wrapped the length of the body, and there's nothing that compares to a contemporary genetic saddle hackle for such work.

There isn't much in the way of surface stonefly fishing in many areas of the country, except for the Rocky Mountains and Pacific states. However, caddis are everywhere. Sometimes the most effective way to fish a caddis emergence is with a larval imitation or an emerger. Nevertheless, there are plenty of dry-fly opportunities, and it can be a very exciting time.

Caddisflies are quite mothlike in appearance, although their wings are in a somewhat more tented posture. Their bodies and legs are both shorter in proportion to the wings than are those of mayflies. They do not go through a final metamorphosis after hatching, so the newly emerged insect and the egg-laying form are the same.

Certain caddis have a unique style of emergence, shooting up out of the water like a missile. Others hop around on the surface. These actions stimulate, and often frustrate, the trout. It's much harder for them to capture the adult insects, and considerably more energy is required. It can also be frustrating for the angler, because visible rises don't always translate into easy pickings. You have to figure out what trout are seeing and how best to deal with it. Circumstances sometimes may mandate subsurface fishing with an emerger, but there are lots of times when the right floater, properly presented, will produce.

Al Troth, a Pennsylvania native who escaped to Montana many years ago, designed a simple yet deadly pattern for his home river, the Beaverhead. It bears his name—the Troth Caddis, or sometimes the Troth Elk Hair Caddis. Not counting color variations, there are two versions: hackled and no-hackle. The no-hackle version is the ultimate in simplicity. It has two components: a dubbed body and an elk-hair wing. The only trick is to configure the wing in such a manner that it aids both flotation and balance. This simply means keeping the wing fairly low over the back of the fly and spread sufficiently to maintain posture.

I've met Al Troth a couple times at fly-fishing events but have never had the opportunity to fish with him, nor have I watched him tie his namesake flies. I've emulated them by looking at the photographs in several books. I'm not sure that my versions are completely faithful to Al's original design, but they do work. This dressing is easily adapted to match whatever caddis may be prevalent in a given region at a particular time, so I'm leaving the color descriptions general. For the wing, I prefer cream-colored elk hair from the animal's rump. It forms a nice-looking wing yet is sufficiently buoyant to facilitate flotation. For smaller-size hooks, it should be of the finer type from a young animal.

Troth No-Hackle Caddis

Hook	Standard dry fly, size 10-18.
Thread	Olive or tan 6/0 or 8/0 Uni-Thread or similar.
Body	Olive dubbing.
Wing	Pale elk hair.

1. Tie on near the front, wrap neatly to the rear, and apply the dubbing.
2. Wrap the body, covering about three-quarters of the hook shank.
3. Wrap to the eye and back a couple times to lay down a thread base.
4. Clean out the underfur from a small bunch of elk hair, and even up the tips in a stacker.
5. Hold the hair atop the hook and measure for length. The tips should extend a little way beyond the rear extremity of the body. Precut the butt ends even with the front of the hook.
6. Tie the hair atop the hook as shown, then whip-finish. Note that the hair at the front is not bound down. This forms a prominent head and contributes to flotation. For stability, I suggest applying a generous drop of Zap-A-Gap on top of the thread wraps, allowing it to penetrate thoroughly.

It doesn't get much simpler than that, but this seemingly underdressed fly works. The key is to keep the wings low over the back and spread the hairs to the sides a bit so that the fly balances properly on the water.

As for the hackled version, I'm not sure just how Al dressed the original pattern or how he's doing them today. My reference books mention fine wire, both gold and copper, but don't clearly explain how this wire is used. If you'd like to include the wire, you tie it as you would any ribbing, and follow it with the hackle, wrap for wrap. Very fine oval tinsel may also be used. I don't think the fly would suffer if this component were left off, but for the sake of completeness, I'll include it here.

The hackle should be undersize because these short-legged insects lie low on the surface, and the imitations look more realistic and balance with shorter-barbed hackles. I tie mine with the barbs equal to or slightly longer than the gape.

The body in place (steps 1–3).

Addition of a simple hairwing completes the basic Troth Caddis (steps 4–6).

Troth Hackled Caddis

Hook	Standard dry fly, size 10-18.
Thread	8/0 or 6/0, tan or light brown.
Hackle	Medium brown, dry-fly-grade saddle, undersize.
Ribbing	Very fine gold or copper wire (optional).
Body	Tan dubbing, fine, tight-packing dry-fly material.
Wing	Light-colored elk hair.

1. Begin the same as for the no-hackle version. At the bend, tie in the hackle and then the ribbing material, if you wish to include it.
2. Dub the body.
3. Estimate how many turns of hackle you want, and wrap an equivalent number of turns of ribbing.
4. Wrap the hackle, with each turn abutting a turn of ribbing at the rear.
5. Tie on the wing in the same way as for the no-hackle version. If you wish, you can cut out a V in the hackle along the back to accommodate the winging hair.

The adult caddis imitations I use are similar to Al's dressing, except for how I finish off the front ends. Here in the Northeast, especially in the Delaware River watershed, we have a major hatch of a caddis known as the shad fly because its emergence occurs with the blooming of the shadbush, which in turn coincides with the shad run in the Delaware. Actually, there are two shad flies, one having a bright green body and tannish wings and legs, and the other a gray-tan body with a hint of olive and gray-tan mottled wings and legs. The two flies are about the same size. If you can tie one of them, you can tie both.

The body in place (step 2).

The ribbing wrapped (step 3).

The hackle wrapped (step 4).

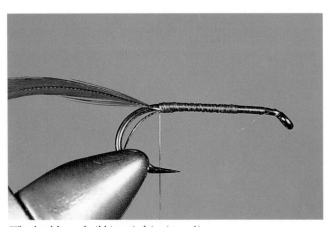

The hackle and ribbing tied in (step 1).

The finished fly (step 5).

Green Shad Fly

Hook	Standard dry fly, size 14-16.
Thread	Tan 6/0 or 8/0.
Hackle	Light ginger dry-fly-grade saddle, undersize.
Body	Apple green dubbing, fine yarn, or Uni-Stretch.
Wing	Very fine tan deer hair.

1. Tie on about one-third of the shank length back from the eye, wrap to the bend, and tie in the hackle.
2. If you're making a dubbed body, proceed with it now, stopping it at the tie-in point. If you're making a Uni-Stretch body, as shown here, wrap the thread forward a little way past the tie-in point, tie in the material, and wrap a two-layered body. The front part of the body serves as part of the base for the wing, which aids in stability and shaping.
3. Spiral-wrap the hackle. When you near the front of the body, secure the feather with a few turns of thread, but don't trim; just let it hang. In fact, if you have a pair of nice, heavy hackle pliers, you can attach it to the feather and simply let it hang, with no thread wraps.
4. Create a base for the wing.
5. Clean out and stack a small bunch of the hair, and tie it on as shown. It should be positioned a little farther to the rear than on the Troth dressings.

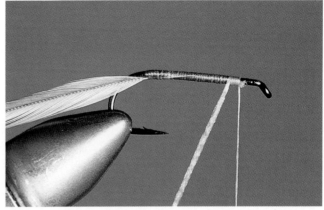

The Uni-Stretch tied in (step 3).

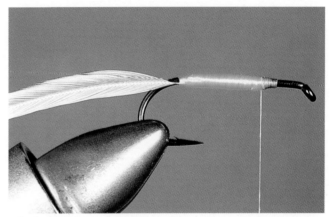

The body wrapped (step 3).

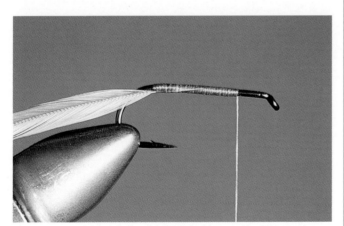

The hackle tied in. Note the thread position (steps 1 & 3).

The body hackle is wrapped, the feather secured, the base for the wing in place (steps 4 & 5).

6. Neatly trim the wing butts on a slope and bind them down, forming a base for the front hackle.

7. Pick up the feather, and complete the fly with a series of three to five turns in front of the wing. These turns abut each other and are not spiraled like the body hackle. Whip-finish.

There's no end to the adult caddis patterns that can be derived from this design.

The wing in place, butts buried (steps 6 & 7).

Wrapping the front hackle completes the Shad Fly (step 8).

Gray-Tan Shad Fly

Hook	Standard dry fly, size 14-16.
Thread	Brown or dark olive 6/0 or 8/0.
Hackle	Medium brown, cree, or grizzly dry-fly-grade saddle.
Body	Dubbing, grayish brown with a hint of olive.
Wing	Fine gray-brown-mottled deer hair.

The wing hair is much finer textured than for the Troth dressings, to accommodate the front hackle. A smaller base is necessary so that the feather can be wrapped around it. Because of the front hackle, I don't rely on the wing for flotation.

Some anglers like a more delicate and detailed caddis dressing. In my opinion, there's none better than the elegant Henryville Special. Here again, color variations reflect adaptations to local and regional hatches. The one presented here is the standard pattern at the Henryville Trout Club on the Paradise Branch of the Brodheads Creek in northeastern Pennsylvania.

You can use cape hackles for this fly, if you wish, as the feathers don't have to be all that long. Be sure, however, that they are of good dry-fly quality, with strong barbs and a high barb count. You have the option of cutting a V down the center of the grizzly body hackle on top in order to create a clear area for the wings. On this particular fly, I find that helpful.

Henryville Special

Hook	Standard dry fly, size 14-16.
Thread	Brown 6/0 or 8/0.
Body hackle	Grizzly, undersize.
Body	Medium olive floss or other body material.
Underwing	Small clump of wood duck flank-feather fibers.
Wings	Two sections from a gray duck or goose flight quill.
Front hackle	Brown, one size larger than the body hackle.

1. Tie on about one-third of the shank length back from the eye, wrap to the bend, and tie in the grizzly feather for the body hackle.
2. Do the body, covering the rear two-thirds of the hook.
3. Spiral-wrap the body hackle, tie it off, and trim.
4. Tie the wood duck fibers on top of the hook, as shown.
5. Cut two opposing sections from left and right flight quill feathers. Hold them convex-to-convex, so that they flare away from each other, with the tips pointed downward.
6. Center the winging sections on top of the hook. Try to avoid crushing the hackle in the process. Tie them in place with several pinch wraps, followed by a few securing wraps, while holding the wings in place with the left thumb and forefinger.
7. Before trimming off the wing butts, check to see that the wings are centered, and adjust if necessary. Then take a few more firm thread wraps while holding the wings in place to prevent them from being moved by thread torque. Trim the butts, and lay down a neat thread base.
8. Tie in and wrap the front hackle in normal dry-fly fashion, trim, and whip-finish.

The main hackle is wrapped palmer-style over the body (step 3).

The wood duck underwing in place (step 4).

The main wing in place (steps 5–7).

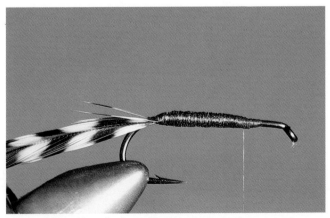

The hackle tied in, body in place (steps 1 & 2).

Wrapping the front hackle finishes the Henryville Special (step 8).

The only difficult thing about tying the Henryville Special is keeping the wings centered and uniform. This may take a little practice. Be sure they are well secured before the front hackle is wrapped, as this can upset them.

Randall Kaufmann is credited with originating a beautiful adult stonefly imitation from the Pacific Northwest called the Stimulator, and I well remember my first encounter with it.

After taking an early retirement from the phone business in 1984, I rented a small cabin not far from the famous Slide Inn section of the Madison River in Montana and spent the summer and early autumn of 1985 enjoying the marvelous waters of that region. In Blue Ribbon Flies in West Yellowstone, I happened onto these elongated dry flies with palmer-hackled bodies. I bought a couple, figuring that I'd imitate them if they worked. And they did. I used them as general attractor patterns and found that they could often bring sizable trout to the surface, at least for a look, if not a take. Soon, the two I'd bought were pretty beat, so I set about tying myself a supply. Immediately, I was confronted by a problem—getting my hackle feathers to span the length of that long body. I had some pretty fair grizzly capes in my kit, but no way would these feathers palmer-wrap the body; in fact, they did well to cover half of it. I was faced with the choice of tying the body and applying the hackle in two separate operations or using a large feather from well back in the cape and trimming the barbs to proper length. Neither method was satisfactory.

I lamented about my problem to Craig and Jackie Matthews, the proprietors of Blue Ribbon Flies, who introduced me to Henry Hoffman's Supergrizzly saddles. End of hackle problems! I began cranking out gorgeous Stimulators by the dozen.

A few years later, I was fishing the San Juan in New Mexico with a very good friend, a lady from California. It was early October, and all we were seeing on the water were midges and tiny mayflies. We 7Xed our way up a long, quiet run, picking up a trout here and there. It was tough, and as the day wore on, it got tougher.

I saw a trout feeding tight to a grassy bank. The riseforms, though occasional and sporadic, were remarkably different—much more animated and aggressive. I decided that there had to be some sort of terrestrial coming down, probably hoppers.

My friend was busily working a line of sipping trout and didn't notice my departure. I cut back my leader and, in the absence of a true hopper pattern, tied on a size 6 Stimulator. I stood across from the fish, about 30 feet away, and waited. Soon he showed again. I hesitated a bit, then dropped the fly 10 feet above the rise. He swam 5 feet upstream to meet it. I found myself engaged in combat with a very angry trout of a strain the locals call a "bright"—a nonhatchery rainbow of almost chrome silver, shaped like a small tuna and just about as powerful.

My friend immediately noticed the commotion and walked down the bank to watch the action. "You're putting an awful strain on that 7X tippet," she commented. I replied, "7X? I cut back to 3X, maybe even 2X!" Eventually the 20-inch fish was subdued and lay gasping in the shallows. My companion's comments, as I removed the gigantic fly from its tongue, were appropriately colorful. I gave her one of my Stimulators, but we never found another hopper eater that day.

This dressing will acquaint you with the convenience and efficiency of bobbin-mounted Uni-Stretch. If you wish, you can tie this fly in the more conventional manner. You can cut a V out of the top of the body hackle, but with this wing, it's not really necessary.

Stimulator

Hook	Long-shanked dry fly, such as the Daiichi model 1280, Mustad model 94831, Partridge model H1A, or Tiemco model 5212, size 6-14.
Thread	Tan or light brown 6/0 or 8/0. If you opt for Uni-Stretch, start with it, bobbin-mounted.
Tail	A short bunch of deer body hair.
Hackle	High-grade dry-fly saddle, grizzly or cree.
Body	Yellow Uni-Stretch, dubbing, or yarn.
Wing	Same as the tail, but more of it.
Thorax	Orange dry-fly-type dubbing.

1. Mount a spool of yellow Uni-Stretch in a regular thread bobbin, and tie on about one-quarter of the shank length back from the eye. Apply just enough turns to secure the material, then stop.
2. Cut the tailing hair from the pelt, clean and stack it, then hold it atop the hook to gauge its length.
3. Tie the hair on top of the hook at this point, perhaps one-third of the shank length from the eye.
4. Hold the bunch taut with your left thumb and forefinger, and bind the hair down along the top of the hook, working to the rear. What you're doing here is creating a level underbody and, at the same time, building up to the desired thickness. If you had tried to do this by tying in the hair at the bend in the traditional manner, you'd find it much more difficult. Trim the tail material butts neatly on a slope.
5. Tie in the hackle at the bend. Then run the Uni-Stretch back and forth a few times until the body is sized as you wish, meanwhile burying the tail butt ends at the front.
6. Spiral-wrap the hackle, and secure it without trimming off the remainder, as in the Green Shad Fly directions. In a moment, you'll use the same feather for the front hackle. The brown thread now replaces the Uni-Stretch.

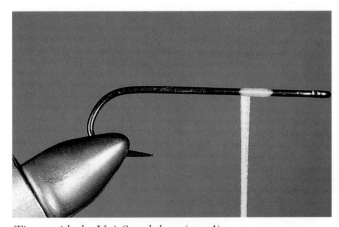

Tie on with the Uni-Stretch here (step 1).

The tailing hair is bound down along the top of the hook (steps 3–5).

The hackle is tied in at the bend, the body formed (step 5).

The body hackle is wrapped and secured, brown tying thread tied on (step 6).

7. Cut off, clean, and stack a bunch of hair for the wing. Don't overdress or the fly will have poor balance.
8. Tie the wing fairly flat over the hook, making sure that it's centered. Trim the butts on a slope, and bind them down neatly.
9. Dub an orange thorax, as shown.
10. Wrap the front hackle. The turns should be slightly spiraled so that some orange shows through, but they should be closer together than the wraps of body hackle. Tie off, trim neatly, and whip-finish.

You now have a fairly comprehensive knowledge of the techniques for tying down-wing dry flies. There are many more patterns, as you'll no doubt discover. Several of these techniques will serve you well in tying other types of flies. For example, the method for tying the tail on the Stimulator has wide application in streamer fly tying.

The wing in place (steps 7 & 8).

The orange thorax is dubbed on (step 9).

Wrapping the front hackle completes the Stimulator (step 10).

CHAPTER 9

Clump-Wing Dry Flies

In the first edition of this book, I devoted a brief chapter to a fly called the Haystack, a pattern shown to me by Francis Betters of New York Ausable fame. I believe it had its roots in the time of his father prior to World War II, which was truly the golden era of that wonderful Adirondack river. The style seemed to catch on immediately and was widely emulated. A similar series of flies appeared in a very useful treatise on aquatic insects, *Hatches,* written by Al Caucci and Bob Nastasi. They called their flies Compara-duns and copyrighted the name.

Call them what you will, these simple patterns are a valuable addition to one's fly box. They don't look very realistic—at least, not to us. In the water, however, viewed from below by the fish, they have a distinct attraction. Given a few basics, they are easily tied, even by relative beginners.

The indistinct silhouette and rather rough appearance of the Haystack or Compara-dun imposes certain limitations on its effectiveness. I haven't found it to be a particularly good choice in slow, placid currents, although there are exceptions to this, especially with smaller sizes. The smaller the fly, the better this sort of dressing seems to work. It doesn't adapt well to large hook sizes; in fact, I don't tie it larger than a 12.

The basic Haystack has no hackle. It consists of an undivided hairwing, a tail of some sort, and a dubbed body and thorax. The fly floats quite low in the surface film on the body, thorax, and tail. The wing provides balance and image. It is suggestive of an emerging form, perhaps a cripple, which trout are quick to identify as an easy mouthful. In *Hatches* and *Hatches II,* Caucci and Nastasi describe hackled Compara-duns, but that's another story. Here we'll explore the basic dressings.

Simple as these flies are, there are a few considerations that directly affect their performance. The first is the choice of hair. There's a bit of a conflict here. Softer, more pulpy hair is lightweight and best for flotation. On the other hand, finer hair is more manageable from a tying standpoint and is more easily formed into a nice-looking wing that will retain its position, especially on the smaller hooks where this style of fly really comes into its own. Thus you find yourself in a balancing act between the two. You need to know how hairs of differing textures perform when winging different-size flies. The Haystack or Compara-dun expert chooses hair as carefully as the Catskill classicist selects hackle.

Fortunately, you have a wide selection of body hairs from which to choose. The hair of the coastal deer, which inhabits areas along the Gulf Coast, is generally very well suited to this sort of work. The hair is quite short, which is desirable, as you don't want to work with just the tips. It represents a good compromise between very fine but slippery and poor-floating hairs and the bulky, hard-to-manage hairs of large deer and elk.

The shape and size of the wing are also important. A wing that's too tall makes for a poorly balanced fly, as does one that's too heavy. A wing that's too sparse results in a less visible image and doesn't help much with flotation.

One problem encountered in tying on the hair bunch is getting it to stay exactly where you want it. When dealing with fairly bulky materials, precision becomes a problem. Thus it's important to establish a good, stable thread base that won't move around when you're wrestling with the hair. I add a tiny droplet of superglue to the thread base while wrapping it in place to ensure that it won't slide forward or backward during the tying-in process. The adhesive must be absolutely dry before the hair is laid in place.

The key to positioning the wing and having it stay in place for the life of the fly lies in the application of the thread and, subsequently, the dubbing. The materials in front of the wing must be sufficient to support it. The tying thread is used fairly generously, balancing out the front-back plane, so that the wraps used to tie on the hair bunch don't make it lean forward. This can be a little tricky. You may think you've properly supported the wing, only to find later that the hair has collapsed and is lying over the top of the thorax. Packing the body material too closely behind the wing contributes to this problem.

There's not a lot of latitude in the shaping of the wing. An upright clump of hair doesn't work well, as it has a negative effect on balance. You can either spread the wing into a 180-degree fan, so that the hair on each side lies flat on the water like a spentwing, or shape it as a deep V as viewed from the front. Either configuration is easily formed by managing the application of the thorax material.

The style of the tail is your choice. You can tie a conventional tail out of hackle barbs or hair, or a spent-type tail. A shuck-dragger tail, which consists of a sparse tag of synthetic yarn, such as Antron, turns the fly into a Sparkle Dun, the name ascribed to it by the folks at Blue Ribbon Flies, who originated this innovation. All work fine, as the fly does not depend much on the tail for flotation and balance.

Clump-Wing Fly, or Haystack

Hook	Standard dry fly, Daiichi model 1180 or comparable, size 14. (Note: Flies of this construction work best in smaller sizes. Size 12 is the maximum.)
Thread	Gray or black 8/0 Uni-Thread or comparable.
Wing	A bunch of fairly soft, short deer hair.
Tail	Your choice, as above.
Body and thorax	Dry-fly-type gray dubbing.

1. Tie on just to the rear of the eye, and begin to wrap the foundation. After wrapping the first layer of thread, rub on a bit of Zap-A-Gap or similar super-glue. Wrap another couple layers of thread over the glue to accelerate the drying process. Let it dry completely before continuing. The thread should be positioned about one-third of the shank length to the rear of the eye.

2. Cut off a bunch of hair, clean out all underfur and short stuff, and even up the tip ends in a stacker. Examine the photograph, paying particular attention to the quantity of hair being used. Note that a size 12 hook is being used here, large for a Compara-dun-type fly.

3. Gauge the length of the wing; it should be no longer than the hook shank. Set the bunch atop the thread base, and tie it in place with several wraps of thread that become progressively tighter. Don't use much tension on the first wrap or two, as this will cause the hair to flare prematurely and become difficult to manage.

4. Inspect the bunch, and make whatever adjustments are necessary to center and evenly distribute the hairs. The bunch should form an approximate semicircle, viewed from the front. Be sure it hasn't slipped forward or backward.

5. Thoroughly secure the wing with a succession of tight wraps immediately behind the tie-in point, again taking care not to allow the wing to move forward or backward.

6. Wrap forward and stand up the wing by building a substantial dam of thread in front of it.

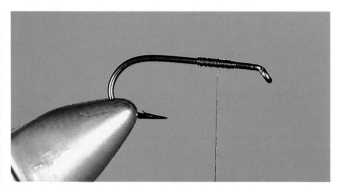

The thread base for the wing in place (step 1).

The winging bunch tied in place (steps 2–5).

The winging bunch standing upright (step 6).

7. Carefully trim the hair butts on a slope, then bind them down to form a tapered underbody as you wrap to the bend.

8. To make a shuck-dragger-type tail, as shown here, tie on a piece of amber or olive-amber Antron or Z-lon yarn, and trim it to approximately the length of the shank or a bit shorter. Trim and bury the tag end. Alternatively, you can tie a conventional tail, as in a regular dry fly, or a spent-type tail, as detailed in the chapter on spinners and spents.

9. Spin on enough dubbing to make the body and thorax. Getting the quantity just right takes a little practice; be prepared to add or remove material as necessary. Apply the dubbing sparingly; you're covering a fairly thick underbody, and you'll need at least two, probably three, X-wraps to form the thorax and position the wings.

10. Wrap to the rear of the wing but don't abut it. Then come underneath, below the wing, and take a tight turn against the front of it.

The shuck-dragger tail in place (step 8).

The dubbed body. Note space to the rear of the wing (steps 9 & 10).

The wing butts trimmed and bound down (step 7).

The first turn of dubbing tight to the front of the wing (step 10).

11. Pass the dubbing back beneath the wing, X-wrapping over the previous wrap. Be sure the dubbing stays tightly packed; respin if necessary.

12. Wrap the dubbing over the hook behind the wing, taking care not to crowd it from the rear.

13. Come underneath again, and repeat the previous steps. Be attentive to how the wing is affected by the formation of the thorax; avoid forcing it into a too-upright position. There is some latitude regarding wing shape. The front view shows how I prefer to configure mine.

14. You may need a third set of X-wraps to complete the thorax, but if two prove to be sufficient, leave it at that. Whip-finish, then tweak the wings with your fingers if repositioning of the hairs appears necessary.

Another interesting fly of similar design, called the Usual, comes from the same Adirondack Ausable source as the Haystack. The story goes that as the little group of regulars who knew and used the pattern were on the river, they would call to each other, "Hey, what did you take that one on?" The answer would resound over the flowing waters, "The Usual!"

One aspect of the fly that is not usual is the wing and tail material. The original dressing calls for hair from between the toes of the hind feet of a female snowshoe rabbit, also known as a varying hare. These are fairly plentiful in the Northeast, but they may be hard to find elsewhere. I have a cigar box full of snowshoe rabbit's feet, but I'm not sure which ones are female. I use them all, regardless of sex or whether they are front or hind feet, and they seem to work satisfactorily. In fact, I find that other, similar hairs, such as those from the feet of large European-strain hares, also work reasonably well, given a little help from an effective floatant. Nevertheless, the real stuff is superior.

The Usual is a rough, nonspecific fly. It's effectiveness lies in its behavior. The properties of the wing and tail material imbue this fly with a certain buoyancy. When properly dressed, it can be skated around on the surface or even pulled under the surface, and it will rise to the top. Its form is nondescript, like that of an emerging insect. In fact, this fly is as much an emerger as a dry fly.

Pass the dubbing back beneath the wing (step 11).

Come underneath again, working forward (steps 12–14).

The finished fly, side view.

The finished fly, front view.

The Usual	
Hook	Standard dry fly, Daiichi model 1180 or comparable, size 12-20.
Thread	8/0 Uni-Thread or comparable, a pale color.
Wing	A bunch of hair from between the toes of a snowshoe rabbit's foot.
Tail	Same as the wing, tied short.
Body and thorax	Dry-fly-type cream dubbing.

The tying procedure is essentially the same as for the Haystack. Keep both the tail and wing short, and spread the wing hairs laterally for better balance. This fly isn't supposed to look neat; in fact, it may be the wildest-looking fly you'll ever tie. The wing material can be tough to handle. If you wish, you can gather it with a few counterclockwise thread wraps around the base of the wing, as though you were preparing a parachute post.

I'm one of those better-living-through-chemistry people when it comes to floating a dry fly. I'm particularly partial to the powder desiccants available today. Don't use a volatile, solvent-based fly floatant on a true Usual. If you're fortunate enough to locate a supply of the hair called for in the original dressing, don't use any kind of floatant when the fly is new and fresh. Later, when it begins to lose its natural floating characteristics, to retain as much as possible of the natural oils, clean the fly by simply swishing it around in the water, then treat it with a powder desiccant. Eventually, you can use a tiny bit of paste-type floatant to extend the life of the fly.

The wing and tail in place.

Dubbing on the body and thorax competes the Usual.

CHAPTER 10

Parachutes

In the early 1960s, I made the acquaintance of an irascible but lovable character named Dudley G. Soper. Dud was born in Bucksport County, Maine, and had an unmistakable Down East accent. When I met him, Dud, who has since passed away, was operating a custom rod-making and repair shop in Delmar, New York, a suburb of Albany.

No one loved dry-fly fishing more than Dud, and few were his equal at presenting a floating fly. He particularly liked quiet pools and placid currents. One evening on a private pool on the Upper Beaverkill, as I stayed in the run at the head, pounding up trout with a large Gray Fox Variant, Dud stood in the shallow, still waters of the tail. He hooked nearly every rising trout that he was able to cover with his long, delicate casts and 14-foot leader. His fly of choice was a nondescript parachute tie or, as he liked to call it, a flat-hackle.

Dud was not a technical tier, but he had a keen eye for fly design, color, image, light pattern, and such essentials. He fished parachutes almost exclusively. His flies weren't pretty, but they certainly looked good to the fish. I learned a great deal about the finer points of dry-fly fishing from Dud, and I'm forever in his debt.

People who have done underwater observation and photography of stream insects and the flies with which we attempt to imitate them tell of a phenomenon called the circular light pattern. When an insect such as a mayfly rests on the surface, its six little feet make an impression in the surface film that is more or less circular or ovate. The quieter the surface, the more distinct this set of impressions. The traditional dry fly, which rests mostly on its tail and hackle, doesn't do a particularly good job of imitating this light pattern. The parachute style emulates it much better, making this fly a wise choice for the glassy pools and glides of such rivers as the Battenkill in the Northeast, the limestoners of Pennsylvania, and the spring creeks of the Rocky Mountains.

This is not to say that standard dry flies don't work. Where the currents are more diverse, they produce very well indeed. It's a matter of choosing the style that fits the environment at hand.

There's been an increasing amount of interest in parachutes in recent years, possibly spurred by a particular pattern that has proven to be universally successful: the Adams Parachute. The components are the same as for the regular Adams except for the wing, which is an upright post of white hair. It's a little harder to tie than most other parachutes, because two hackles are required to obtain the mixed shade of hackle. Even the multi-shaded and quite rare hackle known as cree doesn't produce the alluring effect of the brown-and-grizzly mix.

Before tying the Adams Parachute, let's start with a pattern that calls for only one hackle feather, here a Blue-Winged Olive. Many mayflies are known as blue-winged olives, and they vary widely in coloration and size. Here we'll use a medium to pale gray or dun hackle and a light olive body. This will pass for several important blue-winged olives in various regions, with a little adjustment to the color and size.

With the parachutes, there is a distinct departure from the norm in tail design. In the standard design, the tail helps balance and support the fly on the water. The parachute, on the other hand, floats only on its hackle and body. Thus tails only serve the purpose of imitation. A drifting dun rides on its feet and seldom allows its tails to touch the water. However, a dun that's having trouble getting out of its nymphal shuck has something very visible dragging behind it. Though certainly not a tail, it does lie in that position. This accounts for such designs as the Sparkle Dun, with its shuck-dragger tail of synthetic yarn. The tail also may imitate the set of tails of a spinner. These are very distinctive and clearly visible when a spent mayfly is lying spread-eagle on the water. A parachute serves quite well as a spent-fly imitator, so there's a rationale for adding such a tail if that's the effect you're trying to obtain.

It's up to you to decide what sort of tail, if any, should go on the rear end of a parachute. Often I leave it off, except for the two cases of imitation mentioned above. I'll include directions for a short, sparse tail in the pattern presented here. Mayflies can have either two or three tails. If you're not sure of the count on the bug you're trying to imitate, go with two.

Several special tying problems may be encountered with parachutes. You're going to be wrapping a hackle around something other than a hook shank: an upright wing post of hair, a piece of synthetic yarn, or the butts of the hackle quills themselves. There are two significant differences from the standard hackle: the relative softness of the material around which the hackle is wrapped, and the fact that there isn't a progressive distribution, as there is when a standard hackle is wrapped forward in successive turns. The wing post shouldn't be any thicker than is absolutely necessary. All that's needed is something to wrap the hackle around that's also visible from a distance. Anything more than that becomes counterproductive.

Another vexing problem is that of tying off hackles and doing the whip finish. The flat hackle is simply in the way. This calls for adroit technique with the bobbin, thread, and whip-finish tool, or the prudent use of a superglue.

The Blue-Winged Olive Parachute pattern presented here uses a color that is close to that of the wings of the natural, but I'm not sure that this is important. In recent years, I've been using brighter-colored wings so that I can see them better. A lot of us older guys are doing this. There may be times when being true to wing color is more convincing to trout, but it's hard to prove. The brightness of the day and the type of background might affect a trout's vision of colors, and so might the size of the fly, but how a trout might interpret color is another question entirely, given the creature's minute brain and the relatively low number of cones in the eye, these being the enablers of color vision.

Parachutes don't demand the ultrastiff, strong-barbed hackles that are critical on standard flies. What's important is that the feathers have fine quills and wrap easily and truly. It does not take much hackle to properly dress a parachute, so the shorter neck or cape hackles will work just fine, provided that they have fine quills.

Saddle hackles—or at least, today's top grade ones—usually have finer quills, in comparable sizes, than cape hackles, and they usually have a higher barb count, meaning that fewer wraps are required. They also have another interesting characteristic that can prove useful with flat-hackled flies: The barbs tend to curve, or cup, toward the inside to a greater extent than those on cape hackles. If you can wrap the feather with the dull side facing downward, the natural curvature of the barbs will help create a hackle with a downward slant that touches the surface film in just the right manner.

Blue-Winged Olive Parachute	
Hook	Standard dry fly, such as the Daiichi model 1180, size 10-24.
Thread	Olive or light brown 8/0 Uni-Thread or similar.
Wing post	Gray-dyed calf tail, bucktail, or other hair.
Tail	Pale to medium gray hackle barbs or Micro Fibetts, short and sparse.
Body and thorax	Light to medium greenish olive dubbing of the soft, smooth-packing type.
Hackle	Pale to medium gray.

1. Tie on as you would for any typical dry fly, and create a thread base about one-quarter of the shank length back from the eye.
2. Select and manicure a small bunch of hair as though you were going to make a skinny Wulff wing, cleaning out all of the junky stuff and evening up the tips in a stacker.
3. Tie the wing-post bunch on top of the hook, and stand it up in the conventional manner.

The winging hair tied in (steps 1–3).

4. With the bobbin tube pointed downward, take a few wraps of thread around the base of the hair bunch, working counterclockwise. Then wrap to the bend.

5. Tie a hackle-fiber tail per instructions in the flank-feather wing chapter, but much shorter, as shown.

6. Dub the body per instructions in the same chapter, then pass under the wing post and take a few turns of dubbing tight to the front of the hair. The intent is to level out the plane, front and back.

7. Choose and prepare your hackle feather, keeping in mind the comments above.

8. Tie in the feather with the dull side down, on top of the hook, in front of the wing post, with the tip of the feather hanging off to the rear. You'll actually work the thread back into the dubbing a bit.

9. After securing the feather, hold it upright so that the quill is parallel and adjacent to the wing post, and take a few more wraps of thread around the wing base in a counterclockwise direction, thus binding the quill in with the hair. This strengthens the area where the hackle will go and also creates a little foundation around which to wrap the feather.

10. Use another small wisp of dubbing to cover up the tie-in wraps and reestablish the thorax. Use just a little, as shown.

The tail in place (step 5).

The body and thorax in place (step 6).

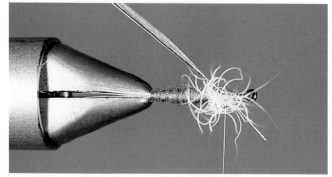

The hackle feather tied in as described (steps 7 & 8).

The wing post standing up, base being reinforced with thread (steps 3 & 4).

Binding the quill in with the wing post (step 9).

11. Grip the tip of the feather with your hackle pliers, and begin the first turn of hackle, wrapping counter-clockwise. On parachutes, each turn of hackle is laid in gently, immediately below the one before, working down the wing post. This causes the hackle to lie flat, as desired. Use just enough tension to keep the feather straight.

12. Three to five turns of hackle should be sufficient, depending on the barb count of the feather and how much hackle you want. When you're finished wrapping, let the feather hang down on the far side of the hook, suspended by the weight of the hackle pliers. At this point, you can follow either steps 13 and 14, using the thread to tie off the hackle, or step 15, finishing the fly with glue.

13. With your left thumb and forefinger, gently lift up the front of the hackle a little so that you can work some thread wraps underneath to tie off the feather, then trim neatly.

14. Here's where a Matarelli whip-finish tool earns its keep. In fact, making a whip finish on a parachute without such a tool is difficult. Mount the thread in the tool, and make the first wrap, sneaking the thread underneath the hackle. Then lift the hackle again, very gently, and finish the knot. You can either lay the bobbin off to the rear and maintain thread tension in that manner or hold the thread with the lower fingers of your left hand.

15. If you had some trouble with those last two procedures, you can make things easier by taking a toothpick and applying a generous drop of Zap-A-Gap or similar adhesive at the base of the wing after completing step 12, allowing the glue to saturate the hackle, thread, and the base of the hair. Rubbing it in with the toothpick aids penetration and accelerates drying. After the glue has dried completely, simply cut off the excess feather and thread. No knots, no fuss, no muss.

Tying off the hackle feather (step 13).

Starting the whip finish (step 14).

Completing the whip finish (step 14).

Wrapping the hackle counterclockwise (steps 11 & 12).

The finished fly, side view.

Is this cheating? If so, I'm a confirmed cheater. True, your vise is occupied for the duration of the drying time. When I'm into parachute production, I have two vises set up so that I can tie another fly while the first one is drying. You can free up your bobbin by simply using the hackle pliers to grip both feather and thread.

Some materials, synthetic yarns in particular, have an annoying habit of wicking up the superglue into the wing post, which makes it pretty stiff. This isn't much of a problem on average-size flies, as it only affects the base, but it's a bit messy on smaller ones. To remedy this, use as little glue as you can get away with; if the problem persists, apply the glue by coming up from the bottom on the rear side of the hook to avoid saturating the base of the wing post.

Another option, if you want to follow the tying-off and whip-finish routine, is to cut a V out of the front of the hackle to allow easier access. Many tiers do this as a matter of course, as they feel that it improves the appearance and performance of the fly.

The Adams Parachute has a mixed hackle that requires two feathers. To tie this pattern, you'll have to learn how to wrap two hackles at once, as well as the superglue finishing method. It's best to use prime-quality saddle hackles because of their length, fine quills, and high barb count. Choose feathers of sufficient lengths that hackle pliers aren't required. This allows the quills to wrap together, yet independently.

The finished fly, bottom view.

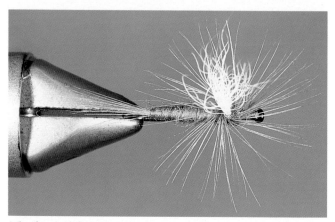

The finished fly, top view.

Adams Parachute

Hook	Standard dry fly, Daiichi model 1180 or comparable, size 10-18.
Thread	Black or dark gray 8/0 Uni-Thread or similar.
Wing post	White calf tail, bucktail, or other hair.
Tail	Use either or both of the hackle colors, or omit.
Body and thorax	Gray dubbing, soft, smooth-packing type, natural or synthetic.
Hackle	Brown and grizzly mixed, as for the standard Adams.

1. Tie everything up to and including the dubbed thorax.

Everything done up to and including the hackle tie-in (step 1).

2. Prepare two hackles, a brown and a grizzly, spoon them, and tie them in together as though they were one. Place them dull sides down, on top of the hook, in front of the wing post, with the tips of the feathers hanging off to the rear. Work the thread back into the dubbing a bit. After securing the feathers, hold them upright so that the quills are parallel and adjacent to the wing post, and take a few more wraps of thread, thus binding the quills in with the hair.

3. As was done with the Blue-Winged Olive, use a tiny bit of dubbing to cover the work area.

4. Using your fingers, wrap both hackles at once, wrapping counterclockwise. Work down the wing post, applying minimal tension. With two feathers going at once, you won't need much; three turns should do it.

5. When sufficient hackle is in place, grip the two quills and the thread with your hackle pliers, and hold them all together. Let everything hang down on the far side of the hook, maintaining tension with the weight of the pliers.

6. Use a toothpick to apply a generous drop of Zap-A-Gap or similar adhesive at the base of the wing, allowing it to saturate the hackle quills, the thread, and the base of the hair. Rub it in with the toothpick to aid penetration and accelerate drying. After the glue has dried, cut off the excess feather and thread.

Dud Soper used a quick and simple method of parachute construction, with the quill or quills of the hackle feathers as a wrapping post. I suggest using cape feathers here, as the quills on saddle feathers are usually too thin to make good hackling posts. Be sure to leave the butt ends of the quills long enough for effective handling during the hackling process. Dud named the fly for the emerging caddis, which are notorious for prancing around on the surface as they attempt to become airborne.

The Zap-A-Gap being applied with a toothpick (step 6).

The completed Adams Parachute, side view.

The completed Adams Parachute, bottom view.

The hackles being wrapped (steps 2–4).

The completed Adams Parachute, top view.

Dud's Kickin' Caddis

Hook	Standard dry fly, Daiichi model 1180 or comparable, size 10-16.
Thread	Brown or tan 8/0 Uni-Thread or similar.
Wing post	The quills.
Tail	None.
Body and thorax	Tannish dubbing, soft, smooth-packing type, natural or synthetic.
Hackle	Brown and gray or, better yet, gray-dyed grizzly, mixed.

1. Tie on just to the rear of the eye, wrap to the bend, and make a dubbed body and thorax, working forward to a position just ahead of where the hackle will be tied in. Then wrap back into the front of the dubbing a bit.

2. Prepare the two hackles and tie them in together as for the Adams Parachute, dull sides down, on top of the hook, with the tips of the feathers hanging off to the rear. Don't cut the butt ends short; you'll need them to hold on to.

3. Stand up the quills as you would a hair post, and take a few counterclockwise wraps around the base.

4. As was done for the Adams Parachute, make a small thorax with a bit of dubbing, covering the tie-in of the hackle feathers.

5. Dud tied off everything with the thread, as was done for the Blue-Winged Olive. If you prefer, you can use the Zap-A-Gap method. You can wrap the feathers one at a time, but it's advisable to wrap both hackles at once, without hackle pliers.

6. Proceed with the tie-in and wrapping as instructed for the Adams Parachute, using the quills as the post. A very soft touch is required here. When switching hands, hold the hackles in a slightly downward attitude so that some of the tension is exerted against the hook rather than the quill post. The hackle will probably flare upward a bit and not lie quite as flat as it does when wrapped around a post. If this is not extreme, it's perfectly okay, and in one sense it's a plus, as it enables you to see the fly better on the water.

7. Tie off with thread as was done for the Blue-Winged Olive, but don't do the whip finish yet. Cut a V out of the front of the hackle, then fold the quills forward, through the cut-away area, and tie them on top of the hook.

8. Trim all tag ends, and whip-finish. Then put a small droplet of Zap-A-Gap onto the center of the wrapped hackle so that it saturates into that spot.

Many tiers use a supplemental device of some sort, such as a gallows tool, to apply tension to the quills when they're used as hackling posts. I have abandoned that in favor of a few turns of thread around the base and a delicate touch when wrapping. The feathers of today are so

The hackles ready to be wrapped. Note the upright quills (steps 1–5).

The hackles wrapped around the quill butts (step 6).

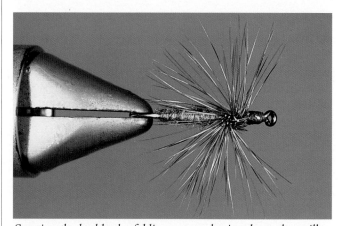

Securing the hackles by folding over and tying down the quills completes the Kickin' Caddis (steps 7 & 8).

much easier to use than the junk Dud and I were using back in the 1960s and 1970s we can get away without such props.

Sometimes Dud and I added wings to parachutes of similar construction. The Gray Fox is one such dressing that incorporates hackle-tip wings. It can be used to imitate lots of different mayflies, including the eastern *Stenonema,* the large *Hexagenia* of the Midwest, and the *Callibaetis* of the Rockies.

Gray Fox Flat-Hackle

Hook	Standard dry fly, Daiichi model 1180 or comparable, size 10-14.
Thread	Cream or tan 8/0 Uni-Thread or similar.
Wing post	The quills.
Tails	None, or your choice as for the parachute flies.
Body and thorax	Pale tan or cream dubbing, soft, smooth-packing type.
Hackle	Straw cream and grizzly, mixed.
Wings	Grizzly hackle tips, soft rooster or hen.

1. Tie everything up to and including the dubbed thorax.

2. Complete the hackle, and tie everything off as for Dud's Kickin' Caddis. Leave a bit of extra space up front, and cut out a V.

3. Select a pair of hackle tips of appropriate size. I prefer quality hen, but soft rooster will work. Strip all material from the quills except that which will form the wings.

4. Set the feathers in place in the delta of the V, convex-to-convex, so that they flare away from each other.

5. Sneak the thread up over the quills, and tie them on top of the hook. With a few tight turns of thread, force the wings back against the front of the body so they stand up to some degree.

6. Trim the butts and do a whip finish, then Zap-A-Gap the center of the hackle and the wing base. You can use the Zap-A-Gap for head cement, but be careful not to get any into the hook eye.

Give these flies a good workout on the streams; they can be amazing producers. There are many other parachute patterns, some of which are given for small flies in the next chapter.

Body and hackle completed as done for the Kickin' Caddis (steps 1 & 2).

The wings tied on (steps 3–5).

Securing and trimming the wing butts completes the fly (step 6).

CHAPTER 11

Small and Smaller

Many people break out in a sweat at the thought of tying mini and micro flies. When tiers first began to appreciate the significance of flies in sizes 18, 20, and smaller, the specialized materials required to tie them efficiently and effortlessly weren't available, hackle in particular. Although very small hooks were available, they were not of proper design. They were simply reductions of larger hooks, with no special consideration given to either tying or fishing these tiny flies.

That's all changed. Today we have everything we need to tie excellent tiny flies with ease and comfort—hooks, threads, dubbings, and so on. We also have come to understand more about minifly design, what needs to be included, and what can be left off. Why struggle to tie some component in excruciating detail when the fish can't see it anyway?

When I first began tying the tiny stuff, I used a hook that was simply a standard dry-fly hook made smaller—a down-eyed hook in which the gape was reduced in direct proportion to the shank length. The problem was that the smaller the size, the poorer the hooking characteristics. In fact, anything below an 18 was pretty bad.

A quick look at the architecture of a standard dry fly clearly illustrates the problems with miniaturization. Look at the size 22 hook in the lower left of the photograph on the opposite page. This is an improved design, but even so, note the proximity of the eye and the point. Adding body would further reduce this clearance, and a stiff hackle becomes a vitual hook guard, getting in the way of the point. This will bounce the hook right out of the jaws of a taking trout without even a scrape.

In an effort to solve this problem, minifly tiers tried straight-eye and up-eye hooks. The straight-eye worked better from an engagement standpoint, but it limited the kinds of knots that could be used, because any knot that is formed behind the eye—including the popular improved and figure eight turle knots—requires a turned-down or turned-up eye.

Eventually hook manufacturers realized that hooks needed to be designed expressly for miniflies. There are now a number of satisfactory hook designs in which the gape is not reduced proportionately to the shank and the points are sufficiently short to allow optimal clearance.

Other developments were in hackle, with suppliers now offering decent small hackles, and dubbing, which has been refined and is now suitable for some miniflies. Quite a few good dubbings are available, some of which will dub down almost to thread diameter. Look for those with the finest possible texture. Synthetics have made a major contribution here, and natural silk also makes excellent dubbing for tiny flies. There's plenty of color selection; you'll be able to come pretty close to what you're trying to match.

Modern threads have also helped. Threads of 8/0 rating and even finer are so strong that you can do just about any operation with them. These threads come in a wide range of colors, so that not only can you match thread color with body material color, but you can dispense with body material entirely on very small flies and use just the thread. I am very much an advocate of the thread-only approach; it's much more practical.

If you can't find the shade you want, a waterproof marker on white thread works wonders. A good artist's supply shop offers an enormous assortment of markers. Keep in mind, however, that when a marker is applied to an absorbent material like thread, the ink darkens, sometimes quite a lot. Take a spool of thread with you to the store and experiment until you find the desired shade. Also, you can't allow a cyanoacrylate superglue to come into contact with marker ink.

The Griffith Gnat is a delightfully simple minifly pattern that often outperforms more complex ones. It is named after the legendary George Griffith, who fished the Au Sable system in Michigan for the better part of a century, as he lived into his nineties. I don't know whether he originated the pattern. He lived on the north bank of the Middle Branch of the Au Sable and is credited with contributing to the development of the unique and pretty drift boats that bear the river's name.

A group of tiny hooks. Upper left: *Daiichi 1330, size 22;* upper right: *Daiichi J220, size 20;* lower left: *partridge L3A, size 22;* lower right: *Daiichi 1480, size 24.*

Griffith Gnat

Hook	Small dry fly with adequate gape, size 16 and smaller.
Thread	Black 8/0 or smaller.
Body	Fine peacock herl.
Hackle	Grizzly, palmer-wrapped over the peacock.

1. Tie on near the eye, and wrap to the bend.
2. Tie in the peacock herl. I usually reinforce peacock bodies by twisting in a piece of thread with the herl. That's still the recommended method here, size allowing. However, when tying on a very small hook, such as 22, you can wrap just the peacock.
3. Tie in the hackle feather in typical dry-fly fashion.

The peacock herl and hackle feather tied in.

4. Wrap the peacock body.
5. Wrap the hackle palmer-style, and whip-finish.

As a variation, you can tie in the hackle about one-quarter of the shank length short of the eye. Then do the body, wrapping behind and in front of the hackle feather. Wrap a few turns of hackle through the front portion of the peacock, and tie off. This causes the fly to drift with the body hanging down below the surface. There are times when this seems to have more fish appeal than the standard version.

Among the most frequently encountered tiny stream insects are the famous *Tricorythodes,* or Tricos, as they're called. Several of these are important. They vary in size, a 20 being a large one and a 28 being the smallest, at least from a practical standpoint. Their bodies are dark brown or black; impregnated females carry a dull green egg mass.

Tricos usually hatch early in the morning, but on overcast days, they may come on later. In the East, we start seeing the hatch in late June through mid-July. On some rivers, it runs on into August and even early September. As the hatch progresses, it generally appears a bit later in the morning, for which I am thankful.

The adult life of the Trico is brief. They come off the water as duns, and go into their final molt almost immediately. Frequently duns are still emerging while spinners from the same hatch are hovering over the water. The trout are liable to take either form.

When imitating the dun, it's wise to consider what sort of water you'll be fishing. Tricos may appear in broken currents as well as calm pools. I like to use different styles as appropriate for the locale. In quiet waters, a tiny standard-style or thorax-style fly with prominent wings or a small parachute works well. In faster, more diffused currents, a hackle-wing thorax tie is effective. Sometimes you can even get away with using the Griffith Gnat.

The duns have prominent silvery white wings. You can use a very pale watery gray or white hen cape to imitate them. It's important that the quills be fine and the texture of the feathers soft, as you'll be fishing with 6X or 7X tippets, and they are easily twisted. For hackles and tails, very pale watery gray is ideal, but if you can't find that in tiny sizes, a pale grizzly will do just fine. For the wing post on the parachute version, I recommend white Antron or Z-lon yarn or, for improved visibility, the yarn in a bright color.

For the body, I prefer to use thread, especially for size 24 or smaller, although you can use dubbing of the softest, finest type on size 22 or larger, if you wish. If you can't find the color you want, use a waterproof marker.

The completed peacock body.

Wrapping the palmer-style hackle completes the fly.

The Griffith Gnat variation in progress. Note the repositioning of the hackle.

The completed Griffith Gnat variation.

Standard or Thorax Trico

Hook	Dry fly, size 20 or smaller.
Thread	8/0 or finer, to match the desired body color.
Wings	White or very pale gray hen tippets.
Tail	White or very pale gray hackle barbs.
Body	Black, dark brown, or bottle green, a dark dull green.
Hackle	White or very pale gray.

This fly is tied just like the Pale Morning Dun standard and thorax, but smaller, so follow the instructions as given in the cut-wing chapter. Be sure to make the tails and hackles in proper proportion so as not to distort the size of the fly. The wings should be prominent, especially on the thorax version.

The hackle feather tied in.

The wings shaped and tied in place.

Wrapping the hackle. When working behind the wings, tip them forward a bit if necessary for clearance.

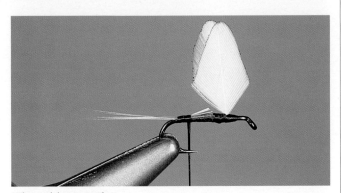

The tail being tied on.

The first turn of hackle in front of the wings resets them in position.

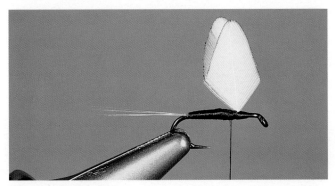

The completed body.

The completed Trico.

The Trico can be tied cut-wing-thorax style. This is a side view.

The Hackle-Wing Trico, side view.

A front view of the Trico tied cut-wing-thorax style.

The Hackle-Wing Trico, front view.

The hackle-wing thorax version is easy to tie and often is just the right medicine when fishing more broken currents. This dressing is a compromise between the dun and the spent. The dressing is the same, except that the hackle is slightly oversize, about one hook size larger than normal. Simply form the thorax as instructed, but leave off the wings. You might consider the dullish green for the body, as the fly may well be taken for an ovipositing female.

The Trico can also be tied as a parachute by following the instructions for the Tiny Olive Parachute, below, but using Trico colors. The problem of wing-post saturation when using superglue to finish off the fly is particularly critical on tiny sizes. It's best to apply the adhesive from the bottom at the rear.

The true spent Trico is tied as in the same manner as the Rusty Spinner, so follow the instructions for that dressing as given in the chapter on spinners and spents. Try to find some very pale gray or white hackle with a distinct sheen. Use a green body and thorax. Tie the tails spent-style after tying in and wrapping the hackle. Wrap thread or dubbing to the bend and make a small ball. Thread is a lot easier. Tie in one hackle barb or Micro Fibett on each side of the hook, fairly long. Force the tail fibers back against the ball so that they spread widely. Then proceed with the rest of the fly.

The Trico Parachute.

The Trico Spent. Note the small ball of thread that spreads the tails.

Parachutes in small sizes can be very effective. In the fall of 1996, Bob Dodge and I were fishing DePuy's. It was mid-October, and the weather varied from pleasant to almost wintry. Every day, a heavy hatch of tiny blue-winged olive mayflies occurred, ranging in size from 20 to 24. There were other fishermen on the stream, most using the same fly—a small Compara-dun, sometimes with a yarn tail to imitate a dragging shuck. It was a good imitation. The trouble was, the trout knew it all too well. Not being admirers of handcrafts, they simply refused to take what they'd been looking at for weeks on end.

After a rather frustrating first day, Bob and I held a council of war over dinner. We decided to try parachutes. We would adhere to proper sizing and not worry too much about color, going for visibility so that we could easily identify our flies among the flotilla of naturals, something we had a lot of trouble doing that first day.

That evening, we tied little parachutes with chartreuse Antron yarn wing posts, some with shuck-dragger or Sparkle Dun tails, and some with regular tails. We used Hoffman Grizzly for the hackles.

The rest of the trip, we did great. The color of the wing post didn't affect the flies' effectiveness, but it did enable us to see our flies and thus control drift and deal with drag. We had the other anglers muttering and glaring, although if they had asked, we would gladly have shown them what we were using.

The Tiny Olive Parachute is presented here. Aside from their size, these flies and other small parachutes are tied in exactly the same manner as their larger relatives, as discussed in the chapter on parachutes. It's important that the wing post be visible. Here I'm using bright fluorescent green synthetic yarn. A thin strand of synthetic floss is used for the body. Because of their small size, I recommend using Zap-A-Gap to secure the hackle and finish off these flies. Be careful to keep it from saturating the wing post.

Tiny Olive Parachute

Hook	Tiny dry fly.
Thread	8/0 or finer, depending on hook size. If the thread will also be the body material, it should match the desired body color.
Wing post	Something slim but very visible: brightly colored Antron or similar yarn, Krystal Flash, or very fine hair.
Tail	A few hackle barbs or a little piece of amber Sparkle Yarn, as shown here.
Body and thorax	On larger sizes, dubbing, floss, or something similar if you wish; on smaller sizes, just thread.
Hackle	Tiny grizzly or gray feather.

1. Tie on up front, wrap a small thread base, then tie on a piece of your chosen material for the wing post about an inch (25 millimeters) in length. Don't stand it up or trim it yet.

2. Wrap to the rear, and tie the tail and body. A Sparkle Dun tail is shown here.

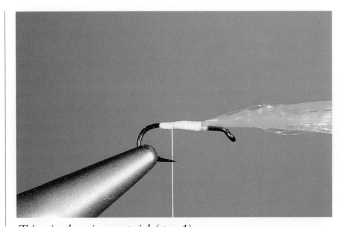

Tying in the wing material (step 1).

Shuck-dragger, or Sparkle Dun, tail in place (step 2).

3. When you reach the place where the wing post is in repose, stand it up with some turns of thread at the base in front.

4. Tie in the feather with the dull side down, on top of the hook, in front of the wing post, with the tip of the feather hanging off to the rear.

5. After securing the feather, hold it upright so that the quill is integrated with the wing post, and take a few more wraps of thread, thus binding the quill in with the yarn. This stiffens the area where the hackle will go and also creates a little base around which to wrap the feather.

6. Use a few thread wraps or a tiny bit of dubbing to cover up the tie-in wraps and to level the body and thorax fore and aft of the wing post.

7. Grip the tip of the feather with your hackle pliers, and begin the first turn of hackle, wrapping counter-clockwise. On parachutes, each turn of hackle is laid in gently, immediately below the one before, working down the wing post. This causes the hackle to lie flat, as desired. Use just enough tension to keep the feather straight.

8. Three or four turns of hackle should be sufficient, depending on the barb count of the feather and how much hackle you want. When you're finished wrapping, let the feather hang down on the far side of the hook, suspended by the weight of the hackle pliers.

9. Follow the finishing steps described for the Blue-Winged Olive Parachute. You can use the thread for tying off the hackle, but I prefer to finish off these small flies with glue. Use it sparingly, and try not to let it run up the wing post. When everything is secured in place, trim the wing post to the desired length.

There are many other small insects that can be imitated, and other techniques for doing so. The ones I've shared with you here are my favorites. I hope they bring you the success they've brought me.

Body and thorax in place, wing material standing upright, hackle tied in (steps 3–6).

The completed fly (steps 7–9).

CHAPTER 12

Variants

The variant is a unique style of dry fly. A variant has no wings; instead, the oversize hackle forms a wing silhouette. Art Flick, who is credited with having originated the variant design, makes this quite clear. In his classic *Streamside Guide to Naturals and Their Imitations,* he uses the Dun Variant to imitate the large slate drake, *Isonychia bicolor,* the Cream Variant for a *Potamanthus distinctus,* and the wonderful Gray Fox Variant for *Ephemera guttulata,* the eastern green drake. The mottled hackle also does a fine job of imitating the wings of certain other large mayflies, notably the *Stenonema,* which include the March Brown and its first cousin, the Gray Fox. In addition, these flies are great general attractor flies for probing pockets and diffused currents.

When Art first started tying these flies, obtaining hackle and tailing material was no problem. Although finding properly sized feathers for hackling anything smaller than a size 12 was a virtual impossibility, large hackles abounded. Now it's the other way around. The integration of the Hoffman and Hebert strains of chickens, along with innovations by master geneticist Dr. Tom Whiting, may solve this supply problem. As a bonus, we would also have really good tailing material at our disposal.

The bodies on these flies use the same material as was described for the Red Quill in the chapter on flank-feather wings; refer to that section for instructions on preparing the bodies. Each pattern calls for a different color. If you believe in accuracy in this department, look for feathers with quills that remain true to color after being stripped of their barbs. Avoid those that darken at the center, unless the darkened shade is what you're looking for. In other words, you wouldn't want to use a furnace hackle for the body on a Dun Variant, even though the outer portions of the barbs might have a rich mahogany coloration.

Stripped quills in strung bundles are a great convenience if you can find them in the color or colors you want. However, you may end up having to strip the quills yourself, as described for the Red Quill.

A pair of typical hackle feathers suitable for tying a variant.

For the hackle, your best bet is to look for long-barbed spade or throat hackles along the sides of capes, as you would for tailing material. You won't find a lot of these on even the most well-endowed capes, so treasure them. Grizzly is the hardest to come by, as it can't be replicated by dyeing, and only a few strains of barred rock, such as the Dominique and Plymouth Rock birds, have long-barbed throat hackles. One positive note is that they don't have to be nicely barred. Practically anything that has some light-dark contrast will suffice.

While the tails need to be somewhat longer than they would be for a standard fly on a particular hook size, they need not be proportionately so. If you're tying a variant on a size 14 hook and are using hackles that are three or four times oversize, which translates to sizes 8 and 6, the tails could be equal to those of a normal size 10. This leans the fly to the rear a bit on the water, which helps prevent it from tipping over on its face. I tie most of my variants on size 14 and 16 hooks, plus a few 12s at Green Drake time.

The ratio of body to hackle is about two-thirds to one-third. Having too much of the hook covered with the hackles will make the flies tip over on their faces.

Two different variants are presented here. The first one, the Dun Variant, is a bit simpler, as it does not have a mixed hackle and tail. The Gray Fox Variant is very productive and is one of my all-time favorite flies.

Art Flick tied the Dun Variant to represent an insect often called the mahogany dun because of its body color. The dressing below calls for stripped quill from a dark coachman brown neck. If you don't have any quills of this shade, you can color a lighter quill with a dark mahogany brown waterproof marker. If you do this, however, you can't use cyanoacrylate superglue, as the thinner in glues turns marker ink into wild colors. As a substitute, I use a high-quality water-base head cement, such as the one offered by BT Products.

Dun Variant

Hook	Standard dry fly, Daiichi model 1180 or comparable, size 8-14.
Thread	Dark brown 8/0 Uni-Thread or comparable.
Tail	Medium to dark gray hackle barbs.
Body	A stripped quill from a dark coachman brown cape.
Hackle	Medium to dark gray, oversize.

1. Tie on just to the rear of the eye, and wrap to about the center point of the hook shank.
2. Select the tailing barbs and gauge them for length, keeping in mind the comments above. See the photo for proportions.
3. Tie on the tailing material, and wrap neatly over it to the bend. Slip two or three turns of thread underneath the base of the tail in order to obtain the desired spread. Trim off the excess material on a gentle slope, as it will be bound down as underbody.
4. Tie in the body quill by the tip end in such a position that the first turn will fall precisely where the tail joins the hook at the bend. Trim the tip on a slant, then wrap over the excess and bury it smoothly as underbody, along with the tail butts.
5. Wrap the quill, with each turn adjacent to the one preceding. Finish just ahead of the original tie-on point.
6. Secure the quill, then slope-cut and trim off the excess. Use whatever thread wraps may be necessary to smooth out the area.

The tail in place (steps 2 & 3).

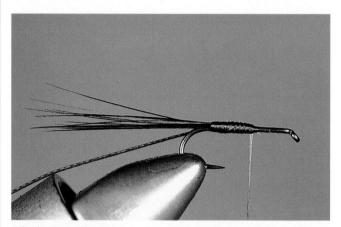
The body quill tied in, underbody formed (step 4).

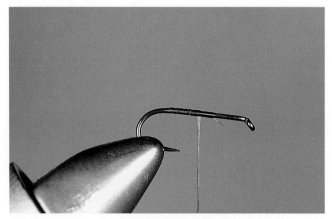
The tie-in. Note the thread position (step 1).

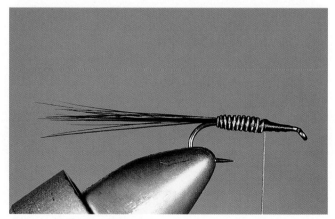
The completed body (steps 5 & 6).

7. Select two large hackle feathers, as described above. Strip to the sweet spots, keeping in mind that you will be using only the outer parts of these feathers, where dry-fly-quality barbs are found. Tie in the feathers by the butt ends of the quills, spoon-style, pretty side forward, leaving a tiny bit of each quill exposed. Advance the thread to where the hackles will be tied off.

8. Wrap whichever feather looks as though it wants to go first, secure it as previously instructed, and trim neatly.

9. Wrap the second hackle, integrating it with the first. Secure it, neaten up, and whip-finish. Either now or later, coat the body with protective adhesive.

10. Remove the fly from the vise and set it on the table. It should rest on the tip of the tail and hackle, with the hook suspended well above the flat plane. When properly dressed, this is how the fly will ride the currents.

Getting Variants to come out neat and pretty is difficult. The large feathers are very obtuse, and the quill body is hard to tie off and trim neatly. Don't worry about it. Do the best you can, trim when you must, and go catch some trout. Remember, this is not an art exhibit. Your flies need only pass the inspection of a hungry fish.

The dressing for the Gray Fox Variant, as set forth in Art Flick's book, calls for three hackles: light ginger, dark ginger, and grizzly. That gets tricky. He tied these flies on relatively large hooks, 10s and 12s, which allowed more space for the three quills. He got very few turns, as the sweet spots on the feathers of that era were quite short.

If you can find a barred ginger that has both the light and dark shades, you can tie a faithful rendition of this pattern with two feathers. If you need to use three, as demonstrated here, look for feathers with fine quills and strip them back to the sweet spots religiously; don't use anything that has any negative attributes. If I'm anticipating fishing the eastern green drake hatch, I might substitute a pale olive green hackle for the dark ginger.

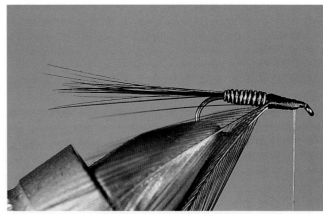

The hackle feathers tied in. Note thread base (step 7).

The first hackle in place (step 8).

The wrapping of the second hackle completes the Dun Variant (step 9).

Gray Fox Variant

Hook	Standard dry fly, Daiichi model 1180 or comparable, size 10-12.
Thread	Primrose, pale olive, or tan 8/0 Uni-Thread or comparable.
Tail	Mixed grizzly and ginger hackle barbs.
Body	A stripped quill from a ginger cape.
Hackle	Dark ginger, light ginger, and grizzly; or dark-and-light barred ginger and grizzly.

1. Refer to the chapter on tippet wings for instructions on making a mixed tail. Then proceed with the tying steps as listed for the Dun Variant.
2. If using three hackles, examine the quills, and when laying the feathers together spoon-style, place the one with the finest quill last.
3. Wrap the hackles sequentially. If you notice that the wrapping of a feather upsets the hackle wrapped previously, back off and do it over with a slightly different positioning and perhaps a bit less tension. Use as few wraps as possible to secure the first two feathers, keeping in mind that the wraps used to secure subsequent feathers also secure those that went before.
4. After wrapping the third hackle feather, secure it, neaten up, and whip-finish. Either now or later, coat the body with protective adhesive.

Now you have in your arsenal one of the truly great styles of dry fly in angling history. The variants have been great producers over the years, especially when fished in the ever-varying currents of our freestone rivers or just at dusk, when the trout can see quite well and feel that they also are less visible. They can get a bit careless at such times, and the variant style can be just the ticket.

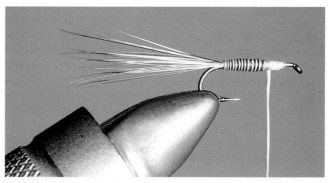

The completed body (step 1).

The three hackle feathers tied in (step 2).

The first two hackles wrapped (step 3).

The tail is in place, the body quill tied in, the underbody formed (step 1).

The wrapping of the third hackle completes the Gray Fox Variant (step 4).

CHAPTER 13

Soft-Hackle Wet Flies

The soft-hackle is a basic fly form that has been part of the history of fly fishing since its origin. The classic *Treatise on Fishing with an Angle,* attributed to Dame Juliana Berners around the end of the 1400s, describes a number of patterns that qualify as soft-hackles and could be fished effectively today. Centuries later, this type of fly became very popular in America, and it remains so today. In 1941, Jim Leisenring gave us a most interesting little book, *The Art of Tying the Wet Fly,* republished in 1971 by Crown with a supplement by Vernon Hidy called *Fishing the Flymph.* More recently, Sylvester Nemes rejuvenated and expanded on the soft-hackle with several books and articles, including *The Soft-Hackled Fly* (Stackpole Books, 1975) and *The Soft-Hackled Fly Addict* (Stackpole Books, 1981).

Soft-hackle wet flies are fairly simple to tie. Their effectiveness lies not so much in a close resemblance to natural insects but in the emulation of their behavior. When properly dressed, these flies can be induced to swim and dance underwater. They virtually come to life, and that's often all it takes to entice a hungry fish.

If there is one overriding discipline in the tying of these flies, it's delicacy. They should not be overdressed, especially the hackle. Often, one turn is enough, as some of the feathers commonly used are webby and heavily barbed. An ancient pattern that continues to take trout is called the Orange Fishawk. The badger hackle called for in this dressing doesn't refer to the fur of the animal of that name. It describes a type of feather that is cream or off-white, with a black or very dark center. If you ever look a badger in the face, you'll understand where the name came from.

Ellis fly.

Orange Fishawk

Hook	Standard wet fly, medium-gauge wire, Daiichi model 1550 or comparable.
Thread	Pale-colored, orange 8/0 or even finer.
Ribbing	Very fine gold tinsel, either flat or oval.
Body	Orange floss.
Hackle	Badger, tied collar-style.

1. Tie on about one-third of the shank length back from the eye.
2. Cut off a short piece of tinsel, and tie it in against the bottom of the hook, gold side inward. If you've chosen flat tinsel that has a gold and a silver side, tie it in with the side you want exposed against the hook shank. This may sound backward, but when you begin to make the first wrap, the tinsel automatically flips over, and the side you want showing is thus exposed.
3. Hold the tinsel with your left hand, and while applying moderate tension, wrap over it to the bend of the hook, keeping your thread wraps neat and smooth.
4. Trim off any tag end of tinsel at the tie-in point, then wrap forward a little way past that point.
5. Tie in a short piece of thin floss and trim off the excess. Tying in soft, floppy materials of this type can be frustrating, as they tend to escape the thread. To overcome this, stretch the floss between the thumbs and forefingers of your two hands and hold it against the back of the hook, immediately in front of the thread. Press the floss against the back side of the hook shank with the middle finger of your left hand. This immobilizes the floss and frees your right hand. Pick up the bobbin and pass the thread around the hook, thus securing the floss in place.
6. Wrap the floss to the bend and back, creating a double layer. Secure and trim the floss, allowing enough room at the front for the hackle and whip finish.

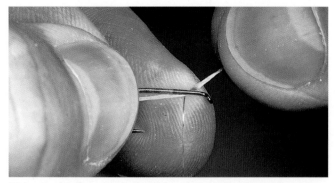
Tying in the floss, per instructions given earlier (step 5).

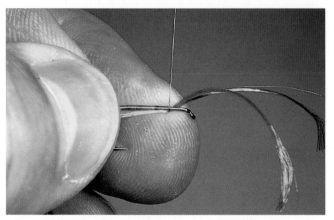
Tying in the floss, per instructions given earlier (step 5).

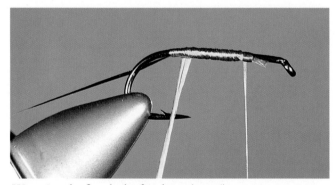
Wrapping the floss body, first layer (step 6).

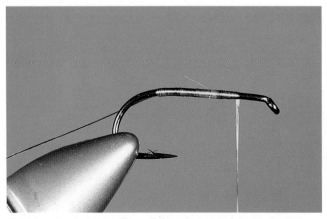
Ribbing tinsel tied in, base of thread wrapped (steps 1–4).

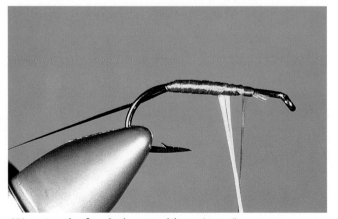
Wrapping the floss body, second layer (step 6).

7. Wrap the ribbing candy cane style. You'll get four or five turns, depending on hook size.

8. If you wish, you can prefold the hackle feather by stroking all of the barbs to one side of the quill. The pretty side of the feather should remain outward during this procedure.

9. Tie in the feather by the tip end, secure, and trim.

10. Begin to wrap the hackle, meanwhile stroking back the barbs with your left hand so that they lie back at an angle and form a sort of cornucopia around the body of the fly. A few turns of hackle are sufficient; the exact number depends on the texture of the feather at hand. Don't overdress. Whip-finish.

11. For a black head, which blends beautifully with the dark center of the hackle feather, touch the thread with a waterproof marker before applying head cement.

Another simple pattern that's tied in the same manner is the Partridge and Green. The quills of Hungarian partridge, or Huns, as they are called, are fairly bulky, which can make things a little tight when tying on, wrapping, and tying off the hackle. To help counteract this, I suggest tying in the feather differently, as described on the next page.

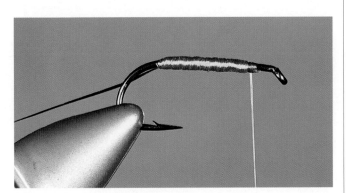

The completed floss body (step 6).

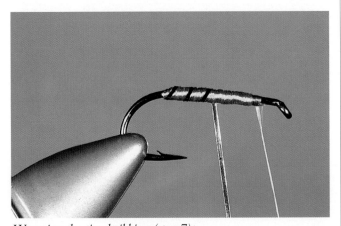

Wrapping the tinsel ribbing (step 7).

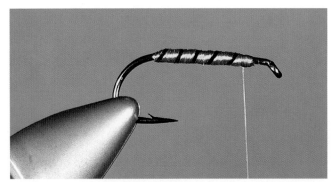

The wrapped tinsel ribbing (step 7).

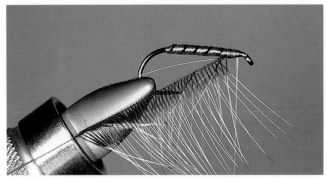

A prefolded hackle feather tied in (steps 8 & 9).

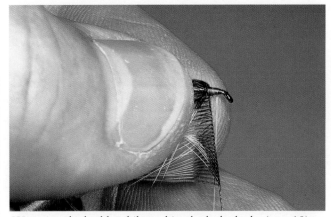

Wrapping the hackle while stroking back the barbs (step 10).

Another turn or two of hackle completes the Orange Fishawk. (Step 11).

Partridge and Green

Hook	Standard wet fly, medium-gauge wire.
Thread	Pale-colored, green 8/0 or even finer.
Ribbing	Very fine silver tinsel, either flat or oval.
Body	Green floss or Uni-Stretch.
Hackle	Hungarian partridge, tied collar-style.

1. Tie on a little way from the eye.
2. Prepare the Hun feather by stripping away all the soft, webby material at the base. Gently flare the barbs to about a 90-degree angle from the quill.
3. Tie in the feather by the tip end with the concave, or dull, side inward. Leave just enough space at the front for a wrap or two of feather and the tie-off. Wrap neatly to the bend, binding down the excess Hun feather as underbody.
4. Proceed as was done with the Orange Fishawk, tying in the ribbing, tying in and wrapping the floss body, then wrapping the ribbing. Meanwhile, the Hun feather hangs out to the front. When trimming off and securing the excess body material and ribbing, be very neat, and don't encroach on the space left for the hackle.
5. Pass the thread in front of the Hun feather. Then gently grip the feather with your hackle pliers and wrap, while stroking back the barbs to form a collar. One turn is usually sufficient; two will give a fuller effect. Secure the quill, trim, and whip-finish.

Hungarian partridge is also used on a somewhat different sort of soft-hackle. This one is the creation of Ellis Hatch of Rochester, New Hampshire, who loves to fish for brookies in ponds. I simply call this fly Ellis.

On the Ellis fly, a bead is used for the thorax. A number of types of beads are available in fly shops. For this fly, I particularly like the kind known as Cyclops Eyes, which are drilled so that the hole is of larger diameter on one end than the other. They come in several sizes and metallic finishes. Even more variety will probably develop as their popularity grows. (I should mention that the original dressing shown to me by Ellis used a little ball of black dubbing to form the thorax. The bead was my idea; I like the added weight. I hope Ellis approves of

The hackle is tied in first (steps 1–3).

Proceed as per the Orange Fishawk. Here's the finished fly (steps 4 & 5).

this innovation, as well as the substitution of moose mane for peacock.)

The bead pretty much eliminates the option of tying in the hackle feather first. It's not impossible to tie it in at the beginning, as done for the previous fly, but it gets a little messy, because you would then have to tie in the hackle, tie off, remove the hook from the vise, slide the bead in place, put the hook back in the vise, tie back on, complete the body and whatever else goes with it, tie off, then tie on again in front of the bead and complete the hackle. With the Ellis, it's better to follow the more conventional procedure, as described on the next page.

Ellis

Hook	Typical wet fly, Daiichi model 1550 or comparable.
Thread	Black 8/0 Uni-Thread or similar.
Tail	Gray-phase mottled Hungarian partridge hackle (optional).
Body	Stripped dual-tone quill from the eyed portion of a peacock tail feather or moose mane.
Thorax	Black or charcoal-gray bead.
Hackle	Gray-phase mottled Hungarian partridge.

1. Debarb the hook, and slide the bead into place. Thread the bead small end first onto the hook, so that the wider end points rearward when the bead is in place.
2. If you opt for a tail, tie it in place now. Bind down the butt ends to form a smooth underbody. The thread ends up at the bend of the hook.
3. If you opt for the stripped-peacock-quill body, pre-pare and create it as described for a Quill Gordon (chapter 4). The effect can also be simulated by using one light and two dark moose mane hairs. Tie them in at the rear by the tip ends, with the white one trailing, and wrap them all together, maintaining this orientation. Finish the body up front, adjacent to the bead, as shown.
4. Wrap some thread at the front until the bead is firmly secured at the front of the body. Then tie off with a whip-finish.
5. Tie on again in front of the bead.
6. Prepare a partridge hackle by stripping off the fluffy stuff at the butt end, then stroking the prime barbs so that they are perpendicular to the quill, as shown. Leave enough for no more than two turns of hackle; this fly fishes best when tied sparsely.
7. Tie in the feather by the tip end, with the outside, or pretty side, of the feather facing forward. Bind it down securely to prevent it from pulling out during wrapping, then trim off the excess.

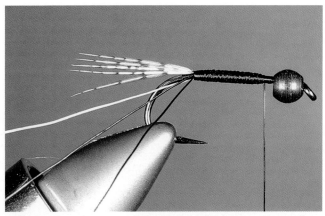

The tail and body material tied in (steps 2 & 3).

The body completed (step 3).

The bead secured in place, the thread reattached in front (steps 4 & 5).

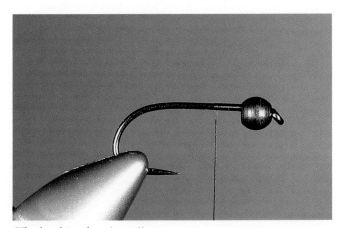

The bead in place (step 1).

The hackle feather tied in (steps 6 & 7).

8. Take one or two turns of hackle, and while doing so, gently stroke the feather with a rearward motion so that the barbs form an attractive cornucopia around the bead.

9. Tie off. Then, while holding the fly in a downward position, coat the body with Zap-A-Gap or similar adhesive. You can also use this glue for head cement, but take care not to get any of it in the hook eye.

If you would like to give the fly even greater durability, you may also apply a thin layer of Zap-A-Gap before wrapping the body. This process is used to protect both peacock-quill and moose mane bodies.

Soft feathers like Hungarian partridge, various types of grouse, hen pheasant, and the like make great soft hackles for these types of flies. The one drawback is that they have a rather limited range of sizes, most of the usable feathers being quite large. Hen capes yield plenty of little feathers suitable for tying soft-hackles down to very small sizes. You won't find the same interesting markings that appear on many of the gamebird feathers, but there is quite a variety to choose from.

The other option is to use just the barbs of larger feathers. This requires removing them from the quill, tying them in as a bunch, using distribution-wrap thread techniques, and making them into a collar in that manner. You may not get quite the esthetic effect of a folded and wrapped collar, but from a fishing standpoint, it's fine. There are two methods for tying such a collar. The fibers can be tied in first, pointing forward, then brought into configuration at the very end, or they can be tied in last, pointing to the rear. The first method is my choice, and it's used on the next fly.

I think it would be appropriate to end the soft-hackle wet-fly chapter with a truly Liesenring-type dressing. I won't put you through the tedious steps in preparing the body materials that Big Jim employed; you'll find all kinds of great dubbing mixes in any well-stocked fly shop. But you should become familiar with the style and character of these flies, because they still work as well as ever.

There are a number of Leisenring dressings I would like to present here. However, I don't know where to obtain such materials as snipe and jackdaw, or if it's even

Hackling and coating the body completes the Ellis (steps 8 & 9).

legal to do so. I also have trouble trying to figure out exactly what he means by colors like rusty blue dun, because there are no color pictures in the book. Thus I've chosen the Blue Dun Hackle, a dressing I believe you can replicate with a fair degree of faithfulness. If I were tying this fly my way, I'd opt for oval tinsel, but I'm using flat tinsel because that's what Leisenring specifies.

If you get around to reading Leisenring, you'll see that he's quite particular and explicit about thread colors. As this book shows, so am I. When a fly is wet and viewed through the denser medium of water, the subordinate color of the thread combines with the dubbing to produce a different, more complex color. Stream insects are imbued with such complex and subtle shading. It's important, believe me.

The dressing calls for a body of mole fur. The fur is short and very soft, and there are no guard hairs. The color runs to a dark, leaden gray. It's usually sold by the pelt. To remove the fur effectively and obtain what length is available, shave it off with an electric beard trimmer or barber's tool. If you'd like to fluff it a bit, which I think improves the texture, zap it in a top-blade blender for a few seconds. Mole fur is used here for reasons of authenticity, and also because it's a very good material. From a practical standpoint, however, substitutions are certainly allowable. One dubbing material you might try is natural silk dyed gray, which produces a molelike effect and is a joy to work with.

Blue Dun Hackle (Leisenring)

Hook	Typical wet fly, size 10-16.
Thread	Primrose 8/0 Uni-Thread or similar.
Tail	A few blue dun fibers (optional).
Ribbing	Very fine flat gold tinsel.
Body	Lightly dubbed mole fur, with a bit of the thread showing at the tail butt.
Hackle	Light blue dun hen hackle.

1. Tie on near the eye. Then cut off a small bunch of barbs from the hen feather, and tie them in at the front, pointing forward, leaving just enough space for the head. Use the soft-wrap or distribution-wrap technique so that the barbs deploy evenly around the hook, like the hair on a Muddler head.
2. Wrap to the rear. If you want to include a tail (not shown here), tie in a few fibers as you bury the butts of the hackle, and cover with thread, working to the rear, to smooth out the underbody. The length of the tail should be one and a quarter to one and a half times the shank of a standard wet-fly hook.
3. Come forward a few wraps, thus creating a small tag of primrose thread. Then tie in the ribbing tinsel.
4. Lightly spin on the dubbing, and wrap the body. Here, the single-thread method is used, but on larger hook sizes that require more dubbing, the spinning-loop method is preferable.

The thread tag in place and the ribbing tied in (steps 2 & 3).

Spinning on the dubbing and wrapping the body (step 4).

Spinning on the dubbing and wrapping the body (step 4).

The hackle barbs in place (step 1).

The completed body (step 4).

5. Wrap the ribbing.
6. Stroke back the hackle barbs. Then come in front of them and wrap a few turns of thread to deploy the barbs in a manner similar to wrapped hackle, collar-style. Whip-finish.
7. Take a look at the finished fly. If you think the body needs to be a little more translucent, fuzz it up a bit with a piece of Velcro, the side with the little hooks.

There is virtually no end to what can be imitated or created using the relatively simple soft-hackle wet-fly design. They can be fished anywhere, from the bottom to the surface film. I've even applied floatant and fished them as funky dry flies. They make very good emergers. Unless you're a devoted purist, you'll want a selection of them in your fly box.

The ribbing in place (step 5).

Tying back the hackle barbs completes the fly (step 6).

CHAPTER 14

Winged Wet Flies

Tying winged wet flies is a school of fly tying that seems to have fallen into relative obscurity. That's unfortunate. Winged wet flies are not only pretty, but they also catch fish, and there's also a great deal to be learned from a tying techniques standpoint.

My early years as a fly-fisher were essentially dedicated to mastering the presentation of wet flies and nymphs. In the freestone streams of the Northeast, this was fairly simple, because the water would fish the flies for you if you'd allow it to do so. The idea was to introduce just enough slack to enable the currents to carry the flies naturally, yet not so much that you were out of touch and unable to recognize or respond to a strike.

It was during this period that I found out just how efficiently and effortlessly trout can feed. Quite often, I'd be fishing a slack line and begin a mend or a pickup, only to find that I was fast to a fish. The take had been so subtle that I hadn't detected it. Later, when I began fishing the spring creeks, I was able to see such phenomena as they occurred. These are the advanced lessons that hone the skills and sharpen the perceptions of the angler.

The winged wet fly was introduced from England early in the nineteenth century. Thus the patterns in the old books are quite British. Some of them were general and nonspecific, and they worked very well over here. A few have survived to the present, such as the Hare's Ear and the Coachman. Other well-known patterns are of American origin, such as the Light and Dark Cahill and the March Brown. The gaudy dressings that were popular in the heyday of the wild brook trout were a combination of the two schools, borrowing heavily from the old salmon flies but simplified and streamlined to suit conditions here. These include the Parmachene Belle and the Fontinalis Fin.

A number of materials have been used for winging these flies. Among the most popular are duck and goose wing quills. Turkey wing quills—the mottled brown ones—are also excellent, but they are no longer the low-cost commodity they were when I began tying. The commercial turkey growers have switched over to the white bird, which is inferior in all respects but is easier and cheaper to raise. So the tiers lost the by-product feathers, and supplies became limited. Today, mottled turkey wing quills are still readily available but a bit pricey. Those of us who use and love them do quite a lot of shopping around and are careful to obtain full utility from those we purchase.

Turkey wing quills are usually sold in matched pairs. The two feathers in the package should be virtual mirror images of each other, as you'll need to match up sections from left and right. One side of each feather should have a nice, neat edge with inward curvature, so that when two opposing sections are laid cupped sides together, the well-marked outer sides are exposed.

The other edge of the feather, which is the trailing edge of the flight quill, is curved in the opposite direction and is usually a little ragged. In the good old days, we used these for nymph wing cases and such. What with today's prices, we've learned to make quite acceptable wings out of them, provided they are well marked.

As with dry flies, tying the wings on winged wets is the most difficult operation. The most common mistakes—and this applies to all quill section wings, not just turkey—include the following:
• Using strips that are too wide or, less frequently, too narrow.
• Poor selection of feathers.
• Failure to lay down a proper thread base before tying on the wings.
• Crowding the front of the body.
• Poor technique with the pinch wrap.
• Failure to mount the winging strips in proper position.
• Tying on the strips upside down.
• Upsetting the finished wings while trimming the butts.

Learning the solutions for one type of feather has general application to all, so the techniques you learn for the March Brown lesson can be applied to patterns that use duck, goose, or other feathers. However, waterfowl flight quills have reverse curvature, so although the same general rules and techniques apply, you'll be exposing the back sides of the feather sections, not the fronts, as with turkey.

Wet-fly wings shouldn't be too long, or you'll end up with a ministreamer instead. They shouldn't be too short, either. A rule of thumb is that they should touch an imaginary line that is tangent to the rear extremity of the bend of the hook. That's a good general rule, but minor variations are allowed in order to accommodate hook design and shape. I like my wings just a bit on the longer side. Trust your eye.

A classic dressing that calls for turkey is the American March Brown (there's also a British version), which is designed to imitate the large mayfly *Stenonema vicarium*. It's also a good pattern for simply fishing the waters.

March Brown

Hook	Wet fly, slightly on the longer side, such as those designated 1XL, size 8-12.
Thread	Tan or brown 6/0 or 8/0 .
Tail	A few mottled barbs from a Hungarian partridge feather.
Ribbing	Heavy brown thread.
Body	Light tan or beige dubbing.
Hackle	Hungarian partridge, tied as a beard or throat hackle.
Wings	Mottled brown turkey sections.

1. Tie on near the front, and wrap to the bend. Then tie on the tailing fibers.
2. Tie in a 5- or 6-inch (125- to 150-millimeter) piece of thread for the ribbing.
3. Make a dubbed body, using either the single-thread or spinning-loop method. Don't crowd the front; refer to the photo for proportions.
4. Spiral-wrap and tie off the ribbing.
5. Gather a small bunch of barbs from a well-marked Hungarian partridge feather, being careful to keep the tips even.
6. Hold the bunch beneath the hook, at the throat, so to speak. Tie it in with a few upside-down pinch wraps, secure with several more tight wraps, and carefully trim off the excess.
7. Working very carefully and neatly, wrap a thread base on which to mount the wings, as shown. End up with the thread a bit ahead of the front of the body but not abutting it.

Wrapping the dubbed body, ribbing and material tied in (steps 2 & 3).

The ribbing in place (step 4).

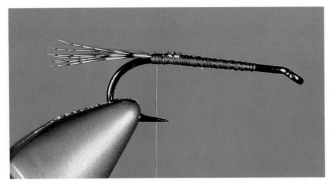

Tying on the tail (step 1).

The beard or throat hackle in place. Note the thread base for the wing (steps 5–7).

8. Cut a section from each of the two turkey feathers—the left and the right. The closer to identical, the better. For a size 10 hook, the strips should be about $^3/_{16}$ to $^7/_{32}$ inch (6 to 7 millimeters) wide.

9. Match the sections with the concave sides facing inward, so that the two curvatures cancel each other out, and the wing strips are straight and flat. They need to be perfectly aligned.

10. Hold the winging set with your right thumb and forefinger, and place it atop the hook with the tips pointed upward. The wings should extend rearward until the tips touch, or barely break, an imaginary line that runs straight upward from the rear extremity of the bend of the hook.

11. With your left thumb and forefinger, hump the winging set slightly by stroking the tips downward. This establishes the desired shape and counteracts the effect the thread will have during tie-on.

12. Transfer the wing set to your left hand. Place the feathers precisely atop the hook, and reestablish the length. Make sure they are perfectly centered and aligned with the hook shank.

13. Sneak the thread up between your fingers, then over the wing set, and between your fingers again on the far side of the hook. Execute your class-A pinch wrap, crushing the wing set down onto the thread base. Repeat this several times. Do not allow the torque action of the thread to move the wings off-center. Keep pressure against the far side of the hook with your left index finger in order to prevent the wings from slipping downward. Some tiers find it helpful, with the first pinch wrap, to come under the hook and sneak the thread up under the fingers a second time, then tighten by pulling upward. If you have trouble, you might give this technique a try.

14. Inspect what you've done. If the wings are not positioned as desired, back off the thread wraps and do the process over again. If they are correctly positioned, grip them in your left hand, hold them steady, and secure them with several firm wraps of thread. Thread torque can still alter the position of the wings. Don't let this happen.

15. Inspect the wings again, and adjust if necessary. Until you have trimmed them off, the wing butts can be used as handles for making subtle adjustments.

16. With the tips of your sharpest scissors, cut off the wing butts flush with the thread wraps. Hold the wings firmly in place while cutting, as the shearing action of the scissors can also upset the wing position. Use several chops instead of trying to cut everything at once, as that exacerbates shearing action.

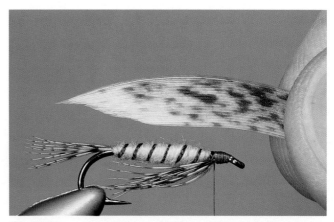

The turkey section being gauged for size against the hook shank. Note how the feather sections have been reshaped (steps 8–11).

The turkey sections tied in place with several pinch wraps (steps 12 & 13).

Securing and trimming the wing butts completes the March Brown (steps 14–17).

17. While still holding the wings, cover the trimmed butts with a few more wraps. Then make a whip finish, and sit back and admire your work.

Here's how to configure a set of wings out of the raggy side of a turkey feather. This works better on some feathers than others.

1. Isolate a section twice the width normally needed for a wing of the size hook you're working on, so that when it's folded, it will be this size you want.
2. Stroke the fibers outward until the tips are even and squared off.
3. Cut the section from the quill and manicure it a bit more, so that its appearance is uniform.
4. Fold the section exactly in half, thus emulating two opposing sections.
5. Stroke the tips into configuration and, if necessary, do a little discreet trimming to improve the shape.

The raggy sides of turkey feathers will vary somewhat in texture and curvature, so go with the flow. When using this part of a feather, it usually works better to mount them with the tips down instead of up.

Another material commonly used for winging wet flies is a waterfowl flank feather. These vary widely in shape and texture. You can work with some in a manner similar to flight quills, whereas others, such as wood duck flank, are best tied on in bunches, almost like a beard hackle, but on top.

You may have noticed that the component being discussed is sometimes referred to as a wing, and other times as wings. Both are accepted in fly-tying parlance. The plural probably would be more proper when referring to feather-winged flies, because there is a back and a front, but most reference materials use the singular.

Barred gray and white mallard flank feathers are a popular winging material, as are those of teal. I consider mallard flank to be interchangeable with teal flank, provided the markings on the teal are not too contrasty and zebralike. There is more variation in teal than in mallard, mainly because there are more kinds of teal ducks. Teal is usually smaller than mallard, except for the large European variety, which is prized for making wing veilings on classic salmon flies.

This type of wing can be a little difficult to tie, unless you're satisfied to simply tie a bunch of fibers on top of a hook and don't care what the fly looks like. Such a fly will probably fish just as well as the neat and pretty version. However, I like a good-looking set of wings, so I'll pass along a couple of techniques here.

A double-wide turkey section from the trailing edge that can be configured into a wet-fly wing (steps 1–3).

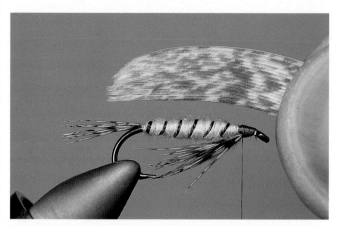

The section doubled over (step 4).

A typical wing formed by this method.

The method that produces the nicest cosmetic effect requires that you find two fairly large flank feathers with neat, well-shaped edges on one side and opposing curvature—that is, a left and a right. They should look like the pair shown for the Grizzly King dressing below. Here's the procedure:

1. Cut two equal sections, one from each feather. Match up the concave sides so that they take the position of a pair of praying hands. You can work with the pointed ends up or down. More often than not, having the pointed ends down works better with these feathers. It's best to go with the flow; let the material do what it wants to do.
2. If you're working with the tips pointing upward, shape the matched sections into a winglike conformation by humping them a bit so that they hug the top of the body and sit low over the back of the fly. This is very similar to the procedure for the turkey sections on the March Brown. What actually goes on during this reshaping process is that the little barbules, the Velcro-like fuzz that holds the fibers together, unmarry and remarry.
3. Set the wing in position, and tie it in place with a series of pinch wraps, keeping the sections centered on the shank and compensating for any rolling to the far side that thread torque might cause.

There's a variation of this method that's easier, faster, and less critical as to the material. It fishes very well and holds its form well in the water because it is double-layered.

1. Select two opposing feathers, but in this case, large ones with long, straight barbs on the good sides.
2. Stroke the barbs in such a manner that they are nicely aligned, with the tips evened up. You'll need wide bunches because they will be folded in half, as done for the raggy turkey wing.
3. Cut two equal bunches from the quills, and lay one on top of the other. Stroke them so that they lie together as one straight bunch made up of two layers. Then fold them in the center, hump them, and tie them in place.

In the case of flank feathers, a limited amount of discreet trimming to improve shape is acceptable. Usually this is a no-no on wings because it results in a very ungraceful appearance, but there are exceptions, and this is one of them.

Feathers of this type vary quite a bit, and you need to learn to be analytical and handle them in accordance with their shapes and innate tendencies. It's up to you to work out the intricate, subtle details that help refine your tying techniques. A fine old pattern that's ideal for learning to tie this sort of wing is the Grizzly King.

Grizzly King

Hook	Wet fly, standard or 1XL shank, size 8-14.
Thread	Ideally, green to match the body; otherwise, some light color, 6/0 or 8/0.
Tail	Opposing red-dyed goose or duck feather sections, narrow.
Ribbing	Fine flat gold tinsel.
Body	Bright green floss, Uni-Stretch, or similar.
Hackle	Soft grizzly.
Wing	Mallard flank feather.

1. Tie on about one-quarter of the hook shank from the eye, and wrap to the rear.
2. The tail is tied just like a wet-fly wing. Match up two narrow, opposing quill sections. Hold them on top of the hook, and establish proper length. Tie the tailing material on top of the hook with a series of pinch wraps. Then work forward and back with gathering wraps, neatly binding down the tail butts. At some appropriate point, taper-cut them for better shaping. End up back at the bend.

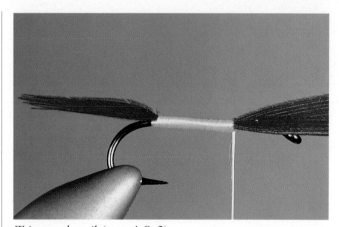

Tying on the tail (steps 1 & 2).

3. Tie in the ribbing tinsel, make a double-layered body with the material of your choice, wrap the ribbing, and trim, as instructed for the Orange Fishawk. There's a little trick that's often useful when making a ribbed body such as this one. While wrapping the body, pass one turn of the body material behind the tied-in ribbing tinsel at the rear of the hook. This better positions the tinsel for the first wrap. Be sure the tinsel is below the hook when you do this, so that the beginning wrap flows properly.

4. Gather a small bunch of soft grizzly hackle barbs, and tie them in at the throat. They should reach to about the hook point or slightly short of it. Neatly trim and bury the butts, while laying down a base for the wing.

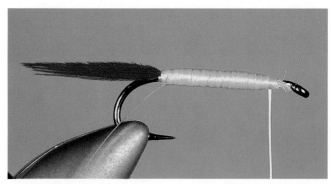

The completed body (step 3).

The ribbing in place, beard hackle tied on (steps 3 & 4).

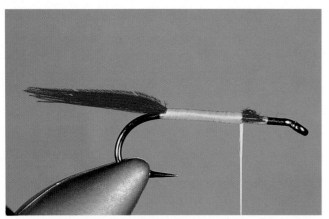

Tail in place, butts trimmed (step 2).

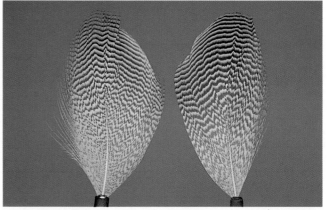

Two opposing flank feathers that will yield a back and a front section.

The ribbing is tied in, and the body is wrapped with Uni-Stretch (step 3).

The winging sections can be mounted tips up, like this.

5. Using one of the methods described earlier, tie the wing. As with the March Brown, the wing should extend rearward until the tips of the fibers touch, or barely break, an imaginary line that runs straight upward from the rear extremity of the bend of the hook. Trim neatly, holding on to the wing to counteract the shearing action of the scissor blades. Cover the trimmed wing butts, and whip-finish.

Another historic pattern, the Catskill, has a simple clump flank-feather wing and a palmered hackle. Unless you hunt wood ducks or have a dependable source, you may want to use a dyed substitute for the wing and tail. There are very good ones available, and for this sort of work, they are at least as good as the real thing. You'll have dyed mallard or teal to choose from, the teal being a bit more distinctly barred. Don't let the regional name of this fly put you off if you're not a northeasterner; this old fly is a good producer everywhere.

The finished Grizzly King (step 5).

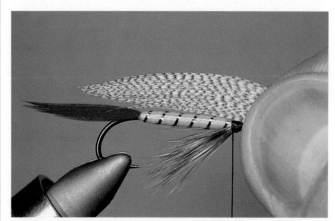

Two bunches of flank feather can be laid atop one another to form a wing in similar fashion to the alternative turkey quill method.

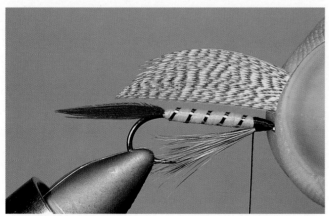

Or, the winging sections can be mounted tips down, like this, which usually looks better.

A wing thus formed.

Catskill

Hook	Wet fly, standard or 1XL shank, size 8-14.
Thread	Tan or brown, 6/0 or 8/0.
Tail	A small bunch of wood duck flank-feather fibers or dyed substitute.
Ribbing and hackle	A brown hackle, preferably a saddle feather, folded and palmered over the body, with a few extra turns at the front.
Body	Brown floss or similar material.
Wing	Wood duck flank-feather fibers or dyed substitute.

1. Tie on just to the rear of the eye, and secure the thread. Hold the tailing fibers on top of the hook, and establish proper length.
2. Tie the tailing material on top of the hook about one-quarter of the shank length rearward of the eye, and while applying tension with the left hand, neatly bind them down, working to the bend.
3. Fold the feather ahead of time, then tie it in by the tip end, with the fibers flowing rearward.
4. Wrap forward, securing the hackle tip. Trim off the excess, and smooth everything out with thread wraps. Note the finishing thread position.
5. Wrap the body.
6. Wrap the ribbing hackle, stroking the barbs rearward as you go. When you get near the front, take two or three stroked-back turns tight together, thus creating a true hackle.
7. Secure the hackle feather, then trim and neaten, as usual.

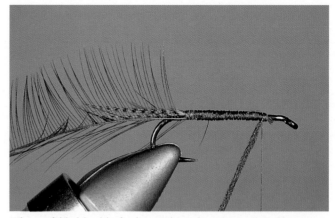

The prefolded hackle feather tied in place (steps 3 & 4).

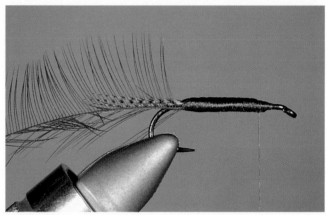

The completed body (step 5).

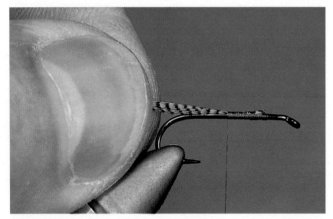

Binding down the tail (steps 1 & 2).

The hackle in place. Note how the barbs are stroked rearward (steps 6 & 7).

8. Prepare a flank feather by stripping off all the junky stuff near the butt end and around the sides—in other words, any material you don't want involved in forming the wing.
9. Gather a bunch of flank-feather fibers, first stroking the tips into a reasonably even position. If the feather suits, you can procure a nicely shaped bunch by snipping out the quill on a centered feather and stroking the remaining barbs into a neat bunch.
10. Set the fibers on top of the hook. If the bunch has gentle curvature, position it in such a manner that the concave side is down, so that the wing hugs the back of the body.
11. Tie the bunch in place, secure, trim, and finish off the fly as usual.

The fly shown here came out very bushy because I used a saddle hackle with an unusually high barb count. In the second example, I stripped the barbs from one side of the feather, thus reducing the amount of hackle that was deployed. I also stroked down the barbs to whichever side of the hook they naturally wanted to go and pruned out the ones that remained on top. This cleared the wing area.

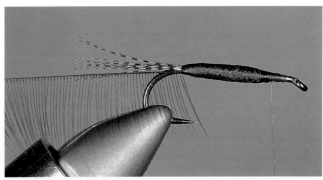

Tying a sparse Catskill. Note that the barbs have been stripped from one side of the quill.

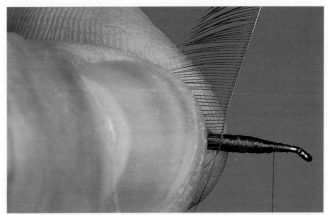

Stroking back the barbs during wrapping results in this effect.

Stroking back the barbs during wrapping results in this effect.

Tying on a simple flank feather wing completes the fly (steps 8–11).

Pruning out the topmost barbs while stroking the rest downward produces this sort of hackle.

Have I converted you into a lover of the subaqueous fly? I hope so. Both of the patterns presented here are beautiful and deadly. If you really become intrigued with the subject, check out Helen Shaw's *Flies for Fish and Fishermen* (Stackpole Books, 1989) which takes you through a progressive course in the art of tying a host of lovely flies. Helen is one of the all-time good-hands people; she eschews the bobbin and wouldn't use anything but real silk thread until I turned her on to Uni-Thread, which has a similar feel. Her methods may seem somewhat archaic, but technique of that level is never really out-of-date.

Pruning out the topmost barbs while stroking the rest downward produces this sort of hackle.

The completed Catskill, sparse version.

CHAPTER 15

Nymphs

I started out as a nymph fisherman. I fished them long before I fished dry flies. A guy told me to pretend they were worms, and that's what I did. It worked, and I was hooked.

The good nympher, in most cases, will outfish everybody else. In a typical trout stream, nymphs constitute the bulk of the fish's diet. They are plentiful and easy to catch. They don't require the fish to rise to the surface, thus expending energy and exposing itself to its enemies, and they don't fly away at the critical moment, like winged flies often do. This makes the odds heavily in favor of the skilled nymph fisher.

There is an enormous array of nymph patterns out there; in fact, there are books, and major sections of books, full of them. I have no dispute with that; however, I don't carry a lot of different nymph patterns as a general practice. There are a few time-tested dressings that produce almost everywhere, if they're the right size and are properly presented. In the main, I focus on those. However, if I'm headed for a stream where I expect to encounter something specific, I'll tie up a supply of imitations of that particular insect.

In a rich stream that has a wide diversity of aquatic insect life, the fish are exposed to quite a number of different nymphs through the year. In a typical freestone stream, there will probably be mayflies, caddisflies, stoneflies, and midges. Within those orders, you're liable to find everything from big burrowing mayfly nymphs to medium-size clingers or crawlers, to miniatures like the Tricos and small Baetidae. Caddis larvae and pupae vary considerably in size and color, as do stonefly nymphs. Midges are usually thought of as tiny flies because of the name, but some members of the order Diptera are very large and can be of considerable importance to the angler. There will probably be some crustaceans in a classic stream also, but that's another subject.

The general patterns can be adapted to imitate what you encounter astream by varying the size and shape. The Pheasant Tail Nymph, also known as the P-T Nymph, can be tied large and elongated, short and squat, or practically anything in between, as can the Leadwing Coachman and Hare's Ear Nymphs. Color variations are also possible; for example, you can now buy at least a half dozen shades of Hare's Ear blend. Cock ring-necked pheasant tails can be dyed olive or other colors. Even peacock herl varies in color; some batches are very greenish, while others have a distinct purplish or bronze cast, which I dearly love.

The Pheasant Tail Nymph is my all-around favorite, and the following is one of several dressings I use. In listing the materials, I specify thin Bugskin, as this material can vary a bit in thickness. The heftier pieces are great for making the Bugskin Crayfish, Hellgrammite, and many other great patterns. For wing cases, however, the thinner the better.

Pheasant Tail Nymph

Hook	Typical nymph design, Daiichi model 1560 or comparable, size 10-16.
Thread	Brown or rust 8/0 Uni-Thread or comparable.
Underbody	Fine weighting wire (optional).
Tail and body	Six to ten long, rust-colored fibers from the tail of a cock ring-necked pheasant, depending on hook size.
Ribbing	Very fine copper wire.
Underbody and thorax	Soft, fine-packing brown or rust-colored dubbing.
Wing case	Dark thin Bugskin or Wapsi Thin Skin, or a strip of goose, duck, or turkey wing treated with an adhesive.
Legs	Pheasant tail fiber tips, or any soft hackle of appropriate color.

1. Tie on at the thorax position, wrap to the bend, and tie in the pheasant fibers to form a short tail. Fold the remainder of the fibers back out of the way.
2. Tie in the copper wire for ribbing, then wrap the weighting wire. Don't crowd either the tail end or the front of the hook; refer to the photo for positioning. Smear on a little Zap-A-Gap.
3. Form the underbody with a thin layer of dubbing that extends forward into the thorax area, creating the shape you want. After completing the dubbing process, wrap the thread back into the material, as shown.

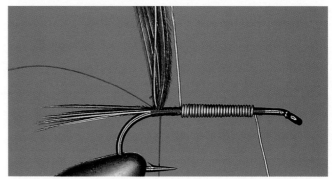

The ribbing wire is tied in, and the wire foundation is being wrapped (step 2).

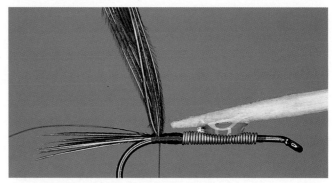

Applying Zap-A-Gap to the wire wraps (step 2).

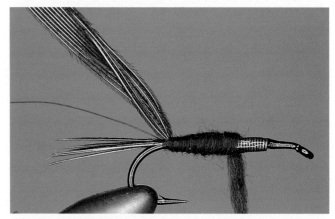

Wrapping dubbing for the underbody (step 3).

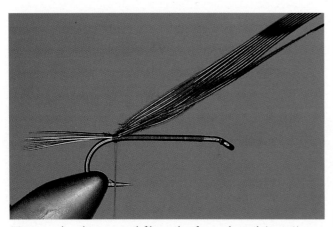

Tying in the pheasant tail fibers also forms the tail (step 1).

The completed underbody. Note the thread position (step 3).

4. Wrap the pheasant fibers to form the body; then re-verse-wrap the copper wire, and tie it off.

5. If it appears to be necessary, spin on a little more dubbing and wrap it in the thorax area, immediately adjacent to the front of the body. This is only a base or foundation on which to mount the wing-case material. Its purpose is to create breadth where the wing-case material will be tied in. Again, wrap the thread back into the material.

6. Tie in whatever wing-case material you have selected; shown here is thin Bugskin. Tie it in upside down and hanging to the rear, as it will be folded forward at the end.

7. Fill out the thorax with more dubbing, leaving adequate space up front for legs and wing-case tie-off.

8. Tie on the legs, fold the wing case forward, and complete the fly with a whip finish.

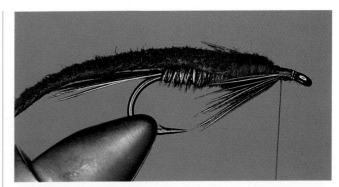

The legs in place (step 8).

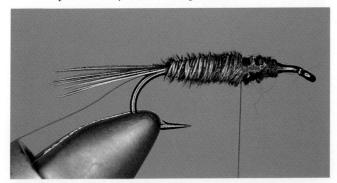

The pheasant fibers wrapped to form the body (step 4).

Folding the wing case forward (step 8).

The copper wire ribbing reverse-wrapped (step 4).

The completed Pheasant Tail Nymph, side view.

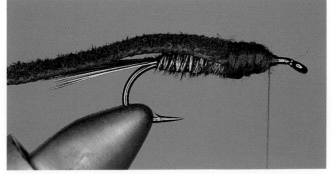

Wing-case material tied in, thorax built up with dubbing (steps 5–7).

The completed Pheasant Tail Nymph, top view.

An interesting and very deadly variation of this nymph employs a bead—not in the common beadhead position, but as a thorax, in place of the dubbing. This design can be incorporated into many other dressings. This dressing is similar to that of the regular Pheasant Tail Nymph, except that a copper bead is substituted for the dubbed thorax, and the weighting wire underbody is omitted. I usually omit the dubbed underbody also. If you choose to include it, keep it thin. Otherwise, simply shape the foundation with thread. If you use thread for the underbody, you can coat it with Zap-A-Gap or similar glue for improved durability. With care, you can wrap the pheasant while the glue is still wet. This makes the ribbing optional, so I'll omit it here.

The wing-case choices are the same. It is critical to use a very thin material for the wing case here as well, as building up too much bulk where the wing case is tied in makes it difficult to seat the bead properly. Very thin Bugskin is fine, but for this design, I prefer Thin Skin. The bead will fill out the wing case and thorax adequately. I have fished this nymph extensively, beginning in the fall of 1995, and it more than fulfilled all expectations. In addition to enhancing its effectiveness, the bead eliminates the need for adding weight.

Bead Thorax Pheasant Tail Nymph

1. Debarb the hook, and slip the bead into place with the larger-diameter side of the hole facing to the rear, as done for the Ellis in the soft-hackle chapter.
2. Tie on just behind the bead, wrap to the bend, and tie in the pheasant tail fibers. When shaping the foundation, be careful not to build up a lot of bulk in front, so that the bead can be slid into position subsequently.
3. Zap-A-Gap the thread base, and wrap the pheasant fibers. After completing the body, tie in the wing-case material as described for the regular Pheasant Tail Nymph. Then tie off with a reduced (three- to four-turn) whip finish.
4. Slide the bead into place as shown, jam-fitting it against the front of the body. There should be enough space ahead of the bead to complete the fly. You can Zap-A-Gap the thread wraps where the bead will be seated if you wish, but do a trial fitting first.
5. Tie on again ahead of the bead.

The completed body, wing-case material tied in (step 3).

The bead is positioned as the thorax, with the thread reattached in front (steps 4 & 5).

The bead is in place, pheasant tail fibers are tied in, and the tail is formed (steps 1 & 2).

6. Tie on the legs, trim, fold over the wing case, and complete the fly with a whip finish.

Although the Hare's Ear Nymph has been written up many times by many fly tiers, I have a few little wrinkles you may not know about, so I'll run through it quickly here. You can buy all kinds of dubbing blends that are labeled as Hare's Ear, but most of them are approximations, as the original is time-consuming to prepare and not as convenient for mass packaging. This is not to disparage these dubbing blends; they all work, some marvelously well.

If you want to use the original material, you'll need a true English hare's mask. On its face and ears is rough, spiky, tweedy fur or hair that is scraped off and mixed together. In small quantities, this can be done by hand. If you wish to prepare a good-size batch, I suggest the water-and-detergent method of blending, rather than using an electric blender method. In a small bowl, mix some lukewarm water with a few drops of liquid dish detergent. Scrape the material off the mask, and place it in the bowl. Stir until well mixed. Pour into a small sieve, and rinse until the detergent is washed out. Squeeze out as much water as you can, then lay the dubbing on a paper towel to dry. Straight hare's ear dubbing can be difficult to work with. If you wish, you can add a little soft body fur of a neutral color to bind the hairs more effectively.

This method of preparing dubbing works for all kinds of furs and hairs. It also is recommended for combining synthetics with natural materials, which is not always feasible in a blender, as some of the synthetics get gooey when zapped by the blades. Don't try to use a conventional bottom-bladed kitchen blender. It won't do the job properly, and the material may get bound up in the blades, which will destroy the motor. Use a top-bladed model, such as a coffee bean or nut chopper.

The Hare's Ear Nymph is commonly tied both plain and gold-ribbed. The purpose of the ribbing is to add a bit of glint. This also can be done with the dubbing itself, as demonstrated here. There are Hare's Ear blends on the market that have some sort of glitz mixed in, so if you'd prefer to simply purchase it, that's fine. If you'd like to prepare your own, follow the mixing procedure above, adding some type of sparkly synthetic material, such as chopped-up Antron. The mixture used here is composed of hare's ear fur and chopped-up copper Lite Brite.

I've listed the legs as optional. The traditional Catskill version of the Hare's Ear wet fly didn't have legs; instead, the dubbing was picked out a little at the front to emulate them. You can do that here, if you wish. I prefer feather barbs for legs on nymphs.

Tying on the legs (step 6).

Forming the wing case completes the fly (step 6).

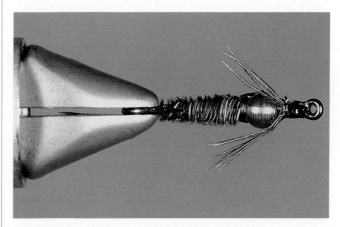

The Bead Thorax Pheasant Tail Nymph, bottom view.

The Bead Thorax Pheasant Tail Nymph, top view.

Sparkly Hare's Ear Nymph

Hook	Wet-fly/nymph model, 1XL, Daiichi model 1560 or comparable, size 10-16.
Thread	Tan or brown 8/0 or 6/0.
Tail	A few barbs from a Hungarian partridge or speckled hen feather.
Underbody	Thin weighting wire, diameter relative to hook size.
Wing case	Same as for the Pheasant Tail Nymph.
Body and thorax	Hare's ear dubbing blend that includes some sparkle.
Legs	Same as tail (optional).

1. Tie on about one-quarter of the shank length to the rear of the eye, and create a substantial base, building up the spot a bit, as shown. The easiest and quickest way to do this is to use some dubbing, then wrap the thread into it.
2. Tie in a narrow strip of Bugskin, pretty side down, over the fur base, and let it hang forward, out of the way.
3. Wrap to the rear, and tie the tail and underbody, as instructed for the Pheasant Tail Nymph. Use the thread to bury the weighting wire, thus creating a smooth foundation.
4. Spin on enough dubbing for the body and thorax, and wrap them in one continuous operation. When you reach the spot where the wing-case material is tied in, fold it back, and crowd the dubbing against the front of it while crossing over. This should be the widest part of the fly.

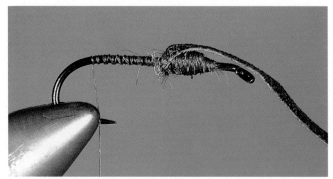

The wing-case material tied in (step 2).

The tail in place. Thin weighting wire is hidden by thread layer (step 3).

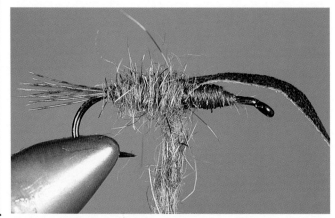

Dubbing the body and thorax (step 4).

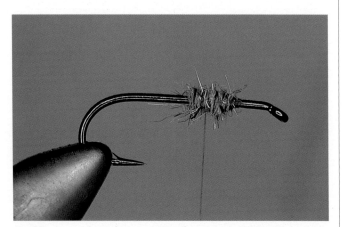

Building up a base for mounting the wing case (step 1).

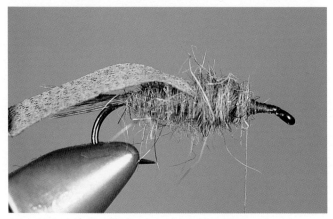

The dubbed body and thorax in place (step 4).

5. Tie on the legs, deploying the fibers around the bottom and sides of the hook. Fold over the wing case, secure it, and trim, then whip-finish.

It's good practice to tie some insect-specific nymphs for occasions when some activity of a particular species is anticipated. A good example is the *Stenonema* emergence that occurs in midspring in the greater Northeast. Two closely related mayflies make up this emergence: *Stenonema vicarium,* the march brown, and *Stenonema fuscum,* the gray fox. The march brown is slightly larger and darker, in both the nymphal and adult forms. Several other mayflies, lighter still than the gray fox, including *Stenonema ithaca* and *Stenacron interpunctatum canadense,* may also be present during this time period, or a little later. All of these can be imitated with the same nymph design simply by varying the size and shade a bit.

These are squat, clinging nymphs with large wing cases, prominent legs, and three long tails. The bellies are much lighter in color than the backs. As hatch time approaches, the nymphs turn a little orangy or amber. This can be matched by using the appropriate shade of dubbing. I'm partial to a product called Scintilla, offered by Ligas. There are several shades that cover the *Stenonema* group nicely.

In order to shape these nymphs, you need to construct the same sort of foundation as for the Perla Stonefly Nymph in the next chapter. The ribbing is also an important part of the shaping process. If you want to get fancy, you can use a thread that's the same color as the dubbing, rather than the Maxima. *Stenonema* nymphs are all rather flat. If you want, you can squeeze your finished flies a bit with flat-jawed pliers, but be very careful.

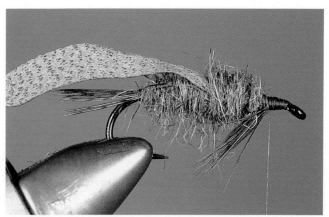

The legs in place (step 5).

The completed fly, side view.

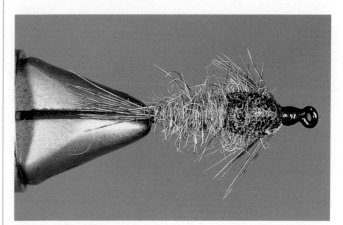

The completed fly, top view.

Dick's March Brown Nymph

Hook	Standard or 1XL wet fly, Daiichi model 1560 or comparable, size 8-12.
Thread	Tan or brown 8/0 or 6/0.
Underbody	Fairly thick, .030- or .035-inch weighting wire, tied in strips along the sides of the hook.
Tail	A sparse bunch of speckled brown mallard, tied long.
Shell	Very thin, brown mottled Bugskin.
Ribbing	Fine Maxima leader material in the original color or thread that matches the dubbing.
Body and thorax	Orangy-amber dubbing, such as Ligas Scintilla #34 fiery amber.
Wing case	Same as shell.
Legs	Brown mallard, speckled hen, or Hungarian partridge, tied fairly long.

1. Tie on near the front, wrap a thread base, and construct the underbody, as shown for the Perla Stonefly Nymph in the next chapter.
2. Tie the tails as you would for a dry fly, with a tiny bump of thread at the bend to make them spread a little.
3. Prepare the Bugskin by cutting it to shape, as shown. Tie it in by the tapered end, upside down and hanging to the rear. Wrap back far enough that when the material is folded forward, there is no gap between it and the tail.
4. Tie in the ribbing near the bend, secure, and trim off the excess.
5. Dub the body as was done with the Hare's Ear nymph, running the dubbing into the thorax area to build up a base for the wing case. Wrap the thread back into it a bit.
6. Fold the shell forward, tie it down, and trim off the excess.
7. Wrap the ribbing, secure it, and trim.

The tails in place (step 2).

The Bugskin and ribbing thread tied in (steps 3 & 4).

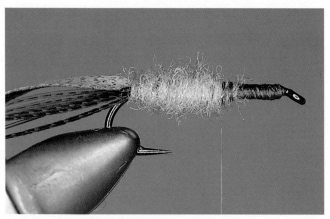

Dub the body as shown (step 5).

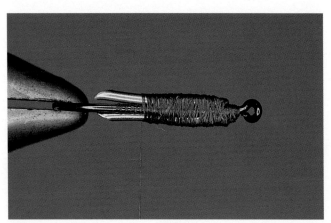

Constructing the underbody, as shown for the Perla Stonefly (step 1).

The Bugskin folded forward, ribbing in place (steps 6 & 7).

8. Prepare another piece of Bugskin for the wing case. It should be just a tiny bit wider than the shell. Tie it in as done earlier.

9. Build up the thorax with a little more dubbing, leaving room up front for the legs.

10. You have a choice for the legs. My preference, as shown here, is to tie in a Hungarian partridge feather by the tip end, as done on a soft-hackle wet fly. Wrap a couple of turns, secure, trim off the excess, then cut off the top barbs. Or you can simply apply bunches of fibers from any of the feathers listed, deploying them around the bottom and sides of the hook.

11. Bring the wing case over the top, secure in front, trim, neaten with thread, and whip-finish.

12. Tease out the dubbing along the sides of the body a little with a Velcro teaser. Unless you used brown thread throughout, darken the head with a touch of waterproof marker.

To try something a little different, tie this nymph as was instructed for the Bead Thorax Pheasant Tail Nymph, but use a cone head or similar product instead. Everything is the same, except for the following procedures:

1. Start by mounting a small cone head or something similar, such as a Fly Head from Umpqua. Gold is okay; copper is even better.

2. Omitting the wire foundation, tie the components as above, using the dubbing and Bugskin to shape the fly.

3. After tying the wing case in place, add just a bit more dubbing where it was tied in.

4. Tie off, slide the cone head back against the wing case, tie back on in front, do the legs and wing case, and whip-finish.

Building up the thorax with dubbing (step 9).

The legs in place (step 10).

The completed March Brown nymph, side view.

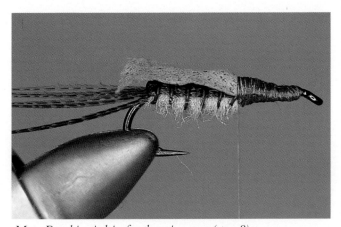
More Bugskin tied in for the wing case (step 8).

The completed March Brown nymph, top view.

Peacock herl makes simple yet effective nymphs. I started out with the Hare's Ear and the Leadwing Coachman Nymph, and they've taken countless numbers of trout for me over the years. I still don't leave home without them.

For variety, I tie some of these flies as Flashbacks, meaning that I substitute a tinsel wing case for the more subdued and traditional type. Here's a dressing that I particularly favor.

Peacock & Copper Flashback

Hook	Typical wet fly or nymph hook, depending on how you want to shape the fly, size 10-16.
Thread	Dark brown or black 8/0 Uni-Thread or comparable.
Tail	Very dark brown, webby hackle barbs, tied short.
Underbody	Fine weighting wire (optional).
Body and thorax	Bronze peacock herl.
Wing case	Wide, flat or embossed copper tinsel. If you can't find tinsel as wide as you want, use two strips, side-by-side and slightly overlapped in the center.
Legs	Same as tail.

1. Tie on near the front and wrap to the rear. Leave a 5- or 6-inch (125- to 150-millimeter) length of thread as a tag; don't trim it off.
2. Tie the tail.
3. Select a few pieces of peacock, about five, and cut back the tips a little to remove the most brittle part. Tie them in as a bunch by the trimmed tip ends at the rear of the hook, where the bend begins to slope off.
4. Wrap the thread forward to where you want the wing case located, and tie in that material. Then continue to where you want the thorax to end.
5. Both the peacock and the thread that was left hanging should be located together at the bend of the hook, with no space between them, or the thread will come across the peacock and may cut it. Pick up the tag end of thread, and start twisting it together with the peacock, forming a chenille effect. Don't take too many twists at first, as the thread might sever the herl. If you accidentally cut off the thread tag, you can either tie in another piece of thread or form a long loop and cut off one side of it.
6. Begin wrapping the herl and thread "chenille" around the hook, working forward, with each wrap abutting the one before it. Continue twisting the thread and herl as you go. If you run into difficulty with twisting, you can grab the bunch with an electronics clip or regular hackle pliers.
7. When you reach the spot where the tinsel for the wing case was tied in, pass in front of it and keep going to where the thread was left hanging. Tie off and trim the peacock.

The tail and reinforcing thread in place (steps 1 & 2).

Peacock and wing-case materials tied in (steps 3 & 4).

The body and thorax are formed with the peacock herl (steps 5–7).

8. Tie on the legs, bring the tinsel over the top, secure and trim it, and whip-finish.

The legs tied in (step 8).

Dick's Wriggler is a pattern I created to imitate the large, burrowing mayfly nymphs indigenous to the Northeast and Midwest. This pattern is a variation of the Wiggle Nymph, which I think was originated by Doug Swisher and Carl Richards. If I'm wrong on that, my apologies to the inventor. The design covers a number of species, including *Ephemera guttulata, varia,* and *simulans; Litobrancha* (formerly *Hexagenia) recurvata;* and the giant *Hexagenia limbata,* which somehow became famous as the Michigan Night Caddis, even though it's not a caddis and its habitat isn't limited to Michigan. Although there are some variations in size and shading among these insects, they are not profound, and a little local knowledge is all you need to make the appropriate adjustments.

Tying this nymph requires two hooks and some fine wire. I like the Monel wire commonly used in making biteproof leader tippets for pike, barracuda, and other toothy fish. For the body and thorax, dubbing works fine, However, on such large flies, it's a lot of work, and you might prefer to use some sort of yarn, such as crewel wool. There are a lot of nice ones for sale in fly shops and knitting supply stores.

The completed fly, side view.

The fly uses two hooks of different designs. The front hook, which accommodates the thorax, wing case, legs, and the wire loop that joins the hooks, is a regular-shank wet-fly hook. The rear hook has a longer shank and can be anywhere from 1XL to 4XL, depending on what you're trying to imitate. A 2XL is a good typical size. I prefer a straight-eyed model, although turned-up or turned-down eyes will work okay, provided the deflection isn't extreme.

Products such as Bugskin and Thin Skin are suitable for the shell and wing case. I like Bugskin better for this application, because it covers the joint better. I also like the texture and the several mottled colors that are available.

When forming the junction loop and working on the other components at that point, keep in mind that the idea is for the rear hook to swing freely. The loop shouldn't be bigger than necessary, but it must be of sufficient size to allow the wriggling action to occur. Be sure the small supplementary wing case that hides the joint doesn't restrict mobility.

The completed fly, top view.

Dick's Wriggler

Hooks	As described above. (Here, Daiichi models 1750 for the rear and 1550 for the front, both size 10.)
Connecting loop	Fine rustproof wire, such as Monel.
Thread	Tan, light brown, or gray 6/0 or 8/0.
Tail	Hungarian partridge, tied short.
Shell	Brown mottled Bugskin.
Ribbing	Fine monofilament; for dark segmentation, use Maxima chameleon.
Body	Tannish gray dubbing or yarn; llama works well for dubbing.
Wing case	Bugskin in two segments, per instructions below.
Thorax	Same as body.
Legs	Hungarian partridge.

1. Put the smaller hook in the vise, and lay down a thread base.
2. Cut off a short piece of the wire. When doubled over, it should be shorter than the hook shank.
3. Tie on the wire just behind the eye, and bind it in place. Then tie off with a whip finish, coat with Zap-A-Gap, and set aside.
4. Put the larger hook in the vise.
5. Tie on the tail, then tie in the shell and ribbing materials, following the instructions in earlier sequences in this chapter and in the next chapter on stonefly nymphs.

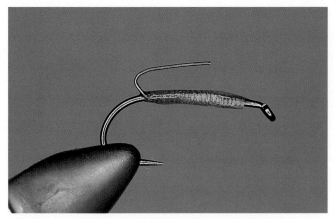

The linking wire secured and bent into position (step 3).

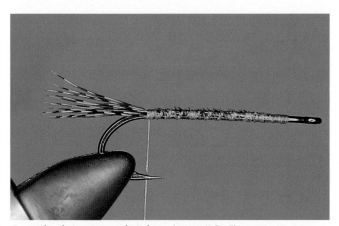

Large hook in vise, tail tied on (steps 4 & 5).

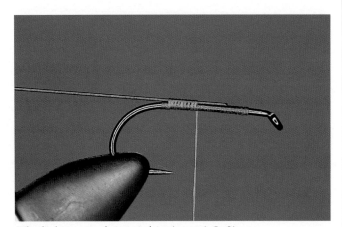

The linking wire being tied in (steps 1 & 2).

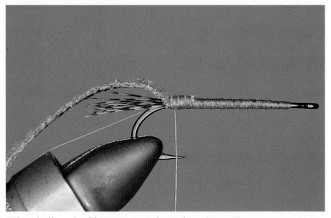

The shell and ribbing materials tied in (step 5).

6. Construct the body out of the material you've chosen. When dubbing such large bodies, a three-layer process is best: forward, rearward, then forward again. This enables you to properly shape the body without having to put massive amounts of dubbing on the thread.

7. Fold the shell forward, secure it, and trim off the excess. Work right up close to the hook eye.

8. Wrap the ribbing and secure it, then tie off with a whip finish. Tease out the dubbing along the sides with a Velcro teaser to simulate the generous gill structure of these burrowing nymphs.

9. Put the smaller hook back in the vise, and insert the wire into the eye of the bigger hook. Form the junction loop, as shown, then close the loop by binding down the other end of the wire. Fine-nosed pliers are very helpful throughout this process. The loop should be vertical (upright) to properly interact with the eye of the rear hook. Coat the windings with Zap-A-Gap or similar glue, and rub dry.

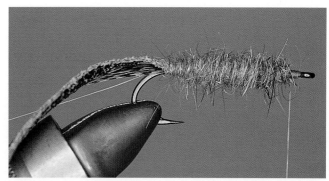

The completed body (step 6).

The shell folded forward and secured, ribbing wrapped (steps 7 & 8).

Constructing the body; the first layer of dubbing (step 6).

Teasing out the dubbing along the sides (step 8).

The second layer of dubbing (step 6).

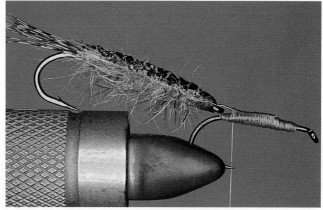

Closing the loop between the two parts (step 9).

10. Wrap on a little dubbing or yarn to build up the diameter where the wing case will be tied in.
11. Tie on a short piece of Bugskin, just long enough to hide the joint.
12. Tie in another piece of Bugskin, upside down and hanging to the rear, in the typical wing-case construction position.
13. Build the thorax with the material of your choice.
14. Tie in the legs in the usual manner.
15. Fold over the wing case, secure, trim, and whip-finish.

Your nymph selection can be as large or as small as you desire, depending on what you feel fills your angling needs. The tying techniques presented in this chapter will allow you to create just about any nymphal, larval, or pupal creature you want.

The wing-case material tie in (step 12).

Building up the thorax (step 13).

Building up the spot where the wing case will be tied in (step 10).

The legs in place (step 14).

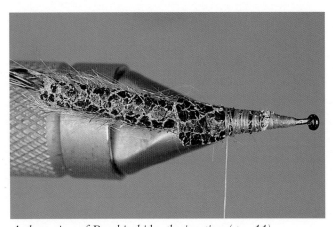

A short piece of Bugskin hides the junction (step 11).

The completed Dick's Wriggler.

CHAPTER 16

Stonefly Nymphs

I have always loved stoneflies. My fledgling fly-fishing stream was the Esopus Creek in the Catskills, which embodies certain characteristics of western freestone rivers and is thus rich in Plecopteran life. It doesn't have the big western salmon fly, but it does have the early brown stone, the gigantic black *Pteronarcys dorsata,* and several species of yellow stoneflies.

Here in the East, we seldom see surface action with stoneflies, and dry-fly fishing to them is a rarity. I've encountered early brown stones on top a few times in early spring and have had a little dry-fly fishing to them. What they were doing there, I have no idea.

Most stoneflies emerge by crawling out of the water and onto rocks or logs. They are fully mature at that time, and there is no metamorphosis to a spinner form, as there is with mayflies. The salmon-fly "hatch" that we hear about out west isn't an emergence; it's an ovipositing flight, in which the egg-laden females drop fertilized eggs into the water. This is enough to attract the attention of even the most shy and reclusive old trout that normally spends its time with its belly rubbing the stream bottom, scarfing up whatever's within reach. The dry-fly fishing continues for a few days after the egg-laying period is over and can be really great, as trout remember these goodies for a little while and are hungry for more.

Such a bonanza doesn't occur with our eastern stoneflies. They do not return in such massive, concentrated egg-laying flights, or at least I've never heard of them doing so. Most of this ovipositing activity is nocturnal, so few anglers encounter whatever surface activity there might be.

What this all adds up to is that stonefly fishing is nymph fishing. Although not everyone likes nymph fishing, nymphing with stoneflies can be extremely productive. And it's not as tedious as other forms, because you're fishing larger flies in moving water, and the trout usually bang them pretty hard. Thus a lot of subtle and sophisticated technique generally isn't needed.

A yellow stonefly nymph dressing called the Perla Stonefly Nymph imitates several important yellowish stoneflies of the family Perlidae. My dressing has evolved over a fairly long period of time, and it now differs considerably from the one shown in the first edition. This dressing is based on a pattern known as the Catskill Curler, which I learned from my old photographer buddy, Matt Vinciguerra. You may have heard it called the Catskill "Coiler," as many New York City guys who fished the Catskills pronounced *curler.* Coiler or Curler, it's the same fly—take my word for it.

For the past several years, I've been using brown mottled Bugskin for the shell and wing cases on this dressing, and it's very good stuff, indeed. Recently, I've been trying out a new product from the Wapsi Company known as Thin Skin. This is a synthetic film that's peeled off a thin backing and cut to shape. It comes in a wide range of colors, including several figured patterns, one of which is ideal for my yellow stonefly. One problem with Thin Skin is that the pattern tends to wear off over time. This can be negated by tying in the strips in such a manner that the underside, which was against the backing, ends up outermost on the fly. Because the material is so transparent, the appearance of the fly is not significantly affected.

Bugskin, which is actually finely shaved leather, makes great stonefly nymphs as well. You get a different effect, because it isn't translucent like some colors of Thin Skin and it's somewhat thicker. It's tough and durable, however, and can be sculpted into realistic shapes. Like Thin Skin, it comes in a myriad of colors, some solid, some mottled. The one I like for the Perla nymph is a mottled brown. It's important to select your Bugskin with some attention to thickness, as this varies a lot. Small to average-size nymphs require very thin Bugskin. On big flies, it's okay if the Bugskin isn't quite so thin.

Uni-Stretch, a product of the company that produces Uni-Thread, serves as thread, body material, and ribbing for this dressing. You'll need to mount Uni-Stretch in a bobbin. The easiest way I know to thread this material is to fish it through the tube with a dental floss threader, available at drugstores and supermarkets. A bobbin with a sharp-edged tube will instantly fray

Uni-Stretch, so it's best to use a ceramic-tubed bobbin. I particularly like the Griffin bobbin, with a ceramic doughnut in the tip.

When laying down wraps of Uni-Stretch, a twist is created in the material with each wrap, preventing it from lying flat and smooth. You can correct this by spinning the bobbin counterclockwise every so often. Conversely, when you want the material to become narrow, semi-round, and threadlike, spin the bobbin clockwise.

The Perla Stonefly is a semirealistic nymph that's relatively easy to tie, durable, and fishable. The tying sequence is important so that the various components will fit together like pieces in a puzzle and won't interfere with each other. The Thin Skin can be tied in either before or after the underbody is created. In either case, the position-

ing and shaping of the wire strips should set things up so that the tails can be tied to the sides of the foundation at the rear. This creates a squared-off spot between the tails, over which the shell material is brought forward later. It's best to prepare a bunch of hooks ahead of time so that the Zap-A-Gap dries completely. You don't want tacky super-glue getting onto the other components or your fingers. Don't tie on the tails before the glue is dry, because you'll need to be able to adjust their position.

It's important to properly shape the Thin Skin strip so that it clears the tails when folded forward and doesn't upset their position. The strip overall should be slightly wider than the body and tapered at the rear. Cut before peeling the material off the backing. The photo below will help you with the shaping.

Perla Stonefly Nymph

Hook	Daiichi model 1750, 2340, or comparable, 4XL to 6XL.
Thread	Yellow Uni-Stretch, then brown 8/0 Uni-Thread or comparable.
Underbody	Thick wire, tied in strips along each side of the hook and coated with Zap-A-Gap.
Tails	Beige or tan biots.
Body	Uni-Stretch.
Shell	Yellow-patterned Thin Skin (Wapsi).
Ribbing	Uni-Stretch.
Wing case	Thin Skin.
Legs	Hungarian partridge or speckled hen.
Thorax	Yellow yarn or dubbing.

1. Prepare the hook by binding a strip of wire along each side. Note that the pieces of wire are squared off at the rear and extend almost to the bend. This helps establish that squared-off spot between the tails.

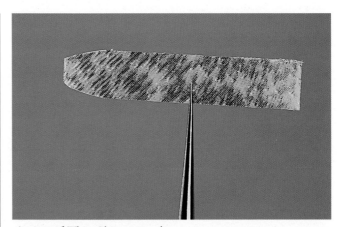

A piece of Thin Skin cut to shape.

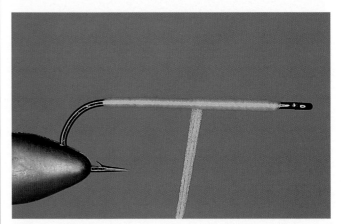

Begin preparing the hook by wrapping a Uni-Stretch base (step 1).

2. After tying in the Thin Skin and covering the wire strips with Uni-Stretch, use a pair of flat-jawed pliers to squeeze the assembly crossways, so that the wires and the hook shank are brought into perfect alignment. Then apply Zap-A-Gap and let it dry. Rubbing with a toothpick helps.

3. Tie in the tailing biots one at a time against the wire strips at the rear. It's easiest to start with the one on the far side.

4. Run the Uni-Stretch forward into the thorax area and back a few times, shaping the body. End up at the rear.

5. Fold the shell strip forward, smoothing out any folds or pleats at the rear. Then spin the bobbin briskly clockwise to render the Uni-Stretch threadlike.

6. Bind the Thin Skin strip on top of the body with spaced wraps, thus creating the segmentation and securing the shell in one operation. Stop at the halfway point or just a bit beyond, tie off the excess Thin Skin, and trim.

The completed foundation, flattened and Zap-A-Gapped (step 2).

The tails in place, body being shaped with Uni-Stretch (steps 3 & 4).

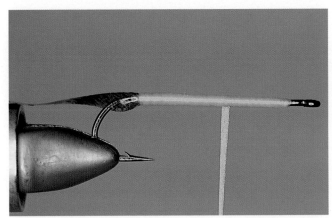

Thin Skin tied in (steps 1 & 2).

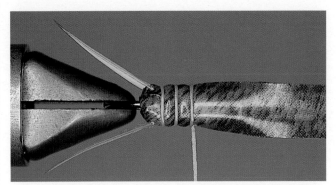

The shell folded forward, ribbing being applied (steps 5 & 6).

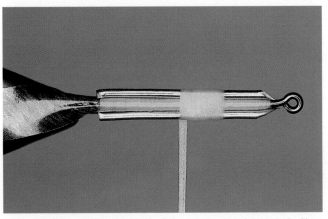

Note shaping and positioning of the wire strips (steps 1 & 2).

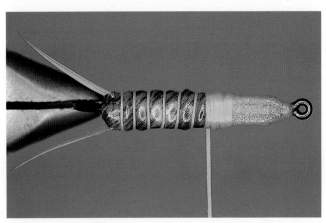

The body and ribbing completed and ready for the wing-case strip to be tied in (step 6).

7. Prepare another piece of Thin Skin, slightly wider than the first one, and tie it in hanging off to the rear. This will be folded forward to form the wing case and thorax assembly.

8. Select a feather from a speckled hen saddle, or any similar feather, for the legs. Tie it in by the tip end, hanging to the rear, pretty side down. When folded forward, it should reach almost, but not quite, to the eye of the hook, leaving space for the tie-down and tie-off.

9. After tying in and securing the feather, tie off the Uni-Stretch, and tie on with brown thread.

10. You have a choice of dubbing or yarn for the thorax. Stoneflies' gills are located in the thoracic area, so fuzzy material is appropriate. With yarn (Uni-Yarn is shown here), tie in near the front, and wrap the yarn rearward to where the wing-case material is tied in, then forward again, forming a double layer. Tie off the yarn and trim the excess. With dubbing, start at the wing-case tie-in point, and cover forward almost to the eye.

11. Fold the speckled feather forward over the thorax, and secure it with thread wraps at the front.

12. This step is optional but recommended. Before folding the Thin Skin forward and completing the fly, rub a little Zap-A-Gap along the center quill of the folded-over feather. This will form a bond and protect the feather during fishing.

13. Fold the wing-case material forward, and tie it off at the front. Trim the excess, whip-finish, and apply lacquer. At this time, you may wish to clip out a few barbs at strategic locations from each side of the feather in order to unclutter the leg area. Do so with great care and discretion; once gone, they're gone forever.

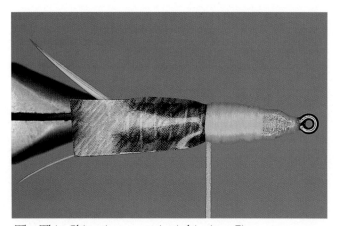

The Thin Skin wing-case strip tied in (step 7).

The Hun feather tied in, Uni-Stretch tied off, brown thread tied on, and yarn for the thorax tied in near the front (steps 8 & 9).

Building up the thorax with the yarn (step 10).

The Hun feather folded forward over the thorax and secured (step 11).

Folding the wing case forward, securing, and trimming completes the Perla Stonefly Nymph (step 13).

This makes a great-looking stonefly nymph. You can vary the size and color to match practically any stonefly you want, including the gargantuan black ones found in our northeastern rivers, such as the Delaware, and the big western salmon fly, *Pteronarcys californica*.

I used to tie my yellow stoneflies with defined wing cases, pronotum, and legs, for greater realism. But I found that the fish didn't care, so now I only do them that way for show. It might make a difference on the great big ones, however, so I'll demonstrate how it's done with the nymph of the Great Western Salmon Fly.

Great Western Salmon Fly Nymph

Hook	Daiichi Model 1750, 2340, or comparable, 4XL to 6XL.
Thread	Salmon orange Uni-Stretch, then dark brown 8/0 Uni-Thread or comparable.
Underbody	Thick wire, tied in strips along each side of the hook and coated with Zap-A-Gap.
Tails	Dark brown biots.
Shell	Dark brown Thin Skin.
Ribbing	Uni-Stretch.
Wing cases and pronotum	Thin Skin.
Legs	Two or three Hungarian partridge or speckled hen feathers, or strips of brown rubber-leg material.
Thorax	Salmon orange yarn or dubbing.

1. The procedure is the same as for the Perla Stonefly Nymph until the rear assembly is completed, the wing-case and leg materials are tied in, and you have switched threads.
2. Form the first set of legs by tying the rubber-leg material in place, as shown.
3. Using the yarn or dubbing, form the first thoracic segment. If you're making the legs from feathers instead of rubber, fold forward as before. Leave only enough for the first set of legs, tie down, and trim off the excess.
4. Fold the Thin Skin forward to form the first wing case. Tie it down, and either trim off the excess or fold it back and use it for the next wing case.

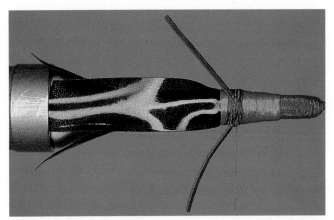

The rear components in place, wing-case material tied in, and the first set of rubber legs mounted and secured (steps 1 & 2).

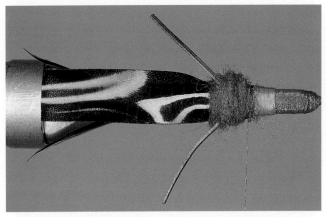

The first segment of the thorax is formed around the legs (step 3).

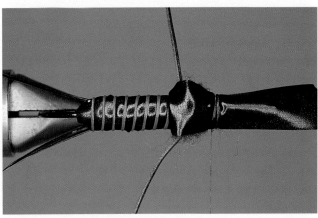

The first wing case being formed (step 4).

5. Tie in the second set of legs, either feather or rubber, and repeat the previous steps, completing the second wing case.
6. The pronotum and third set of legs are tied in the same manner as the wing cases.
7. Tie off everything, trim, and whip-finish.

The Eastern Giant Black Pteronarcys Nymph is another dressing that can be tied following the same procedure.

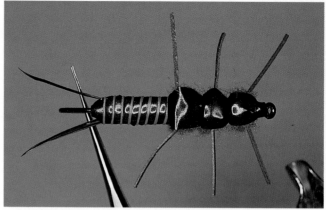

Formation of the final components completes the Great Western Salmon Nymph (steps 5–7).

Eastern Giant Black Pteronarcys Nymph	
Hook	Daiichi model 1750, 2340, or comparable, 4XL to 6XL.
Thread	Black Uni-Stretch, then black 8/0 Uni-Thread or comparable.
Underbody	Thick wire, tied in strips along each side of the hook and coated with Zap-A-Gap.
Tails	Black biots.
Shell	Black Thin Skin.
Ribbing	Uni-Stretch.
Wing case	Thin Skin.
Legs	Black hen cape or saddle, or black rubber-leg material.
Thorax	Black yarn or dubbing.
Head	Black thread.

If you want to tie really huge stonefly nymphs, you can use thin solder for the wire strips. This is a lead composite, however, and thus is illegal in all federal park waters. Several companies, including Mason, make heavy (75- to 125-pound test) shock tippet material that can be substituted for the wire for shaping purposes. Here you won't get the weighting, so a sinker or two will probably be necessary.

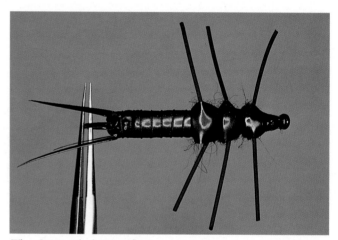

The Giant Black Stonefly.

CHAPTER 17

The Hornberg

The Hornberg is a much-maligned but highly effective quasistreamer pattern that, for some reason, seems to works like crazy everywhere it's fished. It is particularly effective here in the Northeast and is even known to take Atlantic salmon. Years ago, Gene Anderegg, former national casting champion and founding president of the Federation of Flyfishers, used to con me into tying them on double salmon hooks for his annual pilgrimages to the Grand Cascapedia. This was a bit nasty from a tying standpoint, but from his glowing reports, it was well worth the effort, provided the effort was mine, and not his.

When I taught my first weekend tying class at Hunter's Angling Supplies in the winter of 1980, I included the Hornberg in the agenda. When I announced the pattern and began to pass out the materials, one of the class members got up and excused himself. He considered using this fly tantamount to worm fishing and didn't even want to be in the room when it was being tied for fear of pollution by association.

It is my understanding that the Hornberg was originated by a game warden in Wisconsin named Frank Hornberg and that the first model was actually tied as a dry fly, with the wings flat over the top. The story goes that it was even more effective after it got wet and sank, thus the conversion to the dressing that's standard today.

The Hornberg isn't difficult to tie, but there are a few helpful tricks I'll share with you. The hardest part is finding feathers of the right size and shape and sorting them into matched pairs. Mallard flank feathers are generally sold by the bag, in ½-ounce or 1-ounce quantities. There's an awful lot of waste, but fortunately they're quite cheap. In these bags are flank feathers of all sizes and descriptions. If you tie a wide variety of flies, you may find uses for most of them. However, with rare exceptions, only a small percentage are ideal for making Hornbergs.

It would be wonderful if we could buy our mallard flanks on the skin so that we could easily pick out well-paired feathers. If you hunt these ducks, or have friends who do, I recommend preserving them as follows: Skin out the sides of the bird, where the barred flank feathers are found. Scrape the skin well to remove all grease and tissue. Cure with a mixture of salt and borax (not Boraxo, which has soap in it). After they are thoroughly dried out, store them in separate plastic bags, stapled together and marked as left side and right side.

When sorting for Hornberg feathers, I look for those that are more or less almond-shaped. However, I usually have to compromise, as there aren't that many that are ideal. Look for feathers that are fairly elongated in shape and have centered quills. Pair them up as closely as possible.

Typically, mallard flank feathers have a great deal of curvature in the stem. This must be reduced to acceptable levels by making nicking motions along the convex side of the curve of the quill with a fingernail. Work on the bare quill in the area that you have stripped in preparation for tying and on the feathered portion, along the quill. This will not only effectively remove curvature, but it will also help flatten the quill and render it more malleable at the tie-in point.

Hen cape and saddle feathers make the best underwings, provided they are of the right shape. I've found that tying collars on Hornbergs provides me with a practical application for all those larger feathers on the rear ends of my costly grizzly dry-fly capes that I seldom use for anything else. Hoffmans work particularly well. I've also seen hen grizzly used to make collars on Hornbergs. These are much softer, webbier, and darker in shade. Use them if you wish, understanding that the overall effect will be different.

An acceptable substitute for the jungle cock can be fashioned by trimming to shape a single-dotted guinea fowl feather, as shown at the end of chapter 21. Simply select a feather that has a white dot centered on the quill fairly near the tip end, and cut it to shape, as shown in the photo. If you plan on tying a lot of these flies, you can make a jungle cock burner that functions similarly to a wing burner.

In the beginning, I simply tied all the materials in place, working sequentially, which resulted in some problems with getting the feathers properly positioned. However, the real trouble arose during fishing. After a bit of use, the fly would end up with yellow underwings sticking out the sides and top, flank feathers twisting into grotesque positions, and jungle cock being lost. The

solution is preassembly. Preassembling components for flies of this type is nothing new. Carrie Stevens, the legendary Maine streamer tier, prepared her materials in this manner. I like to preassemble at least a dozen pairs at a sitting, laying them out on a sheet of waxed paper until the glue is completely dry. The first four steps below are directions for preassembly.

Hornberg

Hook	Daiichi model 1750 or comparable, 3X or 4X long.
Thread	8/0 black Uni-thread or comparable.
Underbody	Flat silver tinsel.
Underwings	Yellow hackle feathers.
Wings	Mallard flank feathers.
Cheeks	Jungle cock or substitute.
Hackle	Grizzly.

1. After selecting the feathers, strip the quills to remove the fluff near the butt end, until an attractive, almond-shaped silhouette is obtained.
2. Do the same with the yellow underwing feathers. These should be slightly smaller in length and breadth than the mallard flanks.
3. Put a small smear of Zap-A-Gap or similar superglue on the convex side of the yellow feather, near the center, and extending about one-third of the way back from the tip. Then lay the yellow feather inside of the mallard feather, spoon-style, and press them together with the end of a toothpick. Do not use so much glue that it will run through and crust up the outside of the mallard. Do this with both pairs.
4. If you have genuine jungle cock and are wealthy enough to squander it on a Hornberg, prepare two feathers by stripping to the configuration shown in the photo sequence. If they are split, as so many are, they can be repaired very nicely with glue during the assembly process. Apply a small amount of the superglue onto the back of the jungle cock nail, and draw it across a finger. (Wear vinyl surgical gloves when doing this.) Then stick the jungle cock in place on the outsides of the flank feathers, centering the quills with those of the mallard, and copositioning the front ends of the feathers so that they look like the assembly shown in the tying sequence.

A small amount of Zap-A-Gap applied to the inside of the Hornberg wing feathers will seep in and bond them (steps 1–3).

Typical jungle cock nails—one somewhat split, the other extremely so.

The badly split jungle cock can be mended by applying a droplet of Zap-A-Gap to the back side and drawing it across a finger protected by a vinyl surgical glove (step 4).

5. Tie on fairly near the front of the hook, tie in a piece of flat silver tinsel, and wrap to the rear and back. Tie off, and trim the excess.
6. Carefully wrap back and forth to near the eye of the hook once or twice to create a thread base for the assemblies.
7. Tie the assemblies in place, near side first, far side last. They should form mirror images of each other. Bind down the quills securely, then trim the excess.

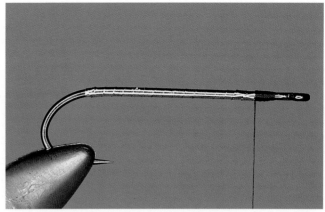

The completed body and thread base (step 6).

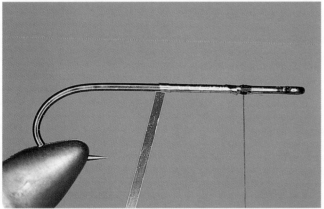

Wrapping the first layer of tinsel underbody (step 5).

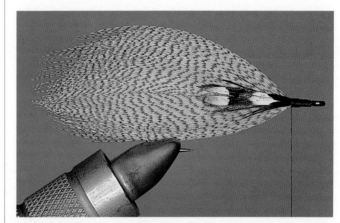

The assemblies in place (step 7).

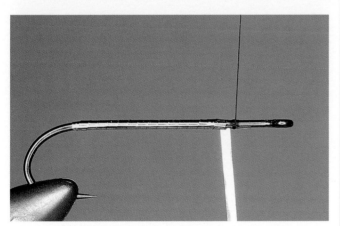

Wrapping the second layer of tinsel underbody (step 5).

A prefolded grizzly hackle feather.

8. Select a grizzly hackle feather from the rear portion of a rooster cape—the finer the quill, the better. I prefer to tie it in tip end first and make a folded collar, in which case prefolding is recommended, although not absolutely necessary. Or you can simply tie it in butt end first and wrap it dry-fly style. In either case, the action of the water during fishing will cause the hackle to be swept back around the front of the fly, cornucopia-style. Whip-finish, and lacquer the head.

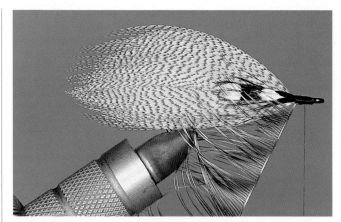

The hackle feather tied in (step 8).

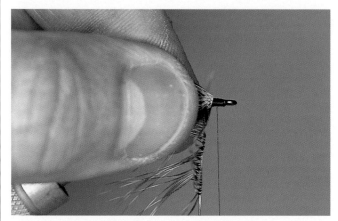

Wrapping and further folding the hackle (step 8).

The completed Hornberg.

CHAPTER 18

New and Novel Woolly Buggers

Over the years, a lot of the instructional writing about fly fishing and tying has been related to the imitation of specific items of food—insects, crustaceans, small fish, and so forth. That's wonderfully useful information, and we should all be thankful to the researchers who have gone to great lengths to collate and present it. However, given today's conditions, it's not the whole story.

Most fly fishers I know would much prefer to pursue their sport in a pristine, wild-trout environment. Oh, that such were available in great quantity! More likely, we find ourselves in compromised circumstances, fishing in tailrace streams below impoundments, or in the stillwaters of the impoundments themselves. Those rivers that are not all dammed up are usually of diminished quality, due to pollution, warming, channelization, bank defoliation, aquifer depletion, or whatever. This is both maddening and saddening, yet we still have a lot of fishing in this country.

Our fishing has changed, and will continue to change. Thus a lot of the more traditional information on aquatic life and fish behavior is no longer entirely valid. Today a lot of our fishing is for hatchery fish—stockers, if you will. With catch-and-release, some of these planted trout survive, grow up, and assume at least some of the characteristics of streamborn fish. This makes things a lot more fun. With hatchery-raised fish being deposited in large numbers in waters where the natural food supply has been depleted, we have a lot of opportunistic trout to fish for, though they may well become selective during an emergence.

Woolly Buggers were probably in existence when I wrote *Mastering,* but I wasn't aware of them. The first time I saw a Woolly Bugger was in the Rockies in 1985, my first summer of what I then thought was early retirement. Craig Matthews, of Blue Ribbon Flies in West Yellowstone, turned me on to Woolly Buggers. After a dozen-fish day on the Madison, I was tying Buggers in near-commercial volumes.

I soon learned that they were highly versatile flies. They worked when drifted out the back of my belly boat in the lakes and when I wade-fished the rivers between hatches. They even worked in the Henrys Fork; all it took was the social courage to tie on these ugly flies in a crowd. I was having a blast catching trout, and I ignored the occasional snide comments from envious purists.

In mid-September, my longtime and highly esteemed companion, Bob Dodge, arrived to spend two weeks fishing with me. I was low on Buggers, which by that time I could tie blindfolded, and set to whipping up a half dozen while Bob watched, mesmerized. At length he said, "I think I can do that." He had never tied a fly before, but he sat down and tied a couple of Woolly Buggers as though he'd been doing it for years.

The next day, we hit the Upper Madison in Yellowstone Park, as I'd heard that the big trout were starting to run up out of Hebgen Lake. Nice guy that I am, I stationed him halfway down the run, ahead of me. Three casts, and he nailed a 19-inch rainbow. He was hooked more firmly than the trout.

Later, at a private club in northern Michigan, I was a guest of Bob's mentor at Ohio State in orthodontics, Dr. Arthur B. Lewis. We were fishing a pondlike area in the stream. After an hour or so of dinking around with soft-hackle wet flies, Bob and I decided to roll out the heavy artillery and tied on the Buggers. Apparently, the Michigan trout hadn't yet been exposed to them, and we began to get smashing strikes on virtually every cast. After a bit, Dr. Lewis strolled over and took a long look at our flies. At length, with a hint of a sly smile, he said, "Don't show those around the club." But the next day, he approached me in private and inquired, "Hey, you got any more of those Woolly Bang-Bangs?"

I carry quite a selection of Buggers, as I find that the trout get used to a particular pattern fairly quickly and I have to throw them an assortment of stuff, like a cagey veteran pitcher. Recently, I began experimenting with a new import called Fur Marabou, which is a by-product from ranch-raised animals in Finland. I love its texture and action, as well as its durability. Here's a dressing that substitutes fur marabou for the usual feather marabou and also explores some new body configurations and other innovations.

There are two methods for preparing the dubbing. First, cut up the Lite Brite so that the fibers are fairly short—about $3/8$ to about $1/2$ inch long. Throw it and the fur into a top-blade blender and zap it. If you don't have a blender, pour some lukewarm water into a bowl and add a few drops of dish detergent. Throw in the materials and stir for a bit; they will blend nicely. Pour the mixture through a sieve, and rinse out the detergent under a faucet. Dry the dubbing by squeezing with paper toweling. If you don't have any fur marabou, follow the same procedure using regular marabou. It's not as durable, and the action isn't as good, but it will work.

The traditional lead wire is being phased out because of its toxicity to wildlife. Acceptable substitutes are now available. For hook sizes 8 and smaller, I use 10 or 15 thousandths inch diameter; for 6s and larger, 15 or 20 thousandths.

Dick's Fur MaraBugger, Psychedelic

Hook	Daiichi model 1750 or comparable, 3X to 4X long.
Thread	Black 6/0 or 8/0 Uni-Thread or comparable.
Tail	Black fur marabou or regular marabou.
Underbody	Lead wire or substitute (optional).
Body	Dubbing mixture of approximately equal parts rainbow Lite Brite and black long-hair dubbing—arctic fox underfur, llama, or similar soft material.
Collar	Black fur marabou.

1. Tie on near the front end of the hook, as you would with any Bugger, and wrap to the bend.
2. Prepare a small clump of fur marabou by removing the fuzzy underfur at the butt end. A fine-toothed comb is useful here. Remove only the short stuff; the rest forms the tail.
3. Tie the fur marabou in place. As a rule of thumb, the tail is about equal in length to the hook shank. After securing the fur, cut off the excess squarely, as this sets up the wrapping of the underbody.
4. With the thread hanging at the rear, wrap some wire around the hook. The thread is not involved at all; the wire simply molds itself in place. Abut the first wrap at the rear against the stubbed-off butt of the tail, and end well short of the eye up front. Smear a thin coating of Zap-A-Gap or other superglue along the top of the wire, as it will run in between the crevices and form a bond.
5. There is no hackle on this particular Bugger, so the next step is to dub the body. You can use either the single-thread or spinning-loop method. I recommend the former. Leave some space up front for the collar.

The fur marabou tail in place (steps 1–3).

Weighting wire in place (step 4).

The body in place (step 5).

6. Tease out the dubbing a bit with a piece of Velcro to obtain a translucent effect. This is optional but, in my opinion, desirable.

7. Make a little thread base between the front of the body and the hook eye, then tie in another bunch of fur marabou about the same length but of somewhat less quantity than the tail. This material is tied in pointing forward, off the front end of the hook. Begin with a soft wrap or two, so that it distributes 360 degrees around the hook. Help it with your finger to effect full and even deployment. Then secure it and trim off the excess.

8. Bring the thread in front of the fur, draw the collar material back, and wrap thread in front of and slightly over the fur bunch, until it assumes a swept-back attitude, as shown in the photo. Whip finish and add lacquer, and you're done.

Here's a variation of this dressing using a cone head. You could use a bead, but the cone is ideal for this application. Not all hook styles will accept a cone head, however. Those with compound bends, such as the Limerick, present too tight a corner. The rounder bends, such as the model perfect and the less extreme sproats, are fine. I suggest that you debarb first. Weighting with wire is not necessary here because of the cone, but if you want a really deep-running Bugger, wrap on some wire.

Teasing out the dubbing (step 6).

The collar material tied in (step 7).

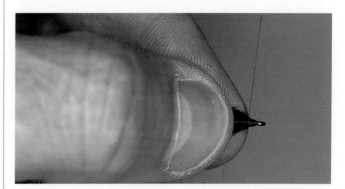

Sweeping back and securing the collar material (step 8).

The finished fly.

Dick's Saturday-Night-Live Fur MaraBugger

Hook, tail, and body	Same as above.
Thread	Black 6/0 or 8/0.
Nose	A cone head, your choice of color (I prefer black nickel).
Collar	Black soft hackle.

1. Slide on the cone by running the point of the hook into the small end. The cone stays up front until later.
2. Tie the tail and body as before. Leave just enough space ahead of the body for the next component, the hackle collar.
3. Make a collar by tying in a black soft-hackle feather by the tip end and taking a series of wraps while stroking back the barbs.
4. After tying off and trimming the hackle butt, fill in with some thread wraps, working right up into the aperture of the cone. Uni-Stretch greatly accelerates this procedure. The idea is to create enough bulk to obtain a snug fit and block the cone from sliding back over the hackle collar, but not so much as to prevent the cone from being slid back over the thread wraps. Test by sliding the cone rearward until you like the fit. Then tie off.
5. If you want, you can further stabilize the positioning of the cone by putting a drop of Zap-A-Gap on the thread wraps. Just make sure you have a good fit first.
6. Using fine thread (8/0 Uni-Thread or similar), tie on in front of the cone and take some wraps, forcing it back against and over the buffering wraps. Tie off and lacquer.

Cone heads come in different sizes and colors, so you can play around with patterns. The White Cone Head MaraBugger is an improbable yet amazingly productive dressing.

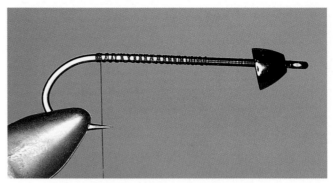

The cone head in place (step 1).

The tail and body in place (step 2).

The soft hackle collar is tied behind the cone head (step 3).

Positioning and securing the cone head completes the fly (steps 4–6).

White Cone Head MaraBugger

Hook	Daiichi model 1750 or comparable, 3X to 4X long.
Thread	White 6/0 or 8/0 Uni-Thread or comparable.
Head	A silver cone.
Tail	White fur marabou or regular marabou.
Underbody	Wire (optional).
Ribbing	Medium silver oval tinsel (optional).
Body hackle	White saddle hackle, palmered over the dubbing (optional).
Body	Dubbing mixture of approximately equal parts clear or pearl Lite Brite and white long-hair dubbing—arctic fox underfur, llama, or similar soft material. Or clear or pearl Krystal Chenille.
Collar	White fur marabou, soft white hackle, or none.

1. Tie on, wrap to the rear, and tie on the tail, as above.
2. Tie in the hackle feather by the tip end, then the ribbing.
3. Dub the body.
4. Wrap the ribbing in even spirals.

The cone and tail in place, hackle feather and ribbing tinsel tied in (steps 1 & 2).

The completed dubbed body (step 3).

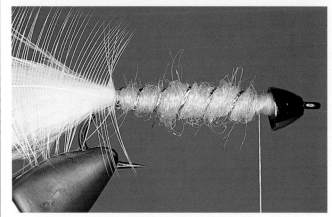

The ribbing is wrapped in even spirals (step 4).

5. Wrap the hackle feather, abutting the trailing edge of the ribbing, and stroking the fibers back as you go. This is classic salmon-fly technique.
6. Use what's left of the hackle to form a collar adjacent to the rear of the cone.
7. Finish off as described for the previous Bugger.

If you do any fishing where damselflies abound, you might try the following Woolly Bugger dressing as a nymphal imitation. I've had considerable success with it in western lakes.

Damselfly Nymph Woolly Bugger

Hook	Daiichi model 1750 or comparable, 3X to 4X long.
Thread	Olive or tan 6/0 or 8/0 Uni-Thread or comparable.
Tail	Pale olive fur or feather marabou, tied short.
Underbody	Wire (optional).
Body hackle	Pale brown or tan saddle hackle with short barbs, palmer-wrapped sparsely.
Body	Pale olive dubbing, with a bit of tan mixed in if you wish.

There is no end to the variations of the Woolly Bugger. Choices of style, dressing, and materials for your Buggers are vast, and you can mix and match: with or without body hackle, with a fur collar or a hackle collar, or with body hackle and no collar other than a few extra wraps of hackle in front. I hope you're not a dry-fly purist, because you'll be missing out on a lot of action.

The hackle follows the trailing edge of the ribbing (step 5).

Finishing the hackle and securing the cone complete the fly (step 6 & 7).

CHAPTER 19

Unmuddling the Muddler

The Muddler Minnow is a special fly, in a number of respects. It was a highly original pattern at the time of its inception, and it created quite a stir. The designer was Canadian tier Don Gapen. He was attempting to imitate a sculpin, which he did, but the fly goes well beyond that. It has been so universally successful over so long a period of time that it deserves consideration as perhaps the greatest all-around fly ever. It has been and still is mass-produced, in a number of versions.

The original Muddler is still a great favorite. It can be fished many different ways, in varying situations, and in all types of water. It has accounted for an enormous variety of fish, including Atlantic salmon. A Yellow Marabou Muddler with a little flash in the body or wing is a fantastic fly for fishing Alaskan salmon.

I used to hate tying this fly. At the time I wrote *Mastering,* I had worked out several techniques that I passed along to help others who struggled with the Muddler, as I did. I have since modified them, so it's time for an update.

I like to think of tying the Muddler as tying two flies on the same hook. The tail-body-wing assembly is a fly unto itself, and the head-and-collar assembly is another. If you can get through the winging of a wet fly as detailed earlier, you can, with a bit more instruction, tie a Muddler. The tail-body-wing assembly is really nothing more than a winged wet fly without a hackle. The head-and-collar assembly is something new and different and is explained below. While they must be totally integrated, they cannot interfere with one another during the construction, or some serious tying problems will result. When you are positioning the thread for the head-collar assembly, keep this in mind, and stay just in front of the wing butt tie-down wraps. That's where the second fly begins.

I won't go into detail on the tying procedures up to and including the wing. You'll probably want to weight your Muddlers, as the deer-hair head-and-collar assembly creates a lot of buoyancy. This is easily done by wrapping lead or lead-substitute wire around the shank and covering it with gold braid, rather than the flat tinsel specified in the original dressing. This is shown in the photo sequence.

Another important factor is proportioning. This involves deciding how large of a head you want on your Muddler. Unless I'm tying really large Muddlers, I try to proportion mine so that I can do the head and collar with one bunch of spun deer hair, as this simplifies that operation. If more hair is required, there are a couple of techniques for supplementing the first bunch, described in this chapter. I've seen a lot of variation, but I don't like long collars on my Muddlers. The original concept was to imitate the prominent pectoral fins of the sculpin. These are fairly good-sized, but they shouldn't overbalance the rest of the fly. The head-collar assembly is best when it's about one-third of the overall length.

Selection of hair is all-important in Muddler making, not only regarding texture, but also length. If you choose hair that's too long for the hook size on which you're working, you'll be using just the outer portion near the tips, which is hard protein and doesn't spin well. The result is that the flaring that enables the formation of the head is compromised. Choose hair of such length that you're working nearer the butts than the tips, and be sure it's soft enough to flare easily under thread tension.

I've seen Muddlers tied on everything from 2XL nymph hooks to long streamer hooks. I feel the design of the fly works best on a 3XL or 4XL.

The thread bears a relationship to the size of the Muddler being tied and to the texture of the deer hair. I try to use the finest thread I can get away with. In fact, when tying small Muddlers, I often use 8/0 Uni-Thread or something similar all the way through. This minimizes bulk when tying the non-deer-hair part of the fly and enables a neat, compact head and collar. On medium-size Muddlers, I like to use the fine thread up until I've completed the wing, then switch to something stronger for the head-and-collar operation. On large Muddlers, where spacing is somewhat less critical, a strong thread may be used throughout.

Things change quickly in the world of threads, but at this writing, I find Dynacord to be a very good hair-spinning thread, as well as Uni Big Fly Thread and Danville Monocord. I don't like Kevlar threads, not only because of their obtuse behavior, but also because of what they do to a pair of scissors.

There's also the question of whether to spin hair over bare hook shank or over a thin thread base. Both techniques will work. It's a little easier to get the hair to spin and distribute evenly over a bare hook, but the assembly comes out a little stronger when done over thread. It's your call.

Muddler Minnow

Hook	A 3XL or 4XL wet-fly model, Daiichi 2220 4XL (down-eye) or Daiichi model 1750 4XL (straight eye) or comparable, size 2-16.
Thread	As described above; here, brown Uni-Thread, 8/0 to start, 6/0 to finish.
Tail and wing	Mottled turkey wing quill sections.
Underbody	Weighting wire (optional, but strongly recommended).
Body	Gold braid or mesh.
Underwing	A small bunch of squirrel tail, either gray or fox.
Head and collar	Spinnable deer body hair.

1. Tie on about one-third of the shank length to the rear of the eye, leaving the front part of the hook bare. Wrap to the bend, and tie the tail as you would a wet-fly wing, using two slim sections of feather, with the pointed ends downward.
2. Chop off the tail butts square, then wrap weighting wire, abutting the tail butts and working forward. Stop well short of where the wing will be tied on. Refer to the photos for spacing. Apply a smear of Zap-A-Gap or similar superglue along the top of the wire wraps, and allow it to sink down among them.
3. Depending on the size of the fly, the gold braid can be tied in either at the rear and wrapped in a single layer or ahead of the wire and wrapped in a double layer, like conventional tinsel. In either case, trim the excess and neaten with a few thread wraps.
4. Tie on a small bunch of squirrel tail hair. It should extend a little way beyond the tie-in point of the tail. Trim, and create a neat thread base for the wing.

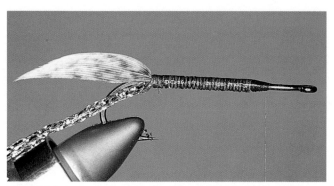

The weighting wire is wrapped, the gold braid tied in at the rear. Note how thread is used to fill in at each end of the wire wraps (steps 2 & 3).

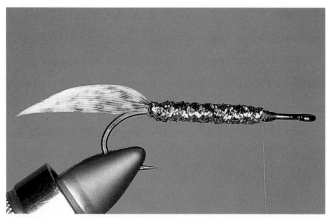

The completed body (step 3).

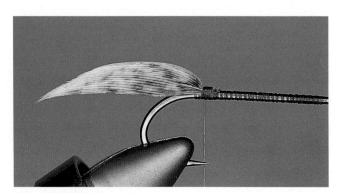

The tail in place (step 1).

The squirrel tail underwing in place (step 4).

5. Tie the wing as you would for a wet fly, but with the tips down. Secure it well, then trim off the butts, leaving the front part of the hook clear. If you're concerned about the stability of the wing, put another droplet of Zap-A-Gap on the thread wraps, and allow it to penetrate and dry completely.

6. You can proceed with the deer-hair operation over bare hook, or you can wrap a smooth, thin layer of thread. In either case, stay away from the wing butts.

7. Prepare a bunch of hair by cleaning out all underfur and shorties and stacking the tips. On a Muddler of this size, the bunch should be about the diameter of an ordinary pencil.

8. Lay the hair atop the hook, and gauge the length of the collar. If necessary, trim the butts a little so that they're long enough to form the head but not overly long, which makes them hard to work with. Then lay the hair back on top of the hook, and work it down around both sides and on top, taking care not to disturb the wing.

9. If necessary, sharpen the thread by spinning the bobbin clockwise so that it isn't strandy. Then take two soft wraps under moderate tension, exactly on top of one another. The hair should begin to flare a little.

10. As you start the next wrap, come over the top and apply very firm thread tension, again keeping the wraps one atop the other. Pull downward on the far side of the hook. The hair will encircle the hook shank and will flare, as you see in the photo.

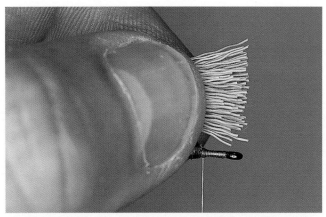

The hair bunch ready to be spun on. Note how the butts are trimmed (steps 6–8).

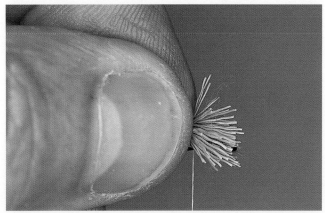

Tension is increased as thread wraps are applied (step 9).

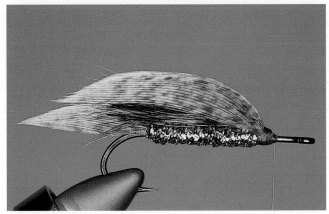

The wing tied on, secured, and trimmed. Note the thread position (step 5).

Maximum tension with third thread wrap causes hair to spin into place (step 10).

11. Inspect the hair from all sides. It should be evenly deployed. If it isn't, help it with your fingers.

12. Take two or three more tight wraps over the others. The hair butts should stand up straight; you can assist them with you fingers if necessary.

13. Make sure the thread is good and sharp, then take several wraps forward, passing the thread through the butts and ending up in front of them. This secures everything.

14. Pack the hair by pushing it gently to the rear. Be careful; you can shove it back into the wing butts and ruin everything. A packing tool is helpful here. Hold on to the collar during this operation.

15. If the hair is deployed as you want it, tie off and start trimming. You can shape the head pretty much as you wish. I cut mine flat across the bottom with either a razor blade or straight-bladed scissors, then shape the top and sides with curved-bladed scissors. Fine serrations on one of the blades are very helpful, as they cause the blades to grip and shear the hair, instead of pushing it ahead. Until the very end, work with the tips of the scissors pointing rearward.

16. If the hair was spun properly, the rear of the head and the collar will be nicely integrated. This can be enhanced by trimming back into the collar just a tiny bit.

17. To get at any butt ends that are buried in the collar, squeeze the tips of the collar hairs flat against the sides of the fly with your left thumb and forefinger. The hidden butt ends will pop out and can be trimmed off.

On larger Muddlers, it's usually necessary to use more than one bunch of hair to form the head-and-collar assembly. There are several methods for doing this. First, let's assume that you have a sufficient amount of hair for the collar and all you need to do is to build out the head. We'll start with the collar in place and unfilled space at the front. Here's the procedure:

1. Cut off and prepare another bunch of hair of adequate size to fill out the head.

2. Cut off the tips of the hair so that when trimming, you'll be able to tell what's head and what's collar.

3. Spin the bunch into place as instructed above, then work the thread through to the front.

4. Pack as necessary, tie off, and trim.

One pattern that employs this technique is the Marabou Muddler, a popular and useful variation. It can be tied in many colors, with many types of bodies and embellishments. Here's the recipe for one of my favorites. It's important to keep the thread sharp throughout this procedure, as you'll be using more wraps than before, and you want them to bury into the hair and not be visible.

The butt ends standing upright, the thread passed through to the front and tied off (steps 11–14).

Beginning the trimming (step 14).

Continuing the trimming (step 15).

Final trimming completes the Muddler Minnow (step 16).

White Marabou Muddler

Hook	Daiichi model 1750 4XL (straight-eye), size 4.
Thread	White 8/0 or 6/0 to start, Dynacord or similar for the hair operations.
Tail	White turkey marabou or fur marabou.
Underbody	Weighting wire (optional, but strongly recommended).
Body	Silver braid or mesh.
Wing	Same as tail.
Wing embellishment	Pearl or rainbow Krystal Flash or similar (optional).
Head and collar	Spinnable deer body hair, natural color or white.

1. Tie on a marabou tail as you would for a Woolly Bugger, but not as long.
2. Tie the underbody and body as was done for the regular Muddler.
3. Tie on the wing. If you want to add the flashy material, tie in a few strands on each side of the wing. Switch threads now.
4. Prepare a bunch of hair per instructions for the standard Muddler. Use as much as you think you can handle.
5. Set the bunch on top of the hook, and spin it as was done on the regular Muddler. Stroke the butts so that they stand straight out at 90 degrees.
6. Sharpen the thread, then walk it through the butts with a few tight, spaced wraps, ending up in front. Pack as necessary.

Tail and body in place (steps 1 & 2).

The wing tied on (step 3).

Flashy material added (step 3).

The first bunch of hair spun into place and being compressed with a packing tool (steps 4–6).

7. Prepare a second bunch, and cut off the tip ends so that they won't get mixed up with the collar material.

8. Spin on the second bunch immediately in front of the first one. Then stroke the butts into an upright position, and march the thread through them with several tight, spaced wraps, ending up in front.

9. If you have enough hair in place for the head, tie off and trim. If not, add another bunch of appropriate size, following the instructions for supplementing the regular type of head. Three bunches is rather extreme, but it can be done with adroit technique. Remember to pack the hair tightly.

The fly is now ready for trimming (step 8 & 9).

The bottom may be trimmed flat with a razor blade (step 9).

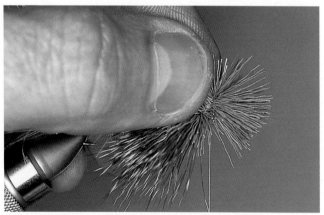

The second bunch consists of butt ends only and is spun on in front of the first bunch (steps 7 & 8).

The completed White Marabou Muddler.

Now let's assume that you want more material in both the collar and the head. This gets a little tricky. You'll need really strong thread, because of the amount of hair you'll be working with. Prepare a bunch that's considerably larger than normal, perhaps even double the amount used on a typical Muddler. Stack the tips, then trim the butts so that when spun in place, they will be short enough to allow the thread to be walked through without matting.

Instead of holding the hair on top of the hook and letting the spinning action deploy it, *encircle the hook with the hair.* Then apply three wraps, getting progressively tighter. Really lean on the third one, then let go of the hair. The entire bunch will spin about one full turn. This means that, in effect, you've lost one turn of thread, which is why it's important to apply three before releasing the hair. Observe the photos of the Marabou Muddler. Notice the well-developed head and collar achieved with this technique.

If you want even more hair in the head, you can supplement with the method described for the Marabou Muddler, spinning on a bunch that has had the tips trimmed off. However, keep in mind that you already have a large amount of hair in place. By trimming back into the collar hair a little, you may well end up with a sizable head without adding any more material and thus complicating the process.

Tying with hair can be carried to highly sophisticated levels. Hair-spinning geniuses like Tim England, Dave Whitlock, Chris Helm, Joe Messinger, Jr., Jimmy Nix, Billy Munn, Carl Bradley, and others, who create incredible replicas of frogs, crustaceans, and baitfish, use these techniques and variations of them. I've never tried anything that complex. If you wish to become a hair-tying maven, try to get into a class with one of the true masters or, at least, watch one at a show somewhere. You'll be amazed at what they can do.

Use very strong thread and lots of tension (step 2).

The result (step 3).

The finished fly, trimmed somewhat differently (step 4).

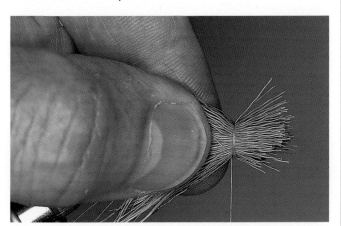

When handling an extralarge bunch of hair, hold it so that it encircles the hook before wrapping the thread (step 1).

CHAPTER 20

The Pseudo Sculpin

At the time I wrote *Mastering,* I was sufficiently insecure about my ability with regard to the Muddler that I passed along a pattern called the Alternative. I did not represent it as being the equivalent of the true Muddler, but it was a no-brainer to tie, and it did catch fish.

Back when I still had a real job, I was often called upon by my boss to take a client fishing. This was not always an unmitigated joy, but it was usually a welcome relief to swap the three-piece suit for a pair of waders and enjoy a day astream on the expense account.

There was one guy in particular who loved to fish with me, and in his case, it was a pleasure, as he was the sort of person you'd want to spend time with on a good river. His first name was Tom; I forget the rest. He was a southerner by birth who had migrated northward, following the corporate trail onward and upward. I doubt that he reached the higher echelons of management, as he was simply too nice. I helped him with his fly fishing and found him an apt pupil.

I had access to several sections of private water in those days, one of which ran through the property of a small club on the Upper Beaverkill that I belonged to for a few years. Tom and I arrived in midmorning on a weekday and found that we had the entire club to ourselves. The water was up a little from recent rains but fishable enough.

Nothing was happening on the surface, so I rigged Tom up for nymphing and positioned him in a prime run. I tied on an Alternative and walked upstream a little ways. I chose a spot where a tiny feeder brook entered the Beaverkill—little more than a spring seepage, actually. In the fall, I had often observed wild trout spawning in this stream, both browns and brookies.

I began to swing the Alternative around in the pool where the little creek entered. About the sixth drift, I felt a hard pull. I was fast to a trout. It turned out to be a brown of about 14 inches—respectable enough. I held it up for Tom to see, and he waved his acknowledgment.

Two more casts, and I got another one—a virtual twin. As I was playing the fish, I thought I saw something swirl at it, as if out of envy. I landed and released the trout, and sat down to rest the pool for a bit. Tom, attracted by the action, waded up and asked if it would be okay for him to watch. I assented, of course.

After about five minutes, I began working the pocket again. I cast across and fed out a little slack, allowing the fly to run deep. The strike came immediately, and I felt the excitement that only a heavy fish can cause. It fought hard but stayed in the pool, as brown trout are prone to do.

But it wasn't a brown! In a few minutes, I was admiring a gorgeous brookie of about 17 inches, gasping at my feet. Yes, there are some fish like that in certain places in the upper river. Tom looked over my shoulder in amazement. He also took notice of the fly, and I was obliged to part with a couple of them.

The Alternative was indeed a successful pattern, but now I have one I like better, which I call the Pseudo Sculpin. It's simpler to tie and promises to be even more productive, although being a recent creation, it hasn't yet stood the test of time and broad exposure.

Dick's Pseudo Sculpin

Hook	A typical 4XL model.
Thread	First, white or cream Uni-Stretch; then brown or tan 8/0 or 6/0 Uni-Thread or comparable.
Tail	A small bunch of well-marked fox squirrel tail hair.
Underbody	Weighting wire—not too thick (optional, but strongly recommended).
Body	Uni-Stretch.
Wing	Well-marked fox squirrel tail in three layers, each a little shorter than the one before. On smaller hooks, use pine squirrel.
Hackle	Speckled hen, tied full and swept back.
Eyes	Gold mylar stick-on.
Head coating	Clear AquaFlex water-based head cement or epoxy.

1. Tie on with the Uni-Stretch as shown, and tie the tail in place.
2. Wrap the wire underbody in the usual manner, and coat it with Zap-A-Gap or similar glue.
3. Build the body out of Uni-Stretch, and in the process, tie on the squirrel tail hair in three or four progressive steps, as shown. Let the hair come down around the sides a bit, thus filling out the body silhouette. Leave plenty of space up front.

Uni-Stretch body being wrapped (step 3).

Tying on the first bunch of squirrel (step 3).

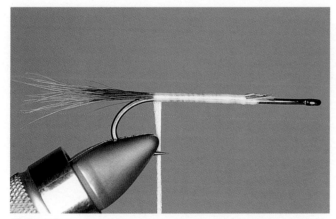

Tail in place (step 1).

Tying on the second bunch of squirrel (step 3).

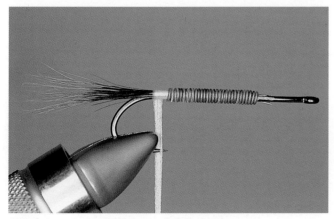

Weighting wire underbody in place (step 2).

Tying on the third bunch of squirrel (step 3).

4. Switch to the brown thread. Tie in a hackle feather by the tip end, and wrap it as a collar. You may need two or three to obtain proper quantities. Again, leave some space up front.

5. Build up the head sufficiently so that a pair of mylar eyes can be affixed. After sticking them in place, cover the entire head with the AquaFlex or epoxy. If you're using AquaFlex, you'll need two layers; allow for complete drying between applications.

The soft, webby collar emulates the movement of the prominent pectoral fins of a sculpin as it scurries about on the bottom of the stream. If you're going to be fishing this fly in very fast water, you might want to use a stiffer feather so that it doesn't get plastered tight against the body by the swift currents. Brown-dyed grizzly rooster works very well.

An interesting variation on this pattern is to tie it as a cone head. Use a good-size gold-plated cone, sliding it into position before mounting the hook in the vise. If you want to add eyes, stick them on with Zap-A-Gap.

The hackle is wrapped, and the head is built up (steps 4 & 5).

Adding the eyes completes the Pseudo Sculpin (step 5).

Brown thread has replaced the Uni-Stretch, and the hackle feather is tied in (step 4).

The cone head version of the Pseudo Sculpin.

CHAPTER 21

Marabou Streamers

arabou is great stuff. Originally, the material came from a huge African stork of that name, one of the most ungainly creatures on earth. They are now included in the list of untouchables. Now what's called marabou comes from white domestic turkeys and certain strains of chickens. Whiting Farms offers a product called Chickabou, which is the marabou from hens. It's excellent for smaller flies. There's also now the product called fur marabou, technically not marabou, but it works the same. This is the soft fur from one of several animals that are ranch-raised in Finland for the garment industry. I particularly like its action and durability.

Marabou is most commonly used on Woolly Buggers and for winging streamers. It also can be substituted for feathers of the same color on streamer fly patterns, where it gives you a different appearance and behavior, as marabou is much more active in the water than are typical streamer wing feathers.

Most turkey marabou is sold in bundles. The feathers vary considerably in size and texture, so you'll need to look them over in the store and determine if they are suitable for what you intend to tie. The characteristics of the feather will dictate just how you handle it. The first thing you should do is discard all the junky, fluffy stuff around the butt. Then, if the feather is fairly large and the fronds are fairly long, you can snip out the center quill back a ways into the feather, stroke the plumes into a neat bunch, and tie in the whole thing at once. If the feather does not lend itself to this method, either because of its limited size or because it has too thick a quill, stroke the longer plumes out to the sides, cut them off where they join the quill, and tie them on in bunches. Use as much as you need to fill out the silhouette, keeping in mind that marabou slims down a lot when wet.

One problem with marabou is that it tends to get tangled around the bend of the hook during casting. There are several ways to counteract this, all of which have to do with the tying of the fly. You can make the wing short but that may compromise action and silhouette. You can tie on a small bunch of stiffer material as an underwing; that's somewhat effective. Or you can tie on a marabou tail of the same color as the wing. When the fly is wet, the wing and tail integrate and appear as one. I like this solution for larger streamers. You can still tie a supplementary tail of some other material and color underneath the marabou tail, if you wish, but on a nondescript pattern like this, I don't believe the tail color makes that much difference.

The Black Ghost is a classic example of the marabou streamer. I don't know why the Black Ghost Marabou works, but it certainly does, and that's all I need to know.

My old friend and colleague Jim Bashline owned a stretch of water on lower Spruce Creek in Pennsylvania. A lover of fun times, Jim occasionally held a fishing contest behind his house. One year, Jim put up a prize of a little antique fly reel—biggest fish takes all. Eight or ten of us were assembled, including Poul Jorgensen and Chuck Furimsky. Jim was the self-appointed arbiter. Each participant got ten casts. They could be taken all at once, one at a time, or whatever. Any fly could be used, provided it was debarbed and passed Jim's inspection, which a number of them did not.

We were about 75 percent of the way through the rotation, and no one had hooked a fish. This was rather amazing, as the place was loaded with them, and big ones at that. Preparing for my eighth turn at bat, I tied on a small Black Ghost Marabou streamer. Jim sort of sniffed at it, but it was allowed.

Halfway through the drift, I worked the rod tip a little and got an immediate strike—a rainbow, and a large one. I played the fish, brought it to the bank, and held it while Jim went to net it. I knew that Jim didn't want me to win, because he considered me a ringer, but the fish seemed well hooked, and I thought I had it made. But I reckoned without my host's resourcefulness; he fumbled around with the net until he knocked the trout loose. No score!

The contest ended without a winner, so Jim declared a fifteen-minute free-for-all. This consisted of him chumming from upstream with large pellets while we fished down below. Immediately the water began to boil. I was prepared: I had tied several deer-hair flies that closely resembled these pellets. I picked out a particularly large riseform and drifted my fly over it. Wham! Five minutes later, I had subdued a brown trout of around 22 inches. Umpire Jim measured the trout, and I released it.

Everyone was into fish now, and Jim was busy making measurements. I should have been watching more carefully. After the time expired, Jim held up some guy's hand and declared him the winner. I hadn't gotten a good look at his trout, but it sure didn't appear to be as big as mine. Oh, well. Jim compensated by mixing me one of the best martinis I ever tasted. I miss that guy.

The Marabou Black Ghost dressing calls for jungle cock, but guinea fowl makes a fishable substitute. Jungle cock eyes, or nails, are smallish, uniquely configured feathers that were widely used in traditional salmon and streamer fly patterns. When I began my tying career, jungle cock was plentiful and cheap; I was able to buy nice capes for $5 to $10.

In 1967, the India gray jungle fowl was banned from import. No acceptable replacement was available. Prices skyrocketed, and a black market developed. For a while, people got away with showing old receipts for capes they had recently acquired under the table, but the Feds soon wised up, and supplies dried up.

Eventually, a Britisher named Ron Taylor developed a strain of farm-raised jungle fowl. He bred in another strain, the Ceylon red jungle fowl, which is close to the gray in many respects, although it lacks the treasured eyed feathers. The cross-breeding rendered the birds somewhat more manageable, and the program has become quite successful. Today this company is licensed to sell jungle cock to the American market. You can buy the product, known as Fisherman's Feathers, in packets of ten, matched for size, or by the cape. Current retail is $5.95 per bag, $125 for grade A capes, and $100 for grade B.

To use guinea fowl as a replacement, simply take a single-dotted guinea fowl feather, with a white dot centered on the quill out near the tip, and cut it to shape. If you wish, you can embellish it by touching the dot with a pale yellow or ecru waterproof marker, which will alter the stark whiteness. Elegant? No. But it's okay for fishing

and quite durable, thanks to the presence of the quill down the center.

Here's another trick, if you're slightly handy with tools. Buy a piece of thin, flat brass stock at a hobby store, and make yourself a guinea-burner! Simply fold the brass in half and cut the two ends into a tear-drop shape with a small pair of tin snips. Then smooth and refine them with a fine file or a grinding wheel mounted in a $1/4$ inch drill or Dremel tool. This process is shown in the tying sequence, so refer to the photograph for details of the shape of the burner. This will enable you to very quickly shape guinea feathers into serviceable fake jungle cock. If you're clever, you can achieve more realism by incorporating part of the next white dot down the quill.

Here's a tying tip. Whether you're using jungle cock or guinea fowl, the eyes may tend to skew if tied in by the quill alone. The solution is to pass the thread over the tiniest part of the front of the feather. This keeps the eyes flat against the head. Be sure to mount them against the thread of the head itself and not against the hair of the wing.

Since marabou is a very forgiving material for winging streamers, the pattern below is tied with what the Brits refer to as a "true" hackle. Instead of simply tying a small bunch of material at the throat, a folded and wrapped collar is tied. Then the fibers along the sides are stroked downward and those on top that refuse to go to either side are pruned out.

The rationale is that true hackles have a more three-dimensional form than simple beards and hold this form better in the current. This is affected by the texture of the feather. Hen cape and saddle feathers make nice true hackles, but because of their softness, they don't have much resistance and as a consequence are swept back along the front of the fly by the flow of the water. Soft rooster generally works out better, but the quill may be so thick that it bulks up the head area and interferes with tying on the wing and finishing the fly. Some hen feathers have the same problem, so beware.

Note that on these larger flies, where access from the rear is no problem, I set the vise at horizontal. This allows me to use the rotational feature to examine and work on the back side of the fly, which helps when you're striving for symmetry.

Black Ghost Marabou

Hook	Typical streamer, Daiichi model 2340 or 2370 or comparable, size 2-12.
Thread	First, black Uni-Stretch; then black 6/0 or 8/0.
Tail	Yellow hackle barbs or very fine marabou fibers.
Ribbing	Narrow to medium flat silver tinsel.
Body	Uni-Stretch or black floss.
Throat and hackle	Yellow, folded and wrapped, or, for a simple throat, use yellow hackle barbs or very fine yellow marabou fibers.
Underwing	Stiff white or crystal synthetic hair.
Wing	White marabou.
Eyes	Jungle cock, single-dotted guinea fowl, or painted or stick-on eyes with protective coating.

1. Mount the Uni-Stretch in a bobbin, and tie on near the front.
2. If you're going to use yellow marabou for the tail, it should be long enough to be tied in about 25 percent of the shank length rearward of the eye. This enables you to bind down the material while pulling rearward on it with your left hand, thus smoothing out the body.
3. Tie in the ribbing tinsel at the rear. Flat mylar tinsel tends to flip over with the first turn, so lay the silver side against the hook; it will end up outermost. Then wrap the body, reverse-spinning the bobbin as necessary to flatten the Uni-Stretch, and applying as many layers as are required, three or four being typical.
4. If you're going to use jungle cock or guinea fowl for the eyes, tie off the Uni-Stretch and switch to black thread. If you're going to use stick-on or painted eyes, stay with the Uni-Stretch, as it will build up the head quickly.
5. Wrap the tinsel with even, well-spaced turns, secure it, and trim the excess.
6. Tie in a yellow feather, and wrap a collar-style hackle. Note the proportions in the photo.

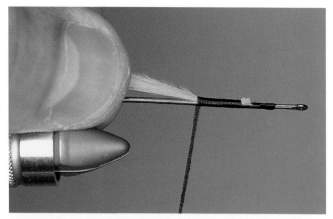

Binding down the tail butts to form a smooth base (step 2).

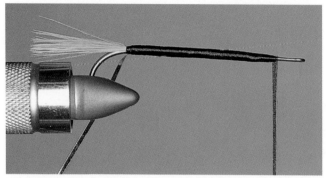

The tail in place, ribbing tinsel tied in, body wrapped (step 3).

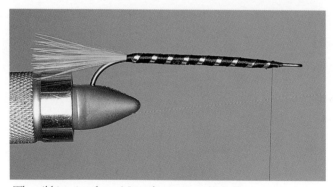

The ribbing in place. Note the spacing (step 5).

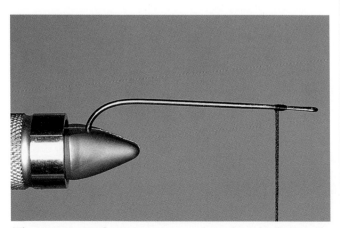

The tie-in covers the return wire on a looped-eye hook (step 1).

Start the true hackle by wrapping a collar. Note the proportions (step 6).

7. Stroke the barbs downward as shown.
8. Prune out all barbs that refuse to lie to one side or the other, until the hackle resembles that in the photo.
9. In some cases, a tiny droplet of Zap-A-Gap applied here helps hold the hackles in place.
10. Tie on the underwing. It should extend just a bit beyond the bend of the hook.
11. Tie on the marabou.

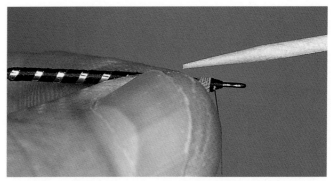

If needed, apply a small drop of superglue here (step 9).

The underwing in place (step 10).

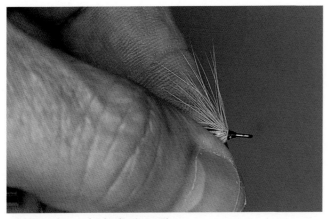

Stroking down the barbs (step 7).

The main marabou wing in place (step 11).

The topmost barbs are removed to form true hackle (step 8).

The butts trimmed (step 11).

12. For the eyes, real jungle cock is best, if you have it. If not, prepare the guinea fowl substitute by hand-trimming a feather to shape or with the aid of a burner, as shown in the series of photographs. Tie one eye on each cheek as mirror images. Alternatively, you can use painted or stick-on eyes with a protective coating as described in the chapters 20 and 22.

13. Whip-finish.

I've included a brief sequence of photos showing the configuration of the combined marabou wing and tail. Here you see the stick-on eye, which gives a nice effect.

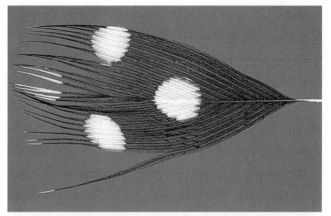

Select a guinea fowl feather configured like this one (step 12).

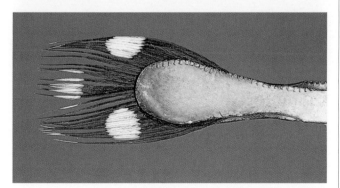

The feather is inserted in the burner (step 12).

The shaped guinea fowl feather tied in place (step 13).

The finished fly.

For a combined tail-and-wing effect, start by tying the tail like this.

The rest of the fly is tied as per the previous instructions.

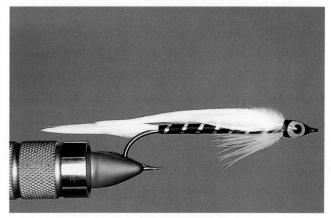

This is how the resulting fly looks when wet.

CHAPTER 22

The Bucktail or Hairwing Streamer

The streamer is the most underutilized type of fly in our arsenal. There's a certain prejudice against such flies, which are considered lures by some. These fishers are missing out on a lot of opportunities, however.

The streamer fly, with its many variations, is perhaps the fly of the twenty-first century. Illusory patterns such as the Woolly Bugger have really come into their own in recent years. One of the reasons may be that we now spend most of our time fishing for hatchery trout, which react to certain stimuli quite differently than fish born in the river.

With the exception of Atlantic salmon flies, there are more attractor flies in the streamer category than any other type. (Of course, the terms "attractor" and "imitator" are misleading. Fish don't make such distinctions. They think attractors are food, or at least something small and conquerable.)

Myself, I love streamers, both the tying and the fishing, and I give them a fair amount of exposure in this book in the hope of winning over some converts.

Hairwing streamers are pretty easy to tie. There are a few problems, but these are easily solved with a little knowledge, discreet selection of materials, and disciplined technique, especially in the application of thread.

The term *wing,* as applied to streamers, is a misnomer. These flies represent small fish, not winged insects. However, the hairs that form the main silhouette of these flies are tied on where a wing would be positioned, thus the term. Everyone in fly tying understands this, so there's no need to change it at this point in history.

Before you get into the actual tying of a hairwing streamer, you need to become familiar with the more common hairs used in their construction. A lot of substitution goes on in streamer fly tying. Materials that are reasonably similar can be used interchangeably. Natural hairs include the following:

• Bucktail, or more accurately, deer tail. Wide variation among strains or subspecies and with geography. Hair is white, with brown in various shades on the back side.

Natural color not bright or shiny. White portion takes dye well. Long to very long. Fairly straight to fairly kinky. Soft and fine to very coarse. Medium to hard in texture. Hair near butt end may flare like deer body hair. A typical bunch has little or no underfur but usually contains many shorties and erratic hairs, and perhaps broken ends.

• Calf tail, once known as kip tail or impala tail. Natural colors are white, brown, and black, with white the most common. Has slightly more brilliance than deer tail. Takes dye quite well. Short to medium in length. Somewhat to very kinky, the latter not being well suited to streamer work. Hard in texture. A typical bunch contains little or no underfur but a lot of short stuff. Needs assiduous cleaning out and combing.

• Gray squirrel tail. Natural shades of gray, tannish gray, and black, with white barring. Amount of white varies considerably. Takes dye reasonably well but is not as easy to dye as softer hairs. Dyed tails retain mottled markings. Hairs are quite straight. Fairly short to fairly long. Slippery and resistant to compression, especially when dyed. A typical bunch contains a little underfur and some shorties. A challenging hair to work with.

• Natural black squirrel tail. Similar to gray squirrel but a little softer in texture. Soft black, running to very dark gray or brown. Black squirrels are rare in most areas but fairly common in parts of Canada.

• Fox squirrel tail. Similar to gray squirrel but not quite as slippery. Natural color is tan or brown, with black barring. Length ranges from medium to fairly long. A very beautiful and useful material. These large squirrels are about the size of a Siamese cat and are common throughout the midwestern states of America.

• Russian or Siberian squirrel tail. Long, lustrous, and medium to dark mahogany in color. Makes a magnificent wing. The animal is common throughout northern Europe.

• Arctic fox tail. Snowy white. Takes dye beautifully. Soft and full of underfur, which can be used for other tying applications. A dream to tie with. The animal is now being raised commercially overseas.

• Arctic fox body fur. Very similar to the tail, but even softer, and with finer guard hairs.

• Badger hair. Usually used dyed. The underfur is the good stuff, very soft and workable. Short to medium in length. This material is getting scarce and may be off the market very soon.

• Bear hair. Various natural shades. Glossy guard hair of black bear is usually not jet black and sometimes is even brown. Very nice sheen. Medium to fairly long. May not tie neatly.

• Polar bear hair. Natural white hair that is uniquely prismatic. Takes dye very well, retaining most of its natural properties. Fairly short to quite long. Was once considered a must-have material but now is illegal, although it may possibly be sold legally under certain conditions. Several new synthetic hairs make fine replacements.

• Monga ringtail. Natural tails have alternate white and very dark brown barring, the white hairs often with dark tips. Takes dye nicely and is a pleasure to work with. Length 1½ inches, give or take ¼ inch.

• Sheep hair. Several kinds are available, mostly Scandinavian and Australian. Nice, soft natural shades of black, gray, brown, and white. Can be dyed easily. Long to very long. Usually quite straight, though some species have a bit of kinkiness. Generally lots of underfur. Ideal for large streamer and tube flies. In water, sheep hair is wonderfully alive and has an almost self-induced action.

• Skunk hair. Black hair from tail has a gorgeous luster and ties neatly, although it tends to be a bit coarse. White hair is beautiful, rather short, but a size 4 is possible. Legal, but availability limited. Just about the nicest hair I've ever used.

• Woodchuck tail. Shades run to dark brown, often flecked with gray. Medium in length, 2 inches being typical. Somewhat stiff.

• Goat hair. Scandinavian goat hair has begun to appear in fly shops. It's wonderful for both salmon-fly and streamer work. Natural color is white. Dyes extremely well. Medium to very long, some measuring 6 inches. Texture similar to fine bucktail. Typically very straight. Some underfur and short stuff that need to be combed out. Watch out for broken ends.

• Yak hair. This material is still on the market, although it may have to be special ordered. Very nice material, long and fairly soft. The Scandinavians designed their elverlike tube flies around it but have now switched mostly to sheep and goat. Natural color is medium to dark brown; often dyed black.

• Polecat. This isn't our native skunk; it's an import from Scandinavia. Hair is very soft and lustrous, similar to arctic fox. Sometimes packaged as fur marabou without being identified as polecat.

Some of these materials may not have a familiar ring. These are recent arrivals in America. We're now getting some interesting materials from other countries, especially Scandinavia. As that part of the world has a long-standing fly-fishing tradition, it comes as no surprise that their materials are well adapted to the tasks at hand.

There are also several worthy synthetics. A long-time favorite of mine is craft fur, which I began using over twenty years ago. It isn't long enough for the huge flies, as the best craft fur maxes out at about 3 inches, but it's plenty long for typical streamer work.

For many years, I purchased craft fur at craft stores, but fly shops now carry a version called Fly Fur, from Mystic Bay Flies. This is an excellent acrylic craft fur available in many colors well suited for flies. Interestingly, it has underfur, just like natural hair. This needs to be removed when you prepare the craft fur for use; you can set it aside for dubbing if you wish. Craft fur should be combed while still on the cloth backing to remove some of the underfur and lay the hairs out straight. A second combing of the butt ends after the bunch is cut from the backing removes the remaining underfur.

This hair is a joy to tie with and has produced very effective flies for me. It is nicely translucent and has excellent action when wet. Craft fur makes multilayered hairwings that are spectacular in their brilliance. It goes nicely with other materials and does not bulk up a lot. It's currently my favorite substitute for polar bear.

Another synthetic that's been around for a long time, and might be considered the progenitor of a number of more contemporary products, is FisHair. It's highly translucent, and the many available colors are quite vivid. The hair is straight, fairly coarse, and doesn't compress very much, which you'll have to compensate for by tying it on in small bunches. You might want to apply a droplet of some adhesive, maybe even a superglue, over the wrappings on each layer. Another little trick is to wrap a few layers of nylon stretch material onto the hook at the tie-in point as a base. This helps affix the hair firmly in place and causes it to behave a little better. FisHair comes in two lengths, 6 inches and 10 inches, so huge saltwater flies can easily be accommodated.

Ultra Hair, from D. H. Thompson, and Super Hair, sold under two labels, Spirit River and Hareline, are very similar to FisHair, except that they seem a bit more crinkly. I consider them to be interchangeable from a practical standpoint, and the tying techniques set forth for FisHair apply. All of these products can be used on really large flies, up to 10 inches. Long, hard-textured synthetic hairs such as these are intended mainly for saltwater flies, however, and do not make great streamer fly materials.

Some slightly softer hairs are available that behave more like sheep hair. Bozo Hair is a rather unkempt sort of material, especially at the tip ends. It's curvy rather than straight, tends to expand or bulk out, and is extremely difficult to comb out. Still, that's not to say you couldn't fashion creditable flies with it. The length is about 10 inches.

Enrico's Sea Fibers, from Enrico Pugliese, is a slightly softer, straighter, more manageable hair that does not expand the way Bozo Hair does. It's considerably more tier-friendly, although it also resists being combed out. The overall length is about 9½ inches.

Big Fly Fiber is distinctly sheeplike in nature and, in fact, appears to have been manufactured with that in mind. It is somewhat bizarre, kinky on one end and straight on the other. This emulates the effect of sheep hair with some of the wool left in. An option is to cut it and use just the straight part, in which case you'd have something very close to goat in a synthetic. The overall length is about 7½ inches, about one-third of which is kinky.

Aqua Fiber, from the McKenzie Fly Tackle Company, is quite tier-friendly, and its tendency to puff out results in a three-dimensional fly. It is translucent without being overly glitzy, which I like. As with most synthetic hairs, trimming at the rear is required to develop a tapered shape, thus avoiding a chopped-off effect. It's available in a wide range of colors. This hair is 100 percent polypropylene, which does not absorb water, meaning that your fly is dry after a false cast or two. This mitigates against the problem of casting large, water-soaked flies, although there is still air resistance to deal with. Unless weight is incorporated in either the fly or the leader, these flies float when they first land on the water, due to air trapped among the fibers, and some manipulation is required to get them to sink.

There are also some soft to very soft synthetics on the market. Polar Aire, from Spirit River, comes in very long hanks, but the individual fibers are actually about 4½ inches in usable length. This material is very soft and compressible and lies quite straight and flat. The colors are brilliant, almost to the point of being glitzy. This product makes a nice highlight when used in combination with other hairs.

Ghost-Fiber, from Roman Moser, is extremely soft in texture. The fibers are very fine, almost cottony. Here again, the maximum usable length is about 4½ inches. The colors are soft and subtle—very pretty. This is a versatile product because of its adaptability to flies of various sizes.

A creative British fly tier named Davy Wotton introduced Synthetic Living Fiber (SLF) several years ago as dubbing. More recently, he has made it available in hank form. It's somewhat slippery but quite soft and manageable, and the colors are brilliant—what might be called high-impact. There are a couple of problems with SLF hanks, however. Though the overall length is about 6 inches, the usable length is only half that, because of the manner in which the fiber is dyed and packaged. In the center of the hank is a plastic tie, and the material apparently is dyed after the tie is attached, which causes a break in the color. Also, the material is stuffed into a very small bag, which introduces kinks. These straighten out when the material is wet but are bothersome during tying. Of course, these are merely packaging and processing problems and thus are solvable. The material itself is most attractive.

A somewhat similar hank material is Hi-Vis, from L&L Products. Its texture is slightly different from that of SLF—it's a little stiffer and just a bit crinkly. The colors are not quite as brilliant, but they're still very attractive. The usable length is just over 3 inches.

In the world of hairwing streamers, there are some do's and don'ts that will help keep you out of trouble. Here are some vital do's:

- Use conservative amounts of materials.
- Use the appropriate thread. Finer thread and more wraps are stronger and smoother than thicker thread and fewer wraps.
- Work in layers when using bulky or slippery hair, even for single-color wings.
- Cover enough hair at the head to ensure an effective bond.
- Create good thread bases, especially between layers of multicolored wings.
- Use a little adhesive in critical areas.

And here are some important don'ts:

- Don't overdress hairwing streamers. You'll create serious tying problems, and the flies will have poor action in the water.
- Don't try to minimize head size for cosmetic reasons. A lot of classic salmon flies tied for framing have artificially small heads. Don't make that mistake with your hairwings.
- Don't stack the tips of the hairs; you'll end up with a poor silhouette.
- Don't allow the front of the body to cock the wing.

The various hairs used in tying streamers differ in their characteristics. This has a direct effect on how you work with these materials. Gray squirrel tail, especially when it's been dyed, is highly resistant to thread and does not readily compress or reduce in bulk under thread pressure. The hair may be tightly packed, but the bunch reduces very little in diameter, no matter how much thread pressure you apply. You may think you've secured the hair effectively, only to have the center hairs, which are not in contact with the thread, loosen after a few casts. A few of them fall out, and soon after, the whole wing disappears. This can be frustrating.

One cause of this is the manner in which the thread wraps are applied. If you start at the front and work rearward, you may cause the center hairs to slide ahead of the thread. This can be avoided by starting at the rear of the head and working the thread forward.

Another useful technique is the encircling wrap. Hold the hair bunch slightly above the hook, and take a full 360-degree turn of thread around only the hair. Then, while tightening the thread, lower the hair into place atop the hook. This also helps with layering in multicolored wings.

Executing the encircling wrap.

With slippery, hard-to-handle hairs, pay strict attention to quantity. Don't use a larger bunch than you can effectively secure. Using two or three layers not only affects durability, but also results in a better-shaped silhouette. And using a little adhesive of some sort on the thread wrap is not cheating.

I've taken the liberty of making some modest alterations to certain traditional hairwing streamer dressings. An example of this is my version of the Black-Nosed Dace, Art Flick's imitative pattern from the golden era of the Schoharie. Art's dressing is as follows:

A Black-Nosed Dace, Art Flick style.

Black-Nosed Dace

Hook	Typical streamer model.
Thread	Black.
Tag	Red yarn.
Body	Flat silver tinsel.
Wing	In three layers: white polar bear, black skunk tail hair, and brown bucktail.

The layering of hairs in this dressing resembles the markings of the baitfish. There were plenty of natural black-nosed daces around in Art's day, and the fly was a credible imitation of that important forage fish. There are still enough of them here in the greater Northeast to make the pattern a worthwhile one, and it also performs well as a general streamer pattern. It's a very good producer on the Big Horn in southeastern Montana, and there isn't a natural black-nosed dace within a thousand miles of there, to my knowledge.

I've created several alternative versions of the Black-Nosed Dace, updating some of the materials and techniques. I'll share one of my favorites with you here. A looped-eye hook, as used here, is not mandatory, but the double wire provides a base on which to tie all the bulky materials. You might do well to give them a try.

If you want to add eyes to your streamer, you need to first build up the head and apply a protective coating of epoxy or other glue. When making painted eyes, the texture of your lacquer or paint must be just right. If it's too thin, it will run around uncontrollably and won't cover well. If it's too thick, you'll get globs that refuse to dry properly. In either case, the result is a mess. Dilute your lacquer or paint to the extent that it dots on nicely but spreads thinly and evenly.

Dick's Dace

Hook	Typical streamer model, Daiichi model 2370 or comparable.
Thread	Black 6/0 or 8/0.
Tag	Red yarn, very short.
Body	Embossed silver tinsel.
Wing	In three layers: white craft fur, dyed black squirrel tail, and brown bucktail or similar hair.
Eyes	Painted or mylar stick-on (optional).

1. Tie on near the front, and wrap rearward a little ways. Then tie in the yarn, trim the excess, and while pulling rearward on the yarn with your left hand, bind it smoothly to the top of the hook. This creates an even base. Cut the yarn off short; all you want is a little red spot.

2. Embossed tinsel can be applied in one layer or two. On very small flies, I use just one, tying in the tinsel at the bend of the hook, wrapping the thread forward, then wrapping and tying off the tinsel. Take great care to cover the hook thoroughly, with no little gaps in between turns. The more conventional, and considerably safer, method is to tie in the tinsel near the front, and wrap it to the bend and back. It's your call.

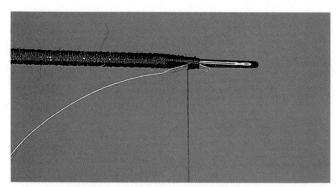

Embossed tinsel tied in as described (step 2).

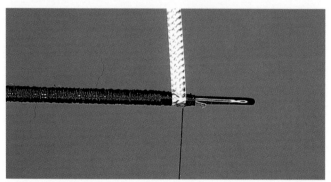

The starting wrap of tinsel forms a pleat to square the material with the hook (step 2).

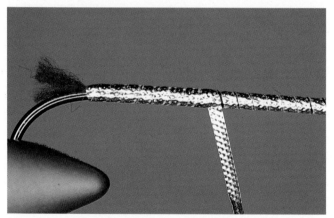

The return layer of tinsel being wrapped (step 2).

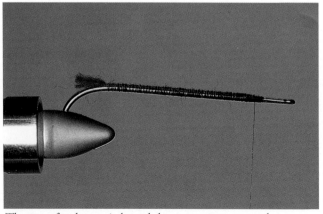

The yarn for the tag is bound down to create a smooth foundation (step 1).

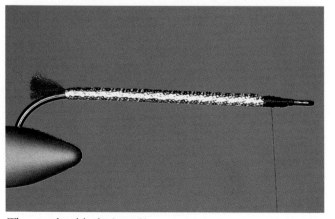

The completed body (step 2).

3. Cut off and manicure a bunch of white craft fur. You can pretrim the butts now or trim them later. In either case, they should be slope-cut a little before being covered with thread.

4. Tie the hair on top of the hook in such a manner that it shrouds down around the sides and veils the tinsel body. It should extend about one-third of the shank length beyond the bend.

5. Use the thread to create a smooth, ample base that will effectively separate the next layer of hair from the craft fur. This begins the layered effect that is the essence of this dressing.

6. Cut off and prepare a small bunch of the black hair, and lay it atop the hook. It should be the same length as the white layer or the tiniest bit shorter.

7. Again, you can pretrim the butts or slope-cut them later. In either case bind the hair in place, and create yet another thread base on which to mount the brown hair.

8. The brown hair should be more generous in quantity—if possible, approximately the amount of the white and black combined. You can tie it on in two bunches if necessary. Here you see that I have pretrimmed the butts to length. Again, slope-cut the butts, but not to the extent that insufficient thread contact results. Note that you must cover plenty of hair, working from the rear of the head, to secure the wing.

9. Secure, smooth out, and shape the head with the thread.

The black hair forms a stripe (steps 5–7).

The brown hair with the butts pretrimmed to length (step 8).

The brown hair in place (step 8).

The white hair shrouds the tinsel body (steps 3 & 4).

The head lacquered in preparation for the painted eyes (step 9 & 10).

10. If you want your fly to have painted eyes, apply one or two coats of head lacquer to create a base for them, and allow to dry thoroughly. Or you can simply leave the fly as-is and go fishing.

11. The painted eyes are dotted on, using small, cylindrical applicators. I use the butt ends of two ¼-inch drill bits, one considerably smaller than the other. Use the larger one for the yellow part of the eye. Get enough lacquer on the end of the applicator to allow you to dot on the eye without actually touching the drill bit to the fly head. Do both sides as mirror images. If you apply too much lacquer, hold the fly suspended on its side with the painted eye facing downward, and carefully remove the excess by touching the globule with your finger.

12. After the lacquer has dried completely, apply the black pupils with the smaller drill bit, following the same procedure. Again, clean off any excess lacquer.

13. After the eyes have dried completely, protect them with a layer of clear head cement or for enhanced durability, a coating of clear epoxy.

If you can get through the Black-Nosed Dace, you can tie just about any hairwing streamer. The improbable Mickey Finn is tied with the same methodology, using different colored hairs and a slightly different body. You'll also find these techniques helpful in tying Atlantic salmon and steelhead flies.

Over the years, streamer fly tiers have been intrigued by the challenge of imitating small trout. Big fish eat little ones, and sometimes those little ones are of the same species. The predator does not discriminate; food means survival. Anglers can turn this instinctive behavior to their advantage by imitating these tasty morsels, and baby trout have not been ignored by the more creative tiers. Sam Slaymaker, of Pennsylvania, designed a three-fly series imitating the fingerlings of the brook, brown, and rainbow. Others did likewise. Some were quite detailed, involving such labor-intensive operations as painting concentric blue-and-red spots on the little brookie. Pretty, but tedious.

I offer here a set of simplified dressings that use several newer materials and techniques. I've found these to be effective representations of the three species we encounter here in the Northeast. The color of rainbow trout fingerlings varies considerably among watersheds and among the various strains. Feel free to adapt the colors to those you see in nature. I like to blend in a little pale green hair with the gray.

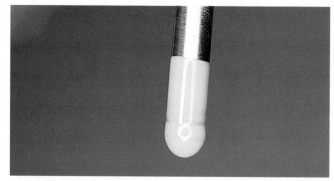

A droplet of yellow lacquer on the tip of an applicator (step 11).

The yellow dot in place (step 11).

The black pupil in place (step 12).

The completed Dick's Dace.

Rainbow Fingerling

Hook	Streamer type, Daiichi model 2370 or comparable.
Thread	White Uni-Stretch, white 8/0 thread, then gray 6/0 or 8/0 thread.
Base	Uni-Stretch.
Underbody	Wide, flat silver tinsel.
Body	Narrow pearl tubing.
Belly	White hair, such as Scandinavian goat or arctic fox.
Stripe	Pale pink or lavenderish pink hair.
Back	Pale gray hair or a composite.
Eyes	Mylar stick-on or painted, with some sort of coating over (optional).

1. Mount the Uni-Stretch in a bobbin with a smooth tube mouth, such as the Griffin model with a little ceramic doughnut inside the tip of the tube. A dental floss threader is ideal for drawing the material through the tube.
2. Tie on up front, and cover the hook shank with the Uni-Stretch, building up the base a little. As you wrap the Uni-Stretch with the bobbin, you're putting twists into it, which interfere with its tendency to go on flat and smooth. This can be counteracted periodically by giving the bobbin a few spins counterclockwise.
3. With your first traverse to the rear of the hook, tie in a piece of flat silver tinsel wide enough to effectively cover the base with one layer. Flat tinsel is usually tied in at the front and double-wrapped rearward and forward, but that's not necessary here.
4. At some point in your traverses up and down the hook, take a few wraps behind the tied-in tinsel. This establishes a small base on which to tie down the rear end of the tubing. When the foundation has attained the desired thickness, which should roughly equal the inside diameter of the tubing, wrap the tinsel forward, secure it, and tie off the Uni-Stretch.

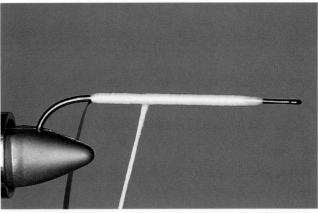

The tinsel is tied in while wrapping the Uni-Stretch foundation (steps 1–3).

Wraps taken behind the tied-in tinsel (step 4).

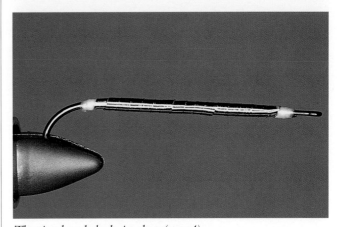

The tinsel underbody in place (step 4).

5. Remove the fiber core from a piece of tubing of appropriate length, and slide it into place on the hook, as shown.

6. Tie on over the tubing at the rear with white 8/0 thread, and secure it. Then tie off with a large-loop whip finish. These wraps need to be protected with something, such as a small droplet of Zap-A-Gap, rubbed until dry with a toothpick.

7. Tie on up front with gray thread, and secure the tubing. If you intend to build up the head a little and affix eyes, position the working thread accordingly.

8. Tie on a conservative-size bunch of white hair along the bottom of the hook.

9. Tie on a conservative-size bunch of pinkish hair along the top of the hook.

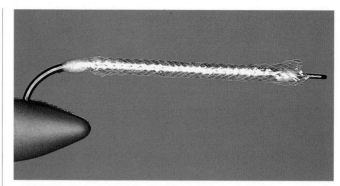

The tubing secured at the rear (step 6).

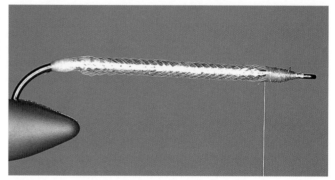

The tubing secured at the front (step 7).

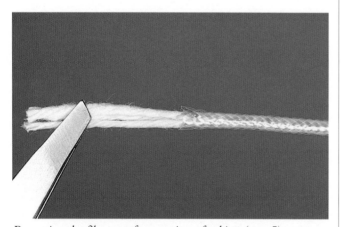

Removing the fiber core from a piece of tubing (step 5).

The white belly hair is tied along the bottom of the hook (step 8).

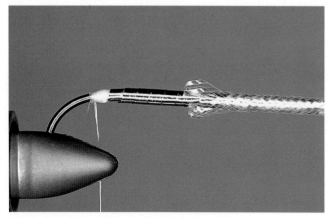

The tubing being slid onto the hook (step 5).

The pinkish hair in place atop of the hook (step 9).

10. Tie on a slightly thicker bunch of gray hair over the pink. If you aren't going to add eyes, whip-finish, and you're done.

11. If you want to add eyes, build up the head sufficiently to accept small stick-on eyes. If you prefer, paint on eyes, per the instructions for Dick's Dace. Coat the head with something tough to protect the eyes, such as epoxy or AquaFlex, a new water-based flexible head cement that works remarkably well. Two coats are required, with thorough drying in between.

The brookie fingerling is tied in a similar manner, except that some additional materials are employed to create an impression of the concentric blue-and-red spots that adorn these gorgeous little fish.

The gray hair is tied over the pink. Here, a little green hair has been blended with the gray (step 10).

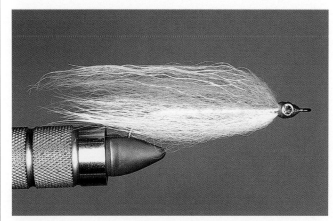

The addition of eyes completes the Rainbow Fingerling (step 11).

Brookie Fingerling

Hook	As for the rainbow.
Thread	Yellow Uni-Stretch, yellow 8/0 thread, olive 6/0 or 8/0 thread.
Base	Uni-Stretch.
Underbody	Uni-Stretch or, if more flash is desired, a layer of gold flat tinsel.
Markings	A few strands each of red and blue Krystal Flash or similar material.
Body	Narrow pearl tubing.
Belly	White hair.
Back	Olive hair.
Eyes	As described for the rainbow (optional).

1. Develop the base as with the rainbow.
2. Tie in the Krystal Flash at the rear. If you want a shiny underbody, tie in the gold tinsel at the rear also.
3. After completing the underbody, either with or without the tinsel, twist the two colors of Krystal Flash together, and spiral-wrap them to the front, twisting as you go. Secure them, and tie off the Uni-Stretch.
4. The rest of the tying steps are the same as for the rainbow, except that there is only one layer of hair above the hook, and the colors are as described.

The German-strain brown trout fingerling can be imitated by following the instructions for the brookie, but using golden yellow hair for the belly and finishing off with light brown hair and thread. Use a more conservative amount of Krystal Flash, as the blue-and-red spots aren't quite as pronounced on the little browns.

The cutthroat trout of the Rocky Mountains and the western states likely eat their progeny as well. There are quite a few strains of cutthroat which vary considerably. The above techniques can be used to create effective imitations, adapting the colors as required.

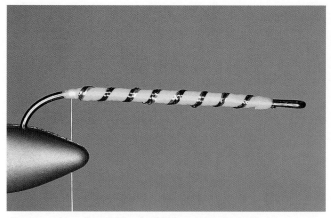

Creating the red and blue highlights (steps 2 & 3).

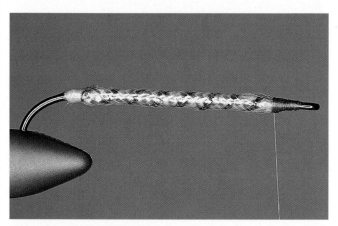

The tubing in place (step 4).

Tying on the belly and back hairs completes the Brookie Fingerling (step 4).

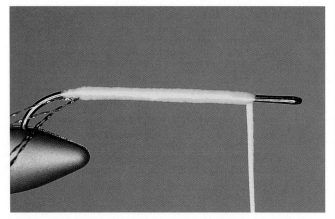

Yellow Uni-Stretch forms the base for this pattern (step 1).

CHAPTER 23

Matukas and Meatballs

A Matuka is a type of streamer. Basically, there are two kinds of Matukas: featherwing and fur (or hairwing). They are tied in much the same manner. With a few little tricks at hand, they are pretty easy to tie. But what are Meatballs? A culinary delicacy, to be sure, but also an interesting fly design that's been a hot producer for me in recent years. We'll get to them in a bit.

Matuka streamers fish very well. They have good action and form in the water and are more tangle-free than classic-style streamers. This is because of the way the materials that form the "wing" are fastened along the top of the body.

Recent developments in the growing of hen chickens for fly tying have produced feathers that are truly ideal for Matuka tying. Rooster feathers of various types are also quite suitable; it's all a matter of what sort of image you want. Webby feathers usually work best,

provided the shaping is as desired. This may extend the utility of your dry-fly capes, as it's an excellent way to use those big feathers nearer the back end of the pelt.

The Matuka is another fly type that allows the tier to be innovative. Many different combinations of materials and colors can be used, and several innovations can enhance the Matuka. One of my favorites is the addition of a cone head. This provides weight and changes the behavior of the fly in the water. Bead chain and dumbbell eyes are also possibilities, but you have to be careful here, as they may turn the fly upside down. But maybe you'd like that. If so, there are techniques for tying Matukas with the hook pointing upward, as demonstrated in the fur Matuka sequence. It's even possible to tie Matukas that are suggestive, if not closely imitative, of actual baitfish. A featherwing Matuka tied with some kind of mottled feathers makes a very credible sculpin.

Lime Fur Matuka fly.

Featherwing Sculpin Matuka

Hook	Typical streamer, 4XL to 6XL.
Thread	Tan or light brown 6/0 or 8/0.
Underbody	Narrow weighting wire (optional).
Ribbing	Narrow oval gold tinsel or plain monofilament thread, mounted in a bobbin.
Body	Fine white or cream yarn, floss, or Uni-Stretch.
Tail and wing	Mottled grayish tan hen or rooster grizzly feathers, one or two pairs, depending on the texture of the feathers and the size of the fly.
Hackle	Same as wing, tied collar-style.

1. Tie on near the front, and wrap to the rear. In the process, tie in the ribbing tinsel. Note that it's bobbin mounted, meaning that you have two bobbins in play at once. The reason for this will become clear a few steps further along.

2. If you're going to apply weight, wrap the wire at this point, being careful to leave some space at both ends of the hook shank. A smear of Zap-A-Gap on the top of the wraps will seep in and form a strong bond. Use the thread to fill in the drop-offs front and back.

3. Wrap forward, and tie in the body material. Don't crowd the eye, as you'll be wrapping a collar hackle later.

4. Wrap the body as shown, secure, and trim off the excess.

5. Match up the tail/wing feathers as you would for any typical streamer; cupped sides opposing each other and facing inward.

6. Prepare the tail/wing feathers by measuring them against the hook to establish the length. Decide how long you want the tail portion to be. Strip off the barbs from the bottom of the quills so that the feathers fit on top of the body, as shown. Note where the front is positioned.

7. Secure the feathers at the front end with some firm thread wraps.

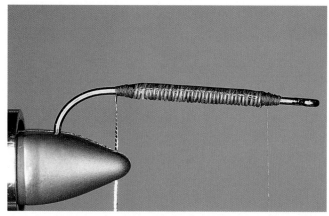

The ribbing tinsel is tied in, and the weighting wire is in place (steps 1 & 2).

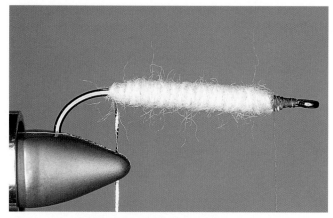

The completed body (steps 3 & 4).

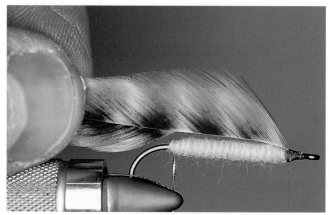

The feathers are prepared and tied in atop the hook (steps 5–7).

8. At the beginning of the bend of the hook, separate the barbs of the feathers so that the first turn of ribbing can pass through them. This anchors the rear end of the wing.

9. Now it becomes apparent why the ribbing material is bobbin mounted: The weight of the bobbin holds the ribbing in place, which frees up your hands to work on the feathers. Create spaces for the ribbing by separating barbs, working progressively forward. The turns should be evenly spaced.

10. When you reach the front, tie off the ribbing and trim the excess.

11. Prepare one or two feathers as required for making a collar hackle. Tie them in by the tip ends and wrap, stroking back the barbs as you go, then tie off, trim, and whip-finish.

The fur Matuka is tied using the same techniques. The tail-and-wing part is formed out of a narrow strip of hide, often called a zonker strip. Rabbit is the most common, but there are others that work very well indeed, including some of the more recent exotic imports, such as arctic fox and Finnish polecat. The main thing is that the hide must be properly tanned, soft textured, and thin; no heavy leather is allowed here.

Various types of heads, or front ends, can be used with fur Matukas. Some people implement a Muddler head-and-collar assembly. A few turns of either a matching or contrasting fur can be used, wrapped as a collar. Cone heads can be added at the beginning. Bead chain or dumbbells can be used, although these may induce the fly to ride upside down in the water. Bead chain probably won't cause this, unless it's disproportionately large in comparison with the fly itself. Dumbbells, being heavier, almost surely will. This can work to your advantage, as Bob Clouser discovered in designing his highly successful Clouser Minnow. An upside-down hook is much less apt to get snagged when fishing the fly deep.

On the Clouser Minnow, Bob simply ties the fly in such a manner that when the hook is turned over, the materials are right side up. The Lime Fur Matuka dressing is a variation in which the dumbbell is tied beneath the hook so that the fly will ride upright. If you want to use the Clouser method so that the fly rides hook-up, all that's required is to cut a small slit into the fur strip so that you can execute the securing wraps with the fur strip positioned along the bottom of the shank. An example follows the tying sequence.

The original dumbbells were made from lead and came in an assortment of sizes. When it became recognized that lead was not a good thing to be throwing into the water, other types of dumbbells quickly appeared. They come in an assortment of sizes and metallic finishes.

The first turn of ribbing, with the bobbin maintaining thread tension (step 8).

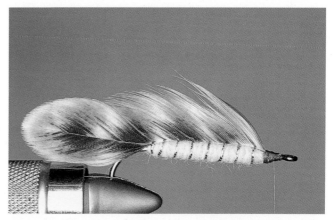

The succeeding turns of ribbing secure the feathers (steps 9 & 10).

Tying a collar hackle completes the fly (step 11).

One clever model, currently distributed by the Spirit River Company, has recesses on the sides where stick-on eyes can be placed.

The Lime Fur Matuka serves double duty in the greater Northeast as a striped bass fly and for fishing brood-stock salmon, breeders from the Atlantic salmon restoration programs that have outlived their usefulness and have been released into the rivers for sportfishing. A number of such programs are being conducted in the coastal rivers of New England.

Lime Fur Matuka

Hook	Typical streamer, 4XL to 6XL, or a saltwater model if you'll be fishing the ocean.
Thread	Lime green Uni-Stretch, bobbin-mounted.
Ribbing	Narrow to medium silver oval tinsel, mounted in a bobbin.
Body	Flat silver tinsel.
Tail and Wing	A lime fur strip.
Head assembly	A dumbbell, figure-eighted into place with Uni-Stretch. Eyes optional.

1. Wrap a base, and secure the dumbbell in place with crisscross wraps between the eyes. Then saturate with Zap-A-Gap or similar glue. Tying the dumbbell on the bottom of the hook will allow the fly to ride in the normal upright position.
2. The subsequent steps are done just as they were with the feather Matuka. The hook is now in the normal position in the vise. Tie on, wrap a base, and tie in the ribbing tinsel. Wrap to the front, tie in the flat tinsel, and wrap a double-layer body.
3. Tie in the fur strip at the front as shown, using crisscross wraps between the ends of the dumbbell.

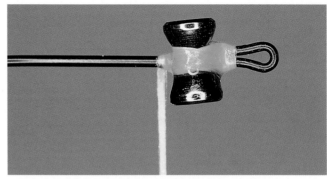

The dumbbell is tied to the bottom of the hook, and the wraps are saturated with Zap-A-Gap (step 1).

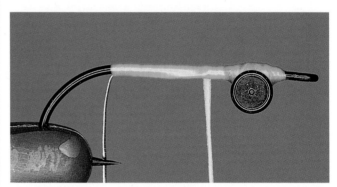

The ribbing tinsel is tied in (step 2).

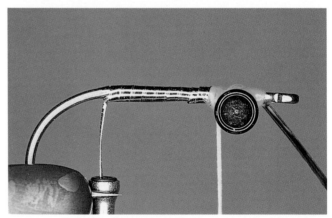

The flat tinsel body in place (step 2).

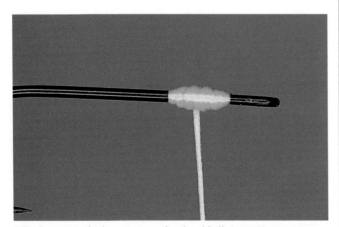

The base on which to mount the dumbbell (step 1).

The fur strip is tied in at the front (step 3).

4. Spread the hairs at the rear in preparation for the first wrap of tinsel. Then proceed with the ribbing process as was done with the feather Matuka. Keep the wraps fairly close, and be careful not to bind down any of the fur.

5. Tie off the tinsel, and finish off the fly by building up the head with crisscross wraps of the Uni-Stretch top and bottom. Apply two or three coats of clear lacquer to the wraps.

6. If you use the type of dumbbell that accommodates stick-on eyes, the eyes must be the proper size to fit into the recesses. The adhesive on the back sides of the eyes may be sufficient to hold them in place, but I don't trust it, so I put a small droplet of Zap-A-Gap into the recesses before pressing the eyes into place.

Following are instructions for making a true Clouser-Style Fur Matuka. The pattern presented here dispenses with the ribbing and body tinsels and uses white Uni-Stretch for both the body and the ribbing. This simplifies matters considerably. If you want some flash, use either or both of the components used in the previous fly.

The ribbing secures the fur strip (step 4).

Applying the eyes completes the fly (steps 5 & 6).

Clouser-Style Fur Matuka

1. Wrap a base, and secure the dumbbell in place with crisscross wraps between the eyes. Then saturate with Zap-A-Gap. In this case, the dumbbell is tied on top of the hook so that the fly will ride upside down.

2. After wrapping a couple layers of Uni-Stretch onto the shank, or after having completed whatever body you have chosen, wrap forward to the rear of the dumbbell.

The Uni-Stretch body is wrapped, the dumbbell in place atop the hook (steps 1 & 2).

3. Measure a piece of fur strip against the hook, and determine where you'll need to cut the slit that accommodates the hook. Make the slit as small as possible to avoid weakening the fur strip unnecessarily.

4. Carefully remove the hook from the vise. Slide the strip into place as shown, with the fur side and the point of the hook both upward. Place the hook back in the vise in that position.

5. The subsequent steps are done just as they were with the previous fly, except that here you rib with the Uni-Stretch. After completing this step, switch to green Uni-Stretch, finish off the head area as before, and apply the eyes per previous instructions.

Fur strips can be purchased ready-cut in two configurations: lengthwise, like the one used here, or crosswise, known as hackling strips. Here the fur lies back at about a 45-degree angle and forms a beautiful collar hackle when wrapped, just like a folded feather. You can also buy tanned pelts and cut your own strips. This is a little tricky. I have devised a method that works quite well. All you need is a piece of soft, smooth board, about 8 or 10 inches wide and a foot or so in length, and a regular single-edged razor blade. Here's the procedure:

1. Stick the razor blade into the board, going with the grain. Position it a few inches in from the front end, at about a 45-degree angle.

2. Turn the pelt skin-side-up, and make a small scissor cut to get the strip started. If you're cutting lengthwise, start at the head end so that you're going with the flow of the fur.

3. Draw the pelt into the blade and pull it through. Make the cut as straight as possible.

4. Make another small scissor cut, thus establishing the width of the strip. Draw the pelt into the blade again, carefully controlling the tension, so that the cut is perfectly parallel to the first one, producing a strip of uniform width.

5. Repeat the process, preparing as many strips as you want.

Crosscut strips, or hackling strips, are cut in the same manner. The only difference is that you need to pull on the pelt at a slightly upward angle so that the fur doesn't become wedged between the blade and the board. This minimizes loss of fur.

The Fur Meatball is a fly that uses both types of strips. I stole the idea from a fly called the Lithuanian Bat, which was popular in Alaska in the early 1980s. Instead of the bead chain or dumbbell head, I've substituted a

The fur strip is tied in place with the hook point passing through it (steps 3 & 4).

Ribbing with Uni-Stretch and adding the eyes completes the fly (step 5).

cone head, which allows the fly to ride upright. If you want it to flip over, use a dumbbell.

My original thought was that this would be a good bass fly, and it is. However, I've also found it to be an excellent trout fly, especially for larger fish. I tie it in a number of colors and shades. I particularly like natural fur colors, such as mink and rabbit. As with the Fur Matuka, it's important that the pelt be well tanned and the skin soft and thin.

Cone Head Fur Meatball

Hook	3XL or 4XL, fairly heavy wire.
Head	A cone head of appropriate size, your choice of color.
Thread	Color to match fur, 6/0 or 8/0.
Tail	A straight-cut fur strip.
Body	A crosscut fur strip, wrapped as hackle.

1. Slide the cone head into place by inserting the point of the hook into the small end of the cone. Then place the hook in the vise, tie on to the rear of the cone head, and wrap several layers of thread, ending up at the bend.
2. Tie on the tail strip as shown.
3. Tie in the crosscut strip so that the fur lies to the rear. Then wrap the thread forward to the cone.
4. Wrap the fur hackle, working up as tight to the cone as possible.

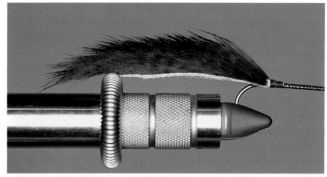

Tie on the tail strip as shown (step 2).

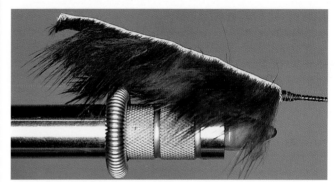

The crosscut strip in place (step 3).

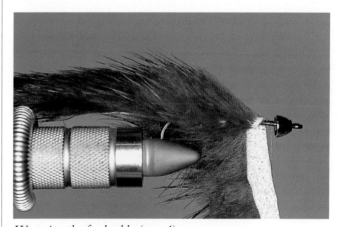

Wrapping the fur hackle (step 4).

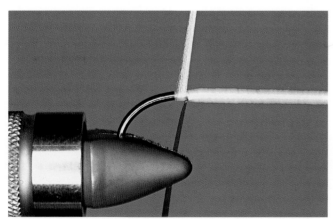

The cone head in place (step 1).

The fur hackle in place (step 4).

5. Secure and trim the fur strip. Put a generous drop of Zap-A-Gap on the thread wraps, allowing it to run forward into the hollow of the cone, then force the cone back over the thread wraps. If you wish, add a little dubbing to fill in any gap that may exist. Tie off with a whip finish.

6. Tie on again in front of the cone. Wrap back against the tip of the cone, securing it tightly in position. Whip-finish again, and coat with head lacquer.

You'll be amazed at the action this fly has in the water. The tail wags, the body pulsates, and the head induces a jigging action. The fish seem to find it virtually irresistible. If you like fishing large subsurface flies, you'll love this one.

The fly is completed by tying off the fur strip, filling in with a little dubbing, tying off behind the cone head, then tying on in front and locking the cone in place (steps 5 & 6).

CHAPTER 24

Featherwing Streamers

The featherwing streamer is a unique style of fly, or fly-rod lure, that's a truly American contribution to the art. The Brits were not into fishing with baitfish imitations; they were more concerned with figuring out how to fool the bug-eating trout of the chalkstreams. But America had a lot of freestone streams with plenty of gullible brook trout swimming around looking for a bite to eat, and the streamer was just the thing.

The hackle-feather wing virtually created itself. Tiers were using rooster capes for hackling dry flies. The larger feathers toward the rear of the neck are shaped much like the body of a small fish, a fact that was noticed by the more perceptive tiers. Soon a new school of fly tying appeared. Many of the early practitioners were from Maine, which offered magnificent brook trout fishing in those days. Tiers of note from that era include Bert Quimby, Herb Welch, William Edson, Joe Stickney, and of course, Carrie Stevens. In southern Vermont, Lou Oatman designed a series of excellent streamers, mainly for the Battenkill.

Many interesting patterns evolved, a few of which are still in use today. Of those, Carrie Steven's Gray Ghost is easily the most popular. I have always loved this fly, and when I've had the opportunity to use it in the proper environment, it has produced very well. This fly is usually tied large—sometimes very large. This presents one vexing problem: wrapping a floss body over a huge hook. Trying to handle long pieces of floss is a nightmare. They get roughed up by constantly being passed through the fingers and may get tangled. This is one case where a full rotary vise might come in handy, as it enables you to feed floss out of a bobbin and sort of "paint" it onto the hook. However, I wouldn't suggest that you go out and buy such a tool just for this. There are other solutions.

The dressing that follows uses the traditional method of making a floss body. If possible, however, I prefer to mount the body material in a bobbin and use it as both floss and thread for the first few operations. This eliminates the need to work with a long strand of material, as well as the need to work around the tying thread and

bobbin. Smooth-tubed ceramic bobbins and strong synthetic floss material, such as rayon, make this method feasible.

In order for floss to be used in a bobbin, it must be single-stranded, packaged on a standard-size spool, and reasonably resistant to fraying. Some flosses qualify in these respects; others don't. There also are floss substitutes, notably stretch nylon, of which I'm enamored. If you can find this material in the color you need, use it; it's much more tier-friendly in a bobbin than floss.

When you wrap bobbin-mounted floss or any such material, you'll be causing twists. To counteract this, you need to spin the bobbin counterclockwise fairly frequently throughout the wrapping process. This is not hard to do, and it's important if you care about the appearance of the finished product. Failure to flatten the floss results in a ridgy body.

The Gray Ghost is an ideal pattern for the floss-in-bobbin technique, because it has no tail or other additional components at the rear of the hook. Thus the only operation required of the floss, besides making the body, is to tie in the ribbing tinsel, which is very simple. I follow this procedure because it allows me to wrap the floss over bare hook shank, and I get smoother results.

When using the conventional technique for wrapping the body material, select your floss relative to the size of the hook so that you can obtain the desired effect with as few layers as possible, preferably just two—one to the rear, one working forward. If you're working on a large hook and need two back-and-forth sequences, cut off only enough floss for the first one, wrap it, tie it off, tie on another length of floss, and wrap the subsequent layers. This way you won't have to work with an overly long piece of floss. If you have rough fingers, try to smooth them a bit with a pumice stone or the fine side of an emery board. If your hands are really rough, wear thin cotton gloves when wrapping delicate body materials. Classic salmon fly tiers often resort to this for cosmetic reasons.

After all your work, it's a good idea to protect the fly's somewhat delicate body. Art Scheck, my editor at

Abenaki Publishers, passed along a technique he picked up from Bob Long, a contributor to *Fly Tyer* magazine. Bob paints his streamer bodies with clear water-based color preserver to protect both color and materials. If you want to do this, you have to make up your bodies ahead of time, apply the color preserver, and let it dry completely. It should be more than worth the effort.

The selection of feathers for the main wing is of great importance. Ideal feathers are not as easy to find as you might think. You need to consider both shape and texture. A fair amount of web is desirable in order to create body and opaqueness. For small flies, two opposing feathers—a back and a front—are usually sufficient. For medium or large streamers, you'll need a pair of each. This means matching up four feathers altogether.

The cheapest way to buy streamer feathers is in strung bundles. This makes precise feather matching tedious, however, and sometimes impossible. If you don't care all that much about the appearance of your flies, you may be satisfied with the results thus obtained; streamer wings don't have to be cosmetically perfect for the flies to fish effectively. But if you want your streamers to look pretty, capes are a better choice. The uniformity is there, and feathers are lying together. Still, you have to know what to look for. The feathers shown in the photos for the Gray Ghost have a distinctive center web and a minnowlike shape.

For freshwater streamers, feathers from capes or necks are usually preferred over saddles, mainly due to their shape. Saddle hackles are used for many saltwater patterns, where longer, more slender feathers are called for. However, certain strains of birds yield suitable saddle hackles for streamer tying; let your eyes be the judge.

Many feathers have some natural curvature, especially if they come from around the edges of a cape. This curvature should follow the flow of the fly, with the convex side up. When matching up feathers in pairs, the curvature should match, as well as the shape and size. Straight feathers, after being tied on, will assume curvature by virtue of their length and weight.

As with hairwing streamers, looped-eye hooks offer an advantage when setting the wings. Select such hooks carefully; some manufacturers do a poor job of tapering the return wire, which causes problems when working in that area of the hook. This can be minimized by tying on over the double wire to bind it tightly against the main shank, but you may still have do a lot of manicuring with the thread in order to smooth out this spot. It's better to choose a well-made hook to begin with.

Many early streamer tiers, notably Carrie Stevens, did a lot of preassembly. Many of them were commercial tiers, and durability was important. According to Joseph D. Bates, Jr., who was perhaps the most authoritative documentary writer on fly tying, Carrie glued together the

The shoulder/cheek assembly.

wing and cheek components of the Gray Ghost in matched sets of fronts and backs. She prepared large numbers of these in advance, then sat down and completed the flies.

I don't like to glue the main winging feathers together, but I do preassemble the shoulders and cheeks—that is, the silver pheasant and the jungle cock. In the process, I do some repair work on the jungle cock, which usually has a split or two, using Zap-A-Gap superglue. This procedure is demonstrated in the Hornberg chapter. I like to tie my Gray Ghosts in groups of a dozen, so I make up two dozen shoulder-and-cheek assemblies beforehand. Steps 1 through 4 of the tying instructions are for preassembly.

As you become more intimately familiar with the feathers, you'll see that both the silver pheasant and the jungle cock pelts yield fronts and backs—that is, feathers that have slight curvature. These should be paired in sets with opposing shape, so that they can be tied on with the curvature pointing downward to fit in with the overall flow of the fly. This is subtle, but with a little practice, you'll see it clearly.

A golden pheasant crest feather is involved as part of the wing-and-body assembly. It's not positioned over the top of the wing, as is the case with Atlantic salmon flies, but is laid flat along the top of the body. This necessitates choosing feathers of the proper length, as golden pheasant crests should be tied in by the butts, where the quill is pithy and more malleable.

For this exercise, select a crest feather of such length that when tied in by the butt, the tip will fall a little short of the end of the wing. To reduce the curvature of the crest, make nicks with your thumbnail, along the outside of the curve of the quill, as demonstrated below. This will also give an attractive "dripping-gold" effect, with the barbs flowing downward from the quill.

Twisting is the worst problem with crest feathers, and unfortunately, it's rather common. For this reason, you should look crests over carefully before buying them. Twisting can be corrected, at least somewhat, via the thumbnail technique or by steam-ironing the feather. Place a damp handkerchief or something similar over the crest during this procedure.

The original pattern calls for silver tinsel ribbing. I like gold better and have thus allowed a small departure from the traditional. It's your choice. In making the head, Carrie Stevens liked to wrap a tiny red band of thread in the center. This was her signature, so to speak. I apply it only when tying for framing.

Gray Ghost

Hook	A long streamer model.
Thread	The body material, then black 6/0 or 8/0. If you prefer to tie in the ribbing tinsel with thread, start with a pale-colored thread, preferably orange, then switch to black.
Ribbing	Narrow flat gold or silver tinsel.
Body	Orange floss, preferably a pale pumpkin color.
Belly, first layer	Four or five peacock fronds.
Belly, second layer	A small bunch of stiff, white bucktail.
Body veiling	Golden pheasant crest.
Wing	Four medium gray hackles, in two matched pairs, front and back.
Shoulders and cheeks	Silver pheasant-jungle cock combination.

1. To preassemble the shoulders and cheeks, start by selecting a silver pheasant saddle feather of the desired size and removing the junky stuff around the butt. If the feather has too much curvature, you can straighten the quill by running your thumbnail along the convex side of it, making little nicks. Lay the feather on a piece of waxed paper.
2. Select a jungle cock nail, as they are called, examine it for splits, and repair if necessary.
3. If you're quick and lucky, the adhesive used in the repair process can also serve to bond the jungle cock to the silver pheasant. If necessary, apply another tiny droplet. Lay the jungle cock nail in position on the silver pheasant feather, centering it on the quill. Be right the first time; you won't get a second chance.
4. Gently pat the jungle cock with your finger to help adhesion. Then set the assembly aside for thorough drying. Unless you are unusually talented and courageous, don't try tying on these assemblies while the glue is still wet.
5. If you're using bobbin-mounted body material, tie it on near the front, and wrap smoothly to a spot about three-quarters of the way down the hook shank. With the conventional method, tie on with the thread, then tie in the floss a little back from the eye. In either case, use the body material to tie in the ribbing tinsel on the first rearward traverse.

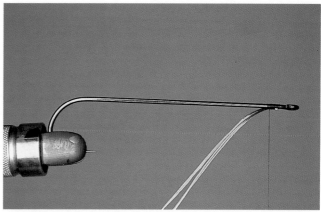

The floss is tied in (step 5).

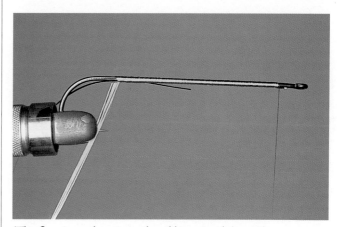

The floss is used to tie in the ribbing tinsel (step 5).

6. Wrap forward, and tie off the floss. If you need another layer, tie in a second piece of floss, and wrap to the rear and forward again, thus completing the body. Don't make it too thick.

7. If you've been using the bobbin-mounted body material, tie it off and tie on with black thread. In either case, note that somewhat less space is left in front of the body as on a hairwing streamer.

8. Wrap the tinsel ribbing, keeping the turns even and well spaced. Tie it off and trim.

9. Select the peacock fronds from the main quill of a tail feather. The ones near the eye work best, as they have strong, flat quills. Try to align them so that the tips match up. Tie them in as a bunch. They should extend a little past the rear extremity of the hook, as shown. Trim the butts up front.

10. Tie in the bucktail so that it supports the peacock from below. Trim neatly.

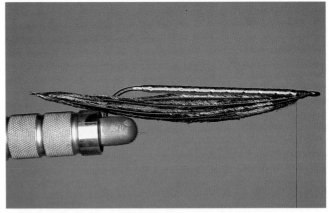

The peacock fronds are tied in place beneath the body (step 9).

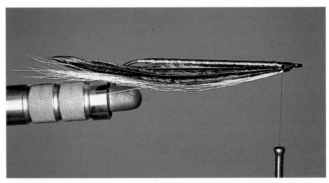

The bucktail supports the peacock from below (step 10).

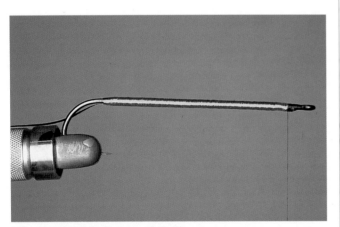

The completed body (steps 6 & 7).

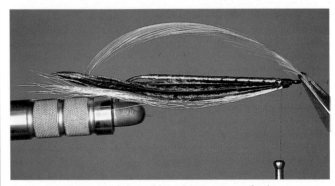

Note the curvature of the golden pheasant crest feather.

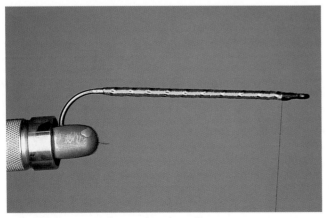

The ribbing wrapped into place (step 8).

Straightening the golden pheasant crest feather.

11. Tie the golden pheasant crest in place along the top of the body. Trim neatly, and wrap a small, smooth thread base for the wing.

12. Form the wing in your fingers, perfectly aligning the two opposing pairs of feathers until they look like the wing shown in the succeeding photos. Measure them for length against the hook; they should extend a little beyond the belly materials. Strip off the stuff nearest the butts until the proper proportion is achieved, then remove a little more from the bottom of the quills than the top. This helps in getting the feathers to lie close along the top of the body. Nick the quills a little with your fingernail to flatten them a bit.

13. Set the feathers atop the hook, centering them. While holding them in place, secure them with very firm thread wraps. The quills should not cross over each other. Trim off the butts, and apply a few more smoothing wraps.

14. Tie the nearmost shoulder-and-cheek assembly in place, covering the front of the wing, as shown. If you have trouble getting it to lie flat, try catching a tiny bit of the delta at the front with the thread, rather than just binding down the quills. Then tie in the other assembly for the back side as a mirror image, secure with very firm thread wraps, trim off the quill butts, form a neat head, and whip-finish.

Learning how to tie the Gray Ghost properly is about as good an orientation in featherwing streamers as you can get. There are many interesting patterns out there—some more complex, some less so. I hope you find them enjoyable to tie and fun to fish.

Setting the winging feathers in place (steps 12 & 13).

The wings in place (step 13).

Tying on the shoulder-cheek assemblies (step 14).

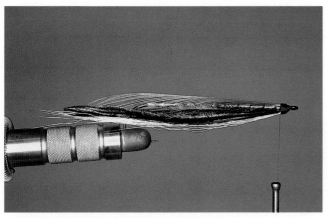

Tying on the golden pheasant crest feather (step 11).

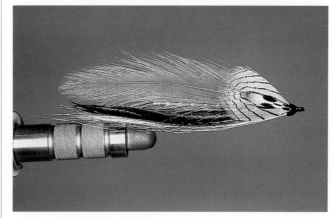

The completed Gray Ghost.

CHAPTER 25

A Very Edible Crayfish

Crayfish, crawfish, crawdads, call them what you will. When my brother lived in southern Louisiana, he ate them all the time. They call them mudbugs down there. For centuries, they have been a favorite bait of the bass fisher. As a northeasterner, I can assure you that trout love them as well. Back when I was a happy bait fisherman, free of guilt and indifferent to protocol, I was a serious mudbug maven—smaller ones for trout, larger for bass. After a while, I learned about shedders, or soft-shelled crayfish. The bass and trout went for them like a Russian diplomat goes for beluga caviar and iced vodka.

Now we seek to imitate these crustaceans using fly-tying materials and techniques so that we can fish them with a fly rod. There are lots of patterns, some very simple and suggestive, others much more complex and imitative. Historically, I've chosen the easy ones; they seemed to work well enough. But that was before Bugskin.

A guy named Chuck Furimsky introduced me to Bugskin. Chuck produces several major fly-fishing shows each year and also owns a leather-goods shop in western Pennsylvania. He's an ingenious tier and first-rate angler. A few years ago, Chuck took me trout fishing on one of his local rivers. Before long, I became painfully aware that he was outfishing me about five to one. Yes, it was the crayfish—a tiny one so small it would barely cover a 25-cent piece. I was hooked. I began tying them and tried them on the smallmouths and trout in my neighborhood in upstate New York. They worked, especially in river fishing.

I've observed that many journeyman tiers are intimidated by imitative tying. Be reassured; it's well within the capability of the average tier to make a strikingly realistic crayfish out of Bugskin. The material comes in many shades, so matching the color of your local mudbugs is no problem. After having tied them now for a number of years, I've reduced the technique to its bare essentials. With a bit of practice, you'll be turning out miniature lobsters that will amaze you by their realistic appearance.

In the chapter on nymphs, I emphasized the importance of finding and using thin Bugskin. For crayfish, the heavier stuff works better, except with very small hook sizes—the quarter-size ones Chuck whacks the trout with.

There are some preparatory steps. First, you need to cut out the Bugskin components—the claws and the shell. The latter extends all the way from the head to the tail. It forms the head, carapace, back, and tail with one continuous piece. Before I had done any of these crayfish, I was apprehensive about the difficulty of cutting out the components, but it turned out to be much easier than anticipated. I got everything just about right the very first time, with no model and no practice.

Take a look at the components in the photo. Then take some light cardboard index cards, or something similar, and practice a little. Small scissors with curved blades are helpful in cutting out the claws, but you can manage with straight ones. Keep in mind that when you're preparing claws out of actual Bugskin, you'll need a right and a left. The easiest way to do this is to cut out a claw, then turn the Bugskin over and cut out another one in exactly the same manner. You need to consider the size of the hook and the finished fly when cutting out the components.

It's a good idea to prepare some hooks ahead of time; I usually make up at least a dozen at a sitting. For crayfish tying, you'll need a fairly long-shanked hook, at least 4XL. Here are the steps for preparing a hook:

1. Put the hook in the vise, and cover it with a layer of tying thread.
2. Cut two pieces of heavy weighting wire, tapering both ends. They should extend from the bend of the hook almost, but not quite, to the eye.
3. One at a time, bind them along each side of the hook so that they lie on a flat plane with the shank. It is very helpful, after you're done wrapping, to use a pair of flat-jawed pliers to squeeze the two pieces of wire and the hook shank crosswise, so they are all on exactly the same flat plane.
4. Coat the assembly with Zap-A-Gap or similar superglue, and set it aside to dry.

The eyes on this fly are also prepared ahead of time. As far as fishing effectiveness, the eyes are optional, but they look so neat that I usually include them. They are made of heavy monofilament. The dark brownish Maxima is my favorite, but for really large crayfish, you may have to use something else in order to obtain sufficient diameter. You need to decide how thick the monofilament should be. For small crayfish, I suggest .030- to .035-inch diameter; for medium-size, .040- to .045-inch, and for large ones, .050- to .055-inch. By large, I mean something on the order of a size 2 streamer hook. Here's the procedure for making eyes:

1. Cut a piece of mono about 2 inches in length.
2. With a butane lighter, singe one end so that it forms a ball. This happens very fast—a second or two. If the mono catches fire, blow it out immediately. Hold the mono with the end hanging down, as this helps the ball to shape itself properly.
3. With fine-tipped pliers, bend the mono so that the eye sticks out at an angle, flattening the mono in the process.

4. Paint the ball with black lacquer, and set it aside to dry.

As with hooks, I usually do up at least a dozen sets of eyes at a sitting. They go very quickly, once you get the hang of it. What with all of the preparation, tying this thing may sound like a real project, but believe me, once you've been through it a few times, there's nothing to it.

In the pattern description, several options are given regarding materials and techniques. One of them has to do with the choice of dubbing versus yarn for the underbody. Dubbing is a bit more precise, but yarn is much easier and faster. As a consequence, I use dubbing on small crayfish and yarn on big ones.

Another choice is whether to tie the fly with the hook in its regular position or upside down. The guideline I follow is based on where I'll be fishing the bug. For river fishing, where I'm letting the fly drift with the currents, I usually tie it with the hook in its normal position. However, if I'm going to be dragging it along the bottom of a pond, I want the hook to ride up.

Bugskin Mudbug

Hook	As described above, prepared in advance.
Thread	6/0 or 8/0 Uni-Thread or similar, color to match shell material.
Foundation	Thick wire, as described above, diameter depending on hook size.
Adhesives	Zap-A-Gap or Flexament, and contact cement, the latter optional.
Antennae	A small bunch of squirrel tail or soft hackle, approximately matching the overall coloration of the crayfish.
Eyes	Singed monofilament, as described above.
Shell and claws	Bugskin cut to shape, your choice of color.
Body	Dubbing or yarn to match or complement the Bugskin.
Legs	Soft hackle, color to match the fly.
Ribbing	Dark monofilament (Maxima) or fine copper wire.
Tail	Formed out of the same piece of Bugskin used for the shell.

1. Begin by cutting out the Bugskin components, preparing the hook, and making the eyes, per foregoing instructions.

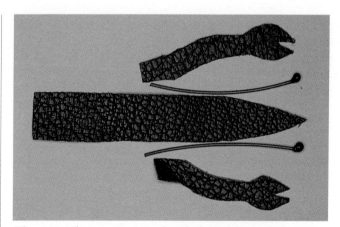

The prepared components, as described (step 1).

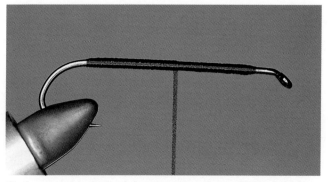

Begin preparing the hook by wrapping a base of Uni-Stretch or thread (step 1).

2. Decide whether you want the hook up or down. (This one is being tied with the hook down.)
3. Tie in the antenna hair, as shown.
4. At that spot where the antenna hair is affixed to the hook, tie in the long piece of shaped Bugskin that will form the head, carapace, rear shell, and tail. It is tied in upside down and hanging to the rear, as it will be folded over later.
5. Apply a little yarn or dubbing to start forming the head. Then tie the eyes in place.

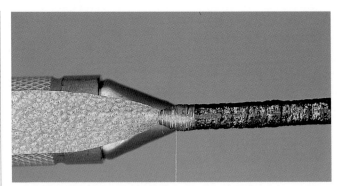

The Bugskin is tied in (step 4).

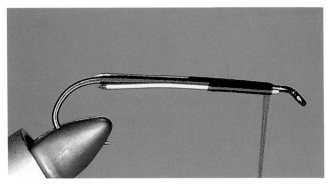

Binding down the weighting strips (step 1).

A little yarn or dubbing starts the forming of the head (step 5).

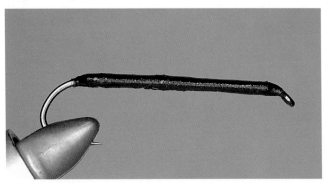

A coat of Zap-A-Gap completes the hook preparation (steps 1 & 2).

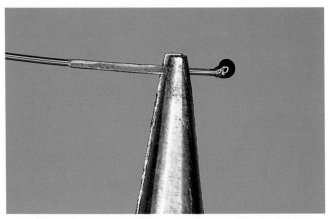

First crimp the Maxima, then tie the eyes in place (step 5).

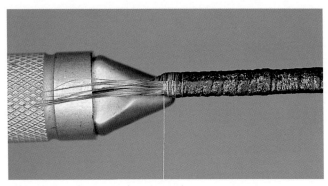

The antenna hair is tied in (step 3).

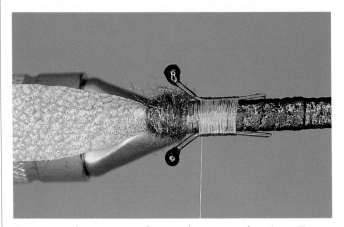

First crimp the Maxima, then tie the eyes in place (step 5).

6. Apply a little more yarn or dubbing around the eyes, ending up just behind them.
7. Tie on the claws one at a time on top of the under-body, in the position shown.
8. Apply some more yarn or dubbing, working around, under, and behind the claws.
9. Tie in the hackle feather for the legs. Then apply a little more body material; enough that two or, at most, three turns of the feather may be palmer-wrapped over it.
10. Wrap and tie off the hackle feather, then cut off the barbs along the top.
11. Tie in the ribbing material, then form the rest of the crayfish by wrapping yarn or applying dubbing al-most to the eye of the hook, leaving enough space for the last couple of tie-off operations and a whip finish.
12. Bring the Bugskin that was left hanging off the front over the entire length of the crayfish, tying it off at the rear. If you wish, you can apply contact cement to the dull side, or underside, of the Bugskin for added strength.

The hackle legs in place (steps 9 & 10).

The ribbing material is tied in, and the body is being formed (step 11).

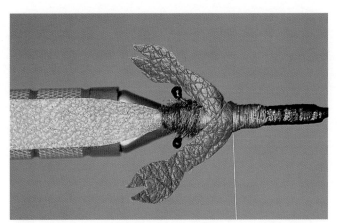

After applying a little more yarn or dubbing, tie on the claws (steps 6 & 7).

The completed body (step 11).

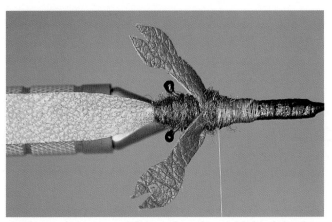

Apply some more material around, under, and behind the claws (step 8).

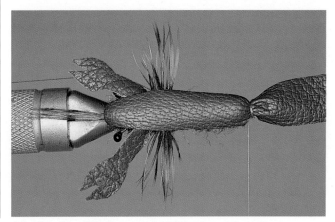

The Bugskin folded over and tied in place (step 12).

13. Spiral-wrap the ribbing, and tie it off at the rear also. Flip the tag of Bugskin up out of the way, and do a whip finish.
14. Pull the tag of Bugskin that will form the tail into place. Observe exactly where the eye of the hook will strike it, then poke a hole through the Bugskin with a scissor tip or other sharp instrument, and pull the tail down, allowing the hook eye to protrude through the hole. Cut the tail to length and shape. Dab a little head cement onto the thread wraps.
15. If you haven't yet painted the eyes, apply a tiny bit of black head lacquer to the ball portion of each eye.

It's possible to put a heavy monofilament weed guard on these flies, but that gets a bit tricky and may interfere with hooking fish. If you absolutely feel that you must have a weed guard, here's how it's made. After tying on the antennae, tie in a length of heavy, stiff monofilament at the bend of the hook, and let it hang off to the rear. Build your crayfish. Then, at the very end, bring the mono around the bend of the hook, just outside of the point, and tie it off at the rear.

One final note: If you have problems forming the tail, don't panic. Though the tail adds a nice touch to the overall image, it isn't essential from a fishing standpoint. So if it doesn't come out very well, just cut it off and head for the water.

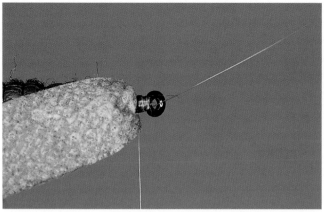

Move the Bugskin out of the way, secure the ribbing, and tie off (step 13).

A top view of the completed Mudbug. The Bugskin has been punctured and slipped over the hook eye, then trimmed to form the tail (step 14).

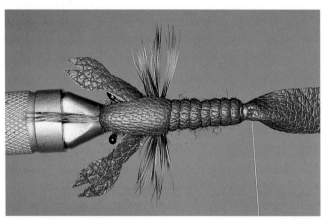

The ribbing in place (step 13).

A side view of the completed Mudbug.

BIBLIOGRAPHY

Berners, Dame Juliana. *A Treatyse on Fysshynge wyth an Angle.* Westminster: 1496.

Caucci, Al, and Bob Nastasi. *Hatches II.* Winchester Press, 1986.

Flick, Arthur B. *A Streamside Guide to Naturals and their Imitations.* New York: Crown, 1947.

LaFontaine, Gary. *Caddisflies.* New York: Nick Lyons Books, 1981.

Leisenring, James, and Vernon "Pete" Hidy. *Tying the Wet Fly and Fishing the Flymph.* New York: Crown, 1971.

Leiser, Eric. *A Book of Fly Patterns.* New York: Knopf, 1987.

Nemes, Sylvester. *The Soft-Hackled Fly.* Harrisburg, Penna.: Stackpole Books, 1975.

——*The Soft-Hackled Fly Addict.* Harrisburg, Penn.: Stackpole Books, 1993.

Schwiebert, Ernest. *Nymphs.* New York: Winchester Press, 1973.

Shaw, Helen. *Flies for Fish and Fishermen.* Harrisburg, Penn.: Stackpole Books, 1989.

Solomon, Larry, and Eric Leiser. *The Caddis and the Angler.* Harrisburg, Penn.: Stackpole Books, 1977.

Swisher, Doug, and Carl Richards. *Selective Trout.* New York: Crown, 1971.

Talleur, Dick. *Mastering the Art of Fly Tying.* Harrisburg, Penn.: Stackpole Books, 1979.

INDEX

Boldface type indicates patterns for which tying instructions are given.

Abby, Ron, 3
Adams, 47, **48–51,** 76, 80
Adams Parachute, 76, **80–81,** 82
Adhesives, 8-10
Alternative, the, 150
Ambroid glue, 9
Anderegg, Gene, 133
Andra Spectrum synthetic fur, 21
Antron yarn, 72, 73, 89, 117
Aqua Fiber, 160
AquaFlex coating, 10, 151, 152, 167
Art of Tying the Wet Fly, The (Leisenring), 34, 95
Au Sable River (Michigan), Middle Branch of, 84
Ausable River (New York), 39, 71, 74
Ausable Wulff, 39-40, **40–44,** 45

Barge Cement, 10
Barracude vise, 3
Bashline, Jim, 153-54
Bates, Joseph D., 178
Battenkill River, 76, 177
Bead Thorax Pheasant Tail Nymph, 116–17, 121
Beaverhead River, 62
Beaverkill River, 21
  Upper, 76, 150
Bergman, Ray, 8
Berners, Dame Juliana, 95
Betters, Francis, 39, 40, 71
Big Fly Fiber, 160
Black Ghost Marabou, 153, 154, **155–57**
Big Horn River, 161
Black-Nosed Dace, 161, 164
Blue Dun Hackle (Leisenring), 100, **101–2**
Blue Ribbon Flies, 22, 68, 72, 137
Blue-Winged Olive Parachute, 76, **77–80,** 81, 82, 90
Bobbin holder, 6
Bobbins, 5-6
Bobbin threader, 6
Bodkin (dubbing needle), 6-7
Bozo Hair, 160
Bradley, Carl, 149
Brodheads Creek, Paradise Branch of, 66
Brookie Fingerling, 168

BT's Flyfishing Products
  coatings, 10
  head cement, 92
Bucktail streamers. *See* Hairwing streamers
Bugskin, 114, 116, 118, 120, 121, 124, 126, 183-86
  described, 113, 123, 127, 182
Bugskin Crayfish, 113
Bugskin Mudbug, 183–86

Catskill, 110–12
Catskill Curler (Catskill Coiler), 127
Catskill Flytier (Darbee and Darbee), 8–9
Caucci, Al, 71
Cellire celluloid varnish, 9
Chickabou, 153
Clouser, Bob, 172
Clouser Minnow, 172
Clouser-Style Fur Matuka, 173–74
Clump-wing dry flies. *See also* Clump-Wing Fly; The Usual
  introduction to, 71
  materials for, 71–72, 74, 75
Clump-Wing Fly (Haystack), 71, **72–74,** 75
Coachman, 103
Coatings, protective, 8–10
Coffin Fly A, 59–60, 61
Coffin Fly B, 61
Comb, fine-toothed, 39
Compara-duns, 71, 72, 89
Cone Head Fur Meatball, 174, **175–76**
Cote, Jean-Guy, 14
Crayfish. *See also* Bugskin Mudbug
  eye-preparation technique for, 183
  hook-preparation technique for, 182
  materials for, 182, 183
Cream Variant, 91
Cyclops Eyes beads, 98

Daiichi hooks
  model 1180, 25, 33, 35, 36, 40, 45, 57, 72, 75, 77, 80, 82,
    83, 92, 94
  model 1280, 59, 69
  model 1550, 96, 99, 124
  model 1560, 114, 118, 120

model 1750, 124, 128, 131, 132, 134, 138, 141, 142, 144, 147
model 2220, 144
model 2340, 128, 131, 132, 155
model 2370, 155, 162, 165
Damselfly Nymph Woolly Bugger, 142
Danville thread, 14, 40
Monocord, 144
Darbee, Elsie, 8–9, 22
Darbee, Harry, 8–9, 22
Dark Cahill, 103
Delaware River, 64, 131
DePuy's River, 89
Dette, Walt, 8, 14, 22
Dette, Winnie, 8, 22
Dick's Dace, 162–64, 167
Dick's Fur MaraBugger, Psychedelic, 138–39
Dick's March Brown Nymph, 120–21
Dick's Pseudo Sculpin, 151–52
Dick's Saturday-Night-Live Fur MaraBugger, 140
Dick's Wriggler, 123, **124–26**
Distribution wrap (thread-management technique), 19–20
Dodge, Bob, 89, 137
Down-wing dry flies. *See also* Green Shad Fly; Green-Tan
Shad Fly; Henryville Special; Stimulator; Troth Hackled
Caddis; Troth No-Hackle Caddis
introduction to, 62
problems/mistakes, 68
Dremel tool, 51, 154
Dubbing needle (bodkin), 6–7
Dubbing twisters, 8
Dud's Kickin' Caddis, 82, 83
Duncan Loop knot, 12
Dun Variant, 91–92, **92–93,** 94
Dynacord, 144, 147
Dyna-King vises, 3

Eastern Giant Black Pteronarcys Nymph, 132
Edison, William, 177
Egg-sac-tying technique, 50
Ellis, 98, **99–100**
England, Tim, 149
Enrico's Sea Fibers, 160
Esopus Creek, 127
Eye-preparation techniques
for Crayfish, 183
painting, 9

Featherwing Sculpin Matuka, 170–71, 172, 173
Featherwing streamers. *See also* Gray Ghost
introduction to, 177
materials for, 177–79
problems/mistakes, 177–79
Federation of Flyfishers, 133
File, 51, 154
FisHair, 159
Fisherman's Feathers, 154

Fishing the Flymph (Hidy), 95
Flank-feather wings
hackle development, history of, 21–23
introduction to, 21
necks, what to look for in, 23–24
tying instructions, 25–37
Flashbacks. *See* Peacock & Copper Flashback
Flexament, 9, 183
Flick, Art, 21, 22, 32, 91, 92, 93, 161
Flies for Fish and Fishermen (Shaw), 112
Fly Fur, 159
Fly Head, 121
Fly Tyer magazine, 15, 178
Fontinalis Fin, 103
Furimsky, Chuck, 153, 182
Fur Marabou, 137–38
Fur-strip-cutting technique, 174

Gallows tool, 82
Gapen, Don, 143
Ghost-Fiber, 160
Gordon, Theodore, 21–22
Grand Cascapedia River, 133
Gray Fox, 82, 91
Gray Fox Flat-Hackle, 83
Gray Fox Variant, 76, 91, 92, 93, **94**
Gray Ghost, 177, 178, **179–81**
Gray Wulff, 38
Great Western Salmon Fly Nymph, 131–32
Green River, 44
Green River Wulff. *See* SteppenWulff
Green Shad Fly, 65–66, 69
Green-Tan Shad Fly, 66
Griffin Company bobbins, 5–6, 128, 165
Griffith, George, 84
Griffith Gnat, 84, **85–86**
Grinding bit, 51
Grizzly King, 107–9
Guinea-burner, 154, 157

Hackle development, history of, 21–23
Hackle gauge, 6
Hackle guard, 8
Hackle pliers, 6, 42–43
Hair evener (stacker), 7, 39
Hair packer, 7
Hair-spinning wrap (thread-management technique), 18
Hairwing streamers. *See also* Black-Nosed Dace; Brookie
Fingerling; Dick's Dace; Rainbow Fingerling
introduction to, 158
materials for, 158–60
problems/mistakes, 160–61
Half-hitch tool, 7
Halford, Frederick, 21
Halford-type dry flies, 38
Halliday, 47

Hansen, Sally (products), 9
Hard-as-Nails head finish, 9
Hareline (brand of synthetic hair), 159
Hare's Ear Nymph, 103, 113, 117, 120, 122. *See also* Sparkly
    Hare's Ear Nymph
Hatch, Ellis, 98
Hatches (Caucci and Nastasi), 71
Hatches II (Caucci and Nastasi), 71
Haystack. *See* Clump-Wing Fly
Head-and-collar-assembly technique, 146
Hebgen Lake, 137
Hebert, Ted, 22, 23
Hebert strains, 91
Hellgrammite, 113
Helm, Chris, 15, 149
Hendrickson, Al, 21
Hendricksons, 21, 24, 32, 56, 57. *See also* Pink Hendrickson
Henrys Fork River, 137
Henryville Special, 66, 67–68
Henryville Trout Club, 66
Hidy, Vernon, 95
Hi-Vis, 160
Hoffman, Henry, 22–23, 68
Hoffman Grizzly, 89
Hoffman saddle hackle, 45
Hoffman strains, 91, 133
Hoffman Supergrizzly, 22–23, 49, 68
Hooks
    design of, 11–12
    finishes of, 12–13
    sizing and classification of, 13
Hornberg, Frank, 133
Hornberg, 134–36
    introduction to, 133
    materials for, 133
    problems/mistakes, 134
Horvath, Dr. Fred, 21
Howard, Herb, 14
Hunter's Angling Supplies, 34, 133
Hunter's Multi Head (HMH) vise, 1

Jennings, Preston, 22
Jorgensen, Poul, 153

Kaufmann, Randall, 68
Kennebec River Fly & Tackle Company vises, 1
Kevlar threads, 144
Krystal Chenille, 141
Krystal Flash, 89, 147, 168

Lac Loon coatings, 10
L&L Products, 160
Leadwing Coachman Nymph, 113, 122
Leisenring, Jim, 34, 95, 100
Leisenring. *See* Blue Dun Hackle
Leisenring-type dressings, 100

Lewis, Dr. Arthur B., 137
Ligas Scintilla dubbing mix, 39, 119
Light Cahill, 103
Lime Fur Matuka, 171, 172–73
Limerick hooks, 139
Lite Brite, 117, 138, 141
Lithuanian Bat, 174
Long, Bob, 178

Madison River, 137
    Slide Inn section of, 68
    Upper, 137
Marabou Muddler. *See* White Marabou Muddler
Marabou streamers. *See also* Black Ghost Marabou
    introduction to, 153
    materials for, 153, 154
    problems/mistakes, 153, 154
March Brown, 91, 103, 104–7, 109
Mason shock tippet material, 132
Mastering the Art of Fly Tying (Talleur), 21, 137, 143, 150
Matarelli whip finisher, 7, 79
Materials clip, 8
Matthews, Craig, 22, 68, 137
Matthews, Jackie, 68
Matukas. *See also* Clouser-Style Fur Matuka; Featherwing
    Sculpin Matuka; Lime Fur Matuka
    fur-strip-cutting technique, 174
    introduction to, 169
    materials for, 169, 171
Maxima
    chameleon monfilament, 124
    heavy brown monofilament, 183
    leader material, 120
    thread, 119
McKenzie Fly Tackle Company, 160
Meatballs, introduction to, 169. *See also* Cone Head Fur
    Meatball
Merg, Bill, 15
Messinger, Joe, Jr., 149
Metz, Buck, 22, 23
Michigan Night Caddis, 123
Mickey Finn, 164
Micro Fibetts, 32, 33, 57, 58, 59, 61, 77, 88
Mini flies/micro flies. *See also* Griffith Gnat; Standard Trico;
    Tiny Olive Parachute
    introduction to, 84
    materials for, 84, 86, 89
    mistakes/problems, 84, 89
Minor, Andy, 22
Monel wire, 123, 124
Muddler Minnow, 144–46, 147, 149, 150. *See also* White
    Marabou Muddler; Yellow Marabou Muddler
    head-and-collar-assembly technique, 146
    introduction to, 143
    materials for, 143–44
    problems/mistakes, 149

Munn, Billy, 149
Mustad hooks, 59, 69
Mystic Bay Flies, 159

Nastasi, Bob, 71
Nemes, Sylvester, 95
Nix, Jimmy, 149
Nymphs. *See also* Bead Thorax Pheasant Tail Nymph; Dick's
    March Brown Nymph; Dick's Wriggler; Leadwing
    Coachman Nymph; Peacock & Copper Flashback;
    Pheasant Tail Nymph; Sparkly Hare's Ear Nymph
    introduction to, 113
    materials for, 113, 116, 117, 119, 122, 123

Oatman, Lou, 177
Orange Fishawk, 95, **96–97,** 98, 108

Pale Morning Dun, 51, **52–53,** 87
Pale Morning Dun Cut-Wing Thorax, 53–55, 57
Parachutes. *See also* Adams Parachute; Blue-Winged Olive
    Parachute; Dad's Kickin' Caddis; Gray Fox Flat-Hackle;
    Tiny Olive Parachute
    introduction to, 76
    materials for, 76–77, 80, 82
    problems/mistakes, 77, 80
Paradise Branch, of Brodheads Creek, 66
Parmachene Belle, 103
Partridge and Green, 97, **98**
Partridge hooks, 59, 69
Peacock & Copper Flashback, 122–23
Perla Stonefly Nymph, 119, 120, 127, **128–31**
Pheasant Tail (P-T) Nymph, 113, **114–15,** 116, 118. *See also*
    Bead Thorax Pheasant Tail Nymph
Pinch wrap (thread-management technique), 15–16
Pink Hendrickson, 25–32, 33
Pink Hendrickson dubbing material, 25
Pliers
    fine-nosed, 125
    hackle, 6, 42–43
Polar Aire, 160
Popovics, Bob, 3
Pseudo Sculpin. *See* Dick's Pseudo Sculpin
P-T Nymph. *See* Pheasant Tail Nymph
Pugliese, Enrico, 160

Quill Gordon, 21–22, 34, **35,** 99
Quimby, Bert, 177

Rainbow Fingerling, 165–67
Rainy's coatings, 10
Rainy's Water-Based Popper Paint, 10
Red Quill, 21, 32, **33–34,** 91
Regal vise, 1
Renzetti, Andy, 2
Renzetti vises, 2, 3
Richards, Carl, 124

Roman Moser, 160
Royal Coachman body, 44
Rusty Spinner, 57–58, 88

San Juan River, 68
Scheck, Art, 177–78
Scissors, 4–5, 144, 146, 182
    metal-cutting (tin snips), 51, 154
Shaw, Helen, 8, 14, 112
Slack loop (thread-management technique), 17
Slaymaker, Sam, 164
Slide Inn section, of Madison River, 68
Smith, Ray, 8
Soft-Hackled Fly, The (Nemes), 95
Soft-Hackled Fly Addict, The (Nemes), 95
Soft-hackle wet flies. *See also* Blue Dun Hackle; Ellis; Orange
    Fishawk; Partridge and Green
    introduction to, 95
    materials for, 98
    problems/mistakes, 95, 97, 98
Soper, Dudley G., 76, 81, 82
Sparkle Dun, 72, 76, 89
Sparkly Hare's Ear Nymph, 118–19
Spents, introduction to, 56–57. *See also* Coffin Fly A; Coffin
    Fly B
Spinners, introduction to, 56–57. *See also* Rusty Spinner
Spirit River Company, 159, 160, 172
Spruce Creek, 153–54
Stacker (hair evener), 7, 39
Standard (Thorax) Trico, 87–88
Stauffer, Chip, 22
Steenrod, Roy, 21
SteppenWulff (Green River Wulff), 44, **45–46**
Stevens, Carrie, 134, 177, 178, 179
Stickney, Joe, 177
Stimulator, 22, 68, **69–70**
Stonefly nymphs. *See also* Eastern Giant Black Pteronarcys
    Nymph; Great Western Salmon Fly Nymph; Perla
    Stonefly Nymph
    introduction to, 127
    materials for, 127–28
Streamside Guide to Naturals and Their Imitations (Flick), 91, 93
Super Hair, 159
Swisher, Doug, 124
Synthetic Living Fiber (SLF), 160

Taylor, Ron, 154
Teal-Winged Adams Quill, 35, **36–37,** 49
Teaser, Velcro, 125
Thin Skin, 114, 116, 123, 128–32
    described, 127
D. H. Thompson products, 159
Thorax Trico. *See* Standard Trico
Thread, choosing, 14–15
Thread-management techniques
    distribution wrap, 19–20

hair-spinning wrap, 18
pinch wrap, 15–16
slack loop, 17
Tiemco hooks, 59, 69
Tin snips (metal-cutting scissors), 51, 154
Tiny Olive Parachute, 88, 89–90
Tippet wings. *See also* Adams
egg-sac-tying technique, 50
introduction to, 47
Treatise on Fishing with an Angle (Berners), 95
Troth, Al, 62, 64
Troth Caddis. *See* Troth Hackled Caddis; Troth No–Hackle Caddis
Troth Elk Hair Caddis. *See* Troth Hackled Caddis; Troth No-Hackle Caddis
Troth Hackled Caddis, 64
Troth No-Hackle Caddis, 63
Tweezerman tweezers, 7

Ultra Hair, 159
Umpqua Feather Merchants, 23
Fly Head, 121
Uni-Stretch, 50, 68, 129, 130, 140
black, 132, 155
brown, light, 69
cream, 151
described, 127–28
green, 65, 98, 107, 172, 174
orange, 131
tan, 69
white, 59–60, 151, 165, 173, 174
yellow, 128, 168
Uni-Thread, 75, 112, 127, 140, 143, 183
Big Fly, 144
black, 36, 72, 80, 99, 122, 132, 134, 138
brown, 36, 57, 82, 114, 128, 144, 151
brown, dark, 92, 122, 131
brown, light, 33, 77
cream, 83
described, 14
gray, 72
gray, dark, 80
gray, light, 25, 35
greenish olive, 35
olive, 77, 142
olive, pale, 94
orange, 40
primrose, 94, 101
rust, 114
tan, 25, 33, 35, 82, 83, 94, 142, 151
white, 141
Uni-Yarn, 130
Usual, The, 74, **75**

Variants. *See also* Cream Variant; Dun Variant; Gray Fox Variant
introduction to, 91

materials for, 91–93
problems/mistakes, 93
Veniard coatings, 9
Vinciguerra, Matt, 127
Vises
design of, 1–2
pedestal base versus C-clamp mount, 2
rotary, 2–3
travel, 3

Wapsi Company, 114, 127, 128
Welch, Herb, 177
West, Howard, 22
Whip finisher, 7, 79
White Cone Head MaraBugger, 140, **141–42**
White Marabou Muddler, 146, **147–49**
White Wulff, 38
Whiting, Dr. Tom, 22–23, 91
Whiting Farms, 23, 47, 153
Whitlock, Dave, 9, 149
Wilder, Leila, 34
Wilder, Nick, 34
Willowemoc Creek, 21
Wing burner, 51
Winged wet flies. *See also* Catskill; Grizzly King; March Brown
flank-feathers techniques, 107
introduction to, 103
materials for, 103, 106, 109
problems/mistakes, 103–4
source of further information on, 112
Woolly Buggers, 147, 153, 158. *See also* Damselfly Nymph Woolly Bugger; Dick's Fur MaraBugger, Psychedelic; Dick's Saturday-Night-Live Fur MaraBugger; White Cone Head MaraBugger
introduction to, 137
materials for, 137–38, 139
Wotton, Davy, 160
Wriggle Nymph, 124
Wulff, Lee, 38
Wulff wings, 21. *See also* Ausable Wulff; Gray Wulff; Steppen-Wulff; White Wulff
introduction to, 38–39
materials for, 38–40
problems/mistakes, 39

Yellow Marabou Muddler, 143

Zap-A-Gap superglue, 34, 63, 72, 79, 81, 82, 83, 89, 100, 114, 116, 124, 125, 128–32, 134, 138, 140, 144, 145, 151, 152, 156, 166, 170, 172, 173, 176, 178, 182, 183
described, 10
Z-lon yarn, 73